Another Kind of Nation

Another Kind of Nation:
An Anthology of
Contemporary Chinese Poetry

edited by Zhang Er and Chen Dongdong

Talisman House Publishers
Jersey City, New Jersey

Published in the United States of America by
Talisman House, Publishers
P.O. Box 3157
Jersey City, New Jersey 07303 - 3157

Manufactured in the United Sates of America
Printed on acid-free paper

ISBN-10: 1-58498-057-5
ISBN-13: 978-1-58498-057-5

05 06 07 7 6 5 4 3 2 1 FIRST EDITION

Chinese typesetting by Frank Chen

Some of the original works were previously published in literary journals, newspapers, unoffical publications, and collections of individual poets in China; some of the translated works were previously published in journals such as *Tinfish*, *Slightly West*, and on-line journals such as *Fascicle*, *Full Tilt*, *Words without Borders* and *How2*. The editor would like to thank the various poets, translators, and publications that granted permission for these works to be reprinted in this volume.

Table of Contents

Contributors

目录

Another Kind of Nation

Preface: A Shimmering Window

A shimmering window might be an unusual metaphor for a book of contemporary Chinese poetry in translation. The work gathered here was collected from twenty-four authors born in the 1960s and 1970s whose work began to appear in publication and gain attention mainly in the 1990s and after. "Shimmering" shows a star, a state of charged energy, of movement and instability, and an existence between a window and a mirror. "Shimmering" evokes tears which well up in rapture and despair. A window lets light in, illuminates the interior as it frames the scene for observers on both sides. . . A window that is shimmering is best admired or gazed at as an object of examination rather than a transparency through which to look for something else, be it political, social or even cultural. Yet, from time to time if one stares long enough with patience and careful gauging, a landscape with scenery and characters emerges from such a window. The occurrence of these scenes and characters, as if seen from a boat on the river of the long tradition of Chinese poetry, mirrors the unique way that tense works in Chinese verbs, at once past, present and future.

The scenery portrayed by contemporary Chinese poets is no longer the natural or bucolic landscape with mountains and rivers, moons and clouds, flowers and birds, vast fields and lonely horses typically found in classical Chinese poetry and are represented in English by the poets Wang Wei (701-761), Li Po (Li Bai, 701-762), Tu Fu (Du Fu, 712-770) and Su Tung-p'o (Su Dongpo, 1036-1101), to name only a few. Contemporary phenomena, urban streets and crowds have replaced the scenes. Let's look at a few lines from the poet Cao Shuying, "Carbohydrate surplus. Calcium deficiency . . . /the smiling candy devours her," "their pile of clay of offspring/their pile of clay Ph.Ds." Han Bo writes: "Snow began to fall, the train entered the station / the director agreed it should begin this way." Jiang Tao states, "but the layout of the suburb was that of a labyrinth, puzzling the nearsighted magpie / whereupon, he ran even more slowly, and almost crept / for fear that he would tread upon the newly-shed shells (from those schoolward kids moments ago)." "I see the photoflash flash and flash, perfectly round, slightly sour / autumn pears copiously occupy the free market, their butts / slapped by long poles. . . ." described Tang Danhong.

3

These lines clearly illustrate a world different before the encounter of Chinese culture with the West. It brought in the dramatic and irreversible modern language / new literature movement at the turn of the last century in the Chinese language world, which bore the fruit of Modern Chinese poetry. Hong Kong poet Huang Canran vividly captures this on-going encounter on a micro-level in his poem, Translation. The encounter is the translation. What to add, what to delete, how to modify, how to convey and how to maintain the vitality of each are all part of the process. This of course is the situation of our time, when cultures developed relatively independently over thousand of years, each with its unique history, now crowded into the same global village, face-to-face, shoulder-to-shoulder. Yet, as Lü De-an puts it, "kids in threes and fives / Skate toward the infinite night of inertia, and when coming back / Already grownups bring more kids with them / More light," "The world never changes much at all." Or has it? And the poetics?

Modern Chinese poetry, over the past hundred years, has broken away from its classical past. In a feverish search it has found versatile forms that are able to assimilate new information, technology and a changed conceptions of the world, which has internalized its relationship with the West.

The experimentation of the 20s and 30s with "free verse" and writing in vernacular was truncated by the anti-Japanese war and the civil war, then the Communist movement in the mainland and the anti-Communist campaign in Taiwan, which lasted from the late 1930s to the 1960s. During the long haul, poetry and all forms of literature and art were subordinated to the demand of the national crisis as vehicles of propaganda messages (with the exception of poets in Hong Kong under British rule, who were paradoxically exempt from such political pressure). Renewed experimentation with poetic language in the 60s in Taiwan was in marked contrast to the unfortunate fiasco of the "Cultural Revolution" on the mainland, during which all traces of culture, be it Western or Eastern, were literally stripped and marred with red paint. Yet, poetry is as resilient as exquisite wild flowers. Disasters of fire, flood, stampede, draught and deep freeze somehow provide nutrients in its slumber, which furnish dream and imagination, deepen its root, strengthening yet sensitizing its nerves, and finally when the spring comes enrich its displays.

For readers who are interested in a closer examination of the contemporary Chinese poetry scene in Mainland China from 1966, as of the eve of the turmoil of the "Cultural Revolution" till now, the introduction in Chinese to this book written by Chen Dongdong, a prolific poet from Shanghai, my co-editor, would be a good place to start.

As there have been two recent anthologies by Michelle Yeh devoted to Taiwan poets, this anthology focuses on Chinese poets who do not live in Taiwan. Although the poets in this anthology were born and grew up in China, several live outside China, or at least have spent a substantial amount of time abroad. Lü De-an is bi-coastal, traveling between Fujian on the coast of South China Sea and New York City on the Atlantic coast. After years of correspondence, I first met Chen Dongdong in New York City when he was a resident at the Yaddo poetry colony. Ma Lan lives in New Haven, Connecticut. Yang Xiaobin completed his Ph.D. at Yale and now teaches at University of Mississippi. Zhang Zhen lived in Europe and Japan after she left China and now teaches film at New York University. Zhang Zao lives in Germany and earned his Ph.D. from Tübingen University. Hu Xudong taught in Brazil for three years. Zang Di is a professor at Beijing University but he taught for a while in UC, Davis, edited the Chinese translation of Rilke and travels widely. Huang Canran, a professional translator of English for a newspaper, makes his home in Hong Kong, as does Cao Shuying. Shu Cai was a diplomat of the Chinese embassy in Senegal and has translated several French authors into Chinese, including Pierre Reverdy, Rene Char, and Yves Bonnefoy. Zhao Xia has translated work of Paul Celan and Gunter Grass into Chinese, writes an English language column for a Chinese newspaper and lives in Stuttgart, Germany and Nanjing. The list goes on. Does this exposure to other cultures and languages contribute to these poets' poetry and alter their poetics? Does it make them somehow similar with poets of the past like Qu Yuan, the first known Chinese poet (around 330 BC in Chu State), Li Po, Tu Fu and Su Tung-p'o, who among their contemporaries traveled widely either by choice or by forced exile, to cultures other than that of the Han Chinese?

One thing is certain: the poets here should not be looked upon as exotic others living in remote corners or from isolated cults. They are very much a part of the contemporary world with a decentralized cultural landscape, linked by Internet, cables and air/land traffic routes, under the shadow of looming globalization. By looking at them, we look at our own world and ourselves.

The American poets involved in this project commented on the literary influences that they recognized in the poems that they were translating:

Ashbery-like in one case, Mallarmé and Rebour in another, Robert Frost in a third. In addition I can also recognize the influences of Stevens, Dickinson, Eliot, Yeats in others — as well as Qu Yuan and the Book of Songs style (600 BC). The Yue Fu style (Ballad-Songs of the Bureau of Music in the Han Dynasty, 200 BC-200 AD) and its mimics from Wei and Jin Dynasty and Six Dynasties (around 300-500 AD) are especially relevant here, perhaps in terms of the narrative nature of certain poems and the abstract lyric quality of others.

Buddhism, Taoism, Christianity and a lingering Communism found their vocabularies and ideology in these poets' work. Yang Jian, a Buddhist monk, wrote about the lost way, " a vivid light — / only few recognize / and walk out on it." In his floating world, a duck with a "calm face" cries out our inside omen and "vague stress." After the wishful declaration, "Life consists of letting days pass . . . / It's over, over, over . . . / Yes, everything will pass," Shu Cai continues, "But there is a little boy wedged between two iron bars. / He is crying. He is struggling. His future." In fisherman Sun Tai's world, "angels," "Cross," "Heaven" and "Hell" entangle, yet "after descending to the sea," Lü De-An tells us in his long poem *Mankato*, "without the sermonic air, we / breathe freely, surrounded by the light of sea stars, deadly quiet for thousand years." Song Ke quotes Hsiang Hsiu's *Lamentations for Bygone Days* and Eugene Pottier's *The Internationale* in the same breath, and then remembers his meeting with a Taoist priest when hiking up the Qian-Mountain at sunrise. Zhang Zhen's *Revolution* (1989) is a far cry from things that the U.S. news media would be interested in, "Revolution and I have parted company / Pour my sangfroid into the refrigerator / God places His hand on my heart, / His face upon the tip of my hair / Says, You made a mistake / Little girl, for you yourself are the Revolution." Zhao Xia's *Stuttgart Christmas* shaped like a Christmas tree, features presents at foot of the evergreen tree: "a brand new portable radio / that perhaps rebuilds us earthlings," together with her contemplation on life, "Everyone would be born a plastic shelled boat in / perpetual motion, sinking and / floating with cool fashion."

Yes, these poets are sponges — lakes and sea absorbing what the world offers from their personal life and experiences, from poetic traditions of their own culture and of cultures they encounter. Their work is complicated, filled with conflicted thoughts and emotions, which demand various writing strategies, as well as a wide range of vocabularies and poetic forms. Their

6

aesthetic stand, if I can speak for the poets who are represented in this anthology, is in stark contrast with the conventional Western view of Chinese poetry's "pure, natural, clean, concise imagism." For sure, they use plenty of images, but they use them in their messy and maximum way, along with many other strategies. Their view of the Chinese language, as reflected by Chinese characters, is holistic: the images of things, the presentation of human perception and understanding of things, and of the human voices that name them. At the root of the Chinese writing system (the characters) live things themselves, not just symbols kept as records but the acceptance of things themselves, things that do not need explanation or even a standard articulated name. Human perspective, reasoning and voice are somehow treated in the Chinese language as secondary or even arbitrary. Yet, as we shall see below, this "thing" is not that "thing" –the objective natural world – so often mistaken by Western poets when reading Chinese poetry.

The poetics represented here fundamentally embrace that system of understanding underlined by the Chinese metaphysical concept of "Heaven and Human are one" – which denies separation of the subject and the object. This knowledge does not involve exclusively human's perspectives dissecting / understanding / observing / experimenting / categorizing / contemplating nature. True knowledge, in this respect, can't be determined, given that mind and matter are the same, and observer and observed are one. Such knowledge is fluid and multi-directional in time and space. The human is not the only active participant in the game of knowledge. "Heaven" is more powerful, more knowing and more ubiquitous. Yet "Heaven" does not equal "God/gods" in the Western sense. "Heaven" entails the universe and the reasoning that embraces us all – and is part of things.

The apparent lack of syntactical structure, the non-directional collages of image and action often found in Chinese poetry including the work collected derive not merely from pure aesthetic considerations for "noninterference with Nature's flow" as the poet and scholar Wai-Lim Yip put it, but more fundamentally from the requirement of such metaphysical understanding. Eza Pound instinctively picked up on this feature of the classical Chinese poetry, and brought it to the West as a new technique to enrich its poetic artillery without realizing the philosophical significance or the distinct difference of the Chinese definition on "things." He was ingenious in attributing the feature to the Chinese writing system and its pictographic aspect – which lead him to invent imagism. Yet he still missed the metaphysical point at the bottom of it all. . . . "No ideas but in things" demonstrates just how narrowly William Carlos Williams and some imagists missed the essence of the Eastern thinking. The philosophical discussion of this fundamental Eastern ideology and its profound influence on the Eastern culture lies beyond the scope of this preface. Martin Heidegger, for one, among the Western thinkers, had a serious dialogue with the East. . . . But here, let me merely focus on how the poetics of these texts manifest these broader issues.

In Chinese, it is perfectly natural for "flowers to share tears" when the poet experiences an emotional moment (Tu Fu), because Heaven/ nature/things can govern, echo or sense human. The separation of two is by no means absolute. It is equally apt when "equipped with the spring's clockwork, the winter moves in the snowfield" (Mo Fei), or when "Some water is unable to stir, / because of its good conscience, or because / the third person tells the second person / that the heart of the first person is dead. / Some water dehydrates them. (Zang Di); After asking "Are you dangling from my eyelashes?" Hu Xudong finds the answer, "Only then do I see it: /the waterfall upstream shines bright, flows clear, / just the way you look when you rush out, shimmering, / from inside this body of mine"; Ye Hui understands "a tree cut down / but its life still extends / it turns into board, is made into a wedding bed / on which people bear sons and raise daughters, so on / and so forth, circling without end"; Ma Lan chooses her seat carefully, " I sit on a block of ice, / Water beneath me. / I sit in his house. / To the left and right are years carried by the wind like confetti. / I touch some books that are crawling across the floor. / They grow thinner as they trek, . . . / I sit outside his house, . . ./ I sit in my own mind, / Remain there so long / I become a package, a bundle of herbs . . . / then return to sit on the block of ice, / The current flowing beneath me." These tenseless lines move in a non-linear, illogical or irrational fashion, vibrating and changing.

The difficulty in translation created by such writing is significant. Translators, who are poets not unfamiliar with imagism or other post-Poundian multi-perspective writing strategies, are nevertheless perplexed by the seemingly arbitrary usage of the personal pronouns in many poets' work, as well as the fluid shifting of perspectives, the animation of thing without any warning, the tenseless transition of events defying linear time line even when the poem is telling a story or following an obvious plot. If nature and human are one, the subjective and objective are one, mind is matter, the conception of the world is not a human-centered activity, then the lack of "I" in many Chinese poets' work becomes perfectly understandable. The absence of "I" is the manifestation of a presence everywhere, by every thing. Things have mind, rather things ARE mind, or in Williams' term, ideas are things. Animation is therefore unnecessary. The lake is the cherished girl, whose presence/absence still affects "you" (See Zang Di's *Weiming Lake*). We don't know whose presence or absence are being discussed here, be it the girl or the lake. Walking around the lake offers sweetness, then saltiness, or is it the lovers' relationship that is hinted at here? Is "you" the poet or the girl or the lake? Who are "they," appearing unexplained and starting to play roles in the passage of the work?

These writers' poems sometimes have the quality of dialogues between interchangeable partners. Everything in a poem, I mean every-thing, is fluid: there is no fixed reference frame. Everything is open to everything else. "I" turns into you, he, she, it, we, they, etc. Time and space are "things" as well as other abstract thoughts and concepts. Things tend to know themselves better than humans, who are simply other "things." The prepositional words used to position them, to pin them down, in turn become meaningless or even misleading. Is pan-perspectival the best word to convey this lack of a human-centered epistemological view?

On the other hand, like other Indo-European languages, English is a phonetic language (i.e. it records the human voice to name things), and therefore it assumes a human perspective and human-centered knowledge. The foundation for such knowledge is the philosophical separation of mind and matter, of subjective and objective. Readers of the English translations of the Chinese poetry in this anthology need to keep in mind that the translators have to make some brave adjustments in English, in order to re-create the energetic fluidity of the internal and external world where these Chinese poets dwell. My postface for the book outlines the work process of this complicated and challenging endeavor.

To say the poets whose work is represented here embrace this Chinese poetic tradition and aesthetics does not mean that they do not investigate other strategies or poetics in their work, nor that the editors intend to define, therefore restrict, what is meant by Chinese poetics and aesthetics. In the Chinese sense, Chinese poetics are constantly changing — they do not "develop" with a linear direction but act more like a wave tracing a cyclic movement over time. The work collected here are themselves the best statements of these writers' poetics.

Many poets whose work the editors admire greatly are not included in the anthology. Works of numerous contemporary poets born before 1960 have been previously translated into English and anthologized or published as individual collections so were not included. Most poets in this anthology have been translated into English for the first time. Poets we feel do not share the poetics delineated above, or poets who have just started their writing career and are beginning to publish interesting work are left for future anthologies.

In a sense, the translation foregrounds the translator more than anything else. The consistent fascination of the American experimental poetry wing with Chinese poetry from Pound on is a phenomenon in itself that needs to be examined in light of what the Chinese can offer here (Eliot Weinberger has written an informative introduction to The New Directions Anthology of Classical Chinese Poetry on the topic). Many American poets involved in the translation have communicated to me that they enjoyed the translation process and gained certain insight into the Chinese poetics.

It is our hope that readers will find that this shimmering window, created by the collective efforts of Chinese and American poets with the linguistic translators, opens onto something beautiful and innovative. Beautiful and innovative, not because it presents exotic scenery on the other side, but because it points a different way to look at ordinary things and to experience the way things look back at us.

Zhang Er
Olympia and Taipei
11/7-25/05

编者序

大陆上的鲁宾逊

作一个历史的大概划分，可以说中国大陆的当代诗歌启于 1966 年开始的无产阶级文化大革命。就实际情况来看，不妨把这片大陆上的当代诗人之名，仅仅授予那些文革以后出道的诗人。那就是所谓的朦胧诗人、后朦胧诗人、新生代诗人、第三代诗人、中间代诗人、晚生代诗人，还有什么 70 后和现在已经现身了的 80 后诗人——也有人将他们统称为先锋诗人——可是又有诗人不愿意自觉戴上上述帽子的任何一项，因为实际上哪一项都不适合。所以，不妨就以几乎算不上命名的当代诗人名之，并且在这一名下，只把他们看作每一个作为个体的诗人，令其超越他可能曾经身在其中的群体和诗歌运动、流派和代际，好让人们真正去关注他写下的诗篇。

这个作为个体的当代诗人是一个无名者，哪怕在简历里写上"著名诗人"的那个人，那些人。逸出诗歌圈，几乎就没有了当代诗人和当代诗歌。在家喻户晓那些风云人物、政经大腕、文体明星直到恐怖分子的当代生活里，诗人实在过于隐秘了。这隐秘，在中国大陆当代诗歌的前三十多年里是一种地下的、有时甚至是"非法"的处境；在加速和差不多已经进入经济和消费社会的最近数年的中国，则成了一种边缘际遇。当然，可以说，当代诗人的地下化和边缘化，并非全然被迫，而往往是出于诗歌尊严的主动选择。但是那种"被抛"感，却是当代诗人都有所体会的。

有人认为中国当代诗歌始于食指（1948—）的短诗《这是四点零八分的北京》：诗人在上山下乡的时代列车开动之际探出车窗，跟母亲和家园诀别。设想一下，那个在诗篇里乘上时代列车奔赴迷惘未来的当代诗人，却因为他的诗而被留在了时代的站台上。可是他并非就不必付出诀别的代价了……他的情形——当代中国这片大陆上的诗人的情形，更像是被遗弃在荒岛上的那个人，被遗弃的原因，既跟鲁宾逊的原型一样——在航行中和船长发生冲突；又跟笛福塑造的那个虚构角色相似——在一次海难后得以幸存。他当时的处境是那样孤绝，被一片红海洋围困，没有援助，没有氛围，没有可能，只有危险。他的写作起于绝望，为生存而拚命，朝希望返回。

在对中国大陆当代诗歌的早期回忆里，总是会提到可以跟鲁宾逊从遇难船上搬往荒岛的有限物资相类比的黄皮书和灰皮书。《局外人》、《变形记》、《麦田里的守望者》、《带星星的火车票》、《人·岁月·生活》……

这些当年的禁书、"供批判用"的"内部发行"的出版物，为中国大陆的当代诗人提供了最初的写作给养。其中，这些翻译作品在文学语言方面的影响是值得玩味的。最近的一篇访谈录里，北岛（1949—）提及，这些翻译作品"创造了一种游离于官方话语的独特文体，……1960年代末地下文学的诞生正是以这种文体为基础的。"在"被抛"背景下将游离的语言当作了根据地，进而，还是用北岛的一行诗来表述，开始了"词的流亡"，这正是当代诗人自觉地下化和边缘化的标志和表现——鲁宾逊转过身去，背对汪洋，到岸上开辟自己的领地。

接下来，一切都是由诗人们自行操办的。大概而言，在中国大陆，当代诗人既是诗歌作者，又是自己诗歌的编者、出版者和推介者，又是热心和够格的读者。当代诗人还是自己诗歌的批评者，而且充任过几回自己诗歌的授奖者……这种自给自足的隔绝状态，的确令诗人们不安，认真探寻着解决之道，但久而久之似乎也就无所谓了。反正，当代诗人遵循自己的诗歌理想，确立自己的写作规范和评判标准，并且，打算或已经由自己来刻写自己的文学史墓碑了——这种鲁宾逊式的开拓、建功、立业，不止于把文明世界从制度律令到生活方式的一整套玩艺儿移植了过来——当代诗人更从文革废墟中催生培育了全新的、令现代汉语拔节招展的现代汉诗。

现代汉诗渐渐地、却又是迅疾地自主和成熟，除了可以列出一份它的优秀诗人名单和一串它自己的经典，主要还在于，它产生了只属于它自己的困惑和问题，并且它有能力自行克服和解决。现代性贯穿着它的诗性、汉语性和中国性，而这些又跟诗人的生存状况和内心生活纠缠在一起，同古典和西方这两大诗学传统对照、对话着，砥砺于当代的历史、政治和文化语境。

在1980年代初的中国大陆，一种被称作"朦胧诗"的新诗歌正在引人关注。在经历了程度相对低浅的诸如"懂"与"不懂"的诗学论争和更多政治色彩的话语交锋以后，"朦胧诗"被主流诗坛不太情愿地接纳，也恰好带给再不能恬不知耻地惯用其"红色转喻符号系统"的主流诗坛一种泛朦胧诗风。探究起来，"朦胧诗"有一个在文化大革命的斗争疯狂和政治愚昧里沉潜和觉悟的启蒙主义渊源，其先驱诗人（譬如食指）在红色主流之下，神奇地令现代诗的艺术精神借道血脉，潜流般推进，直至涌现出一派新诗潮。朦胧诗人以饱经磨难的历史感、使命感和责任感，去成为文革后社会批判、主体意识和人道主义的代言人；但它跟它所反对的国家意识形态及其政治抒情诗，却又有着一种以抗衡结成的亲眷关系。

因为他们所经历的，朦胧诗人集体性地困挠于文革噩梦和别的政治和历史噩梦。比他们年轻的一代诗人，对文化大革命，则有着更多印象式的象征性记忆，却少有刻骨铭心的创伤记忆。1960 年代出生和比之更晚出道的 1970 年代出生的诗人，于是就像是从海难和呼救里转过身去，打量只属于他的新岸的鲁宾逊，甚至愿意把自己的诗人角色置换为更为原始、单纯和本能的礼拜五。那种更注重生命形态、生存境况和生活方式的个人化、自白化的体验之诗，一下子铺张开来，背向了朦胧诗人的幸存之诗。

那是一些倡导回到本来面目的自身，直到回到一次性的身体本身的诗人，那还是一些企图回到前文化和非文化世界的诗人，那也是一些想要让诗歌仅仅在鲜活和被无数张嘴说滥了的口语层面上发生（发声）的诗人……他们似乎造就了一场以诗歌名义展开的青年运动：一连串的联络、串通，假想和实际的诗歌江湖，一些小恩怨，几次小狂欢……上海、北京、四川和江浙汇集了比较多的诗人，出现了"海上"、"圆明园"、"他们"、"非非"、"莽汉"、"大学生诗派"等等诗群名目，不久被统摄在了"第三代"的名下。秘密传阅集结着"朦胧诗"的《今天》杂志曾是这些诗人获罪的由头，回过头来，他们也编印了传达自己的诗歌主张、美学理想，直到价值观、人生观和世界观的地下刊物：《次生林》、《现代诗内部交流资料》、《汉诗》、《海上》、《大陆》、《他们》、《非非》……这些刊物常常被执法部门侦察和取谛，加之经费来源无非是几个同道诗人自己凑钱，所以总是不定期而且短命。

诗歌青年运动趋于迷乱和晕眩，其中几乎有红卫兵的狂热激情回光返照……这种诗歌行为的红卫兵症候，后来在不少当代诗人身上周期性、非周期性地发作，不知道是否因为中国大陆的当代诗歌，刚好就发生在红卫兵运动席卷神州大地的年代。但是连算是被官方半推半就地接受了的朦胧诗人，也还是难以正常发表作品和公开表达其思想观念，更年轻的诗人们则还要没机会。压抑带来的窒息感，不能不让诗人们时有夺（话语）权的冲动而欲爆发。

《深圳青年报》和《诗歌报》举办的"中国诗坛 1986 现代诗群大展"，为当时的诗歌运动提供了一个喷射的机会。它让人们检阅了现代诗"最空前的数量繁荣"、对红色诗歌和毛式语言的反叛，也让人看到了群情激昂的趋同写作行为里，真正意义上的诗歌文本的缺失，以及作为一种艺术方式的现代汉诗的失范和无序。退潮从高潮迭现处开始，那场诗歌青年运动，实际上，在 1986 年宣言纷飞的诗歌大展以后就告结束了。尽管，还是不断有诗人用写作去撩拨身体和语言，去挑衅，去颓废，去划开诗的皮肤作自残式的对抗。但当代诗人开始更自觉地从身体和语言出发写下诗篇，去抵及精神宇宙和大生命之魂。

1988 年，一种叫作《倾向》的自印诗刊创刊，到 1992 年，出版了 3 期即被迫停刊，而后，一种承接其倾向的《南方诗志》又出版了 5 期，到 1994 年再告停刊。《倾向》和《南方诗志》，以及跟它们倾向相近的《红旗》、《写作间》、《象罔》、《九十年代》、《发现》、《阿波里奈尔》、《北门》、《偏移》和《翼》等民间诗刊宣扬一种或数种人本主义而文本主义，现实主义而理想主义的现代汉诗，它们的出现，现在看来，是现代汉诗写作自觉的又一个信号，又一次表达了写作自律和汉语自律的那番渴意。这种自律的愿望，显然是针对那场诗歌青年运动里泛滥开来的非理性、破坏欲、低级粗俗平庸和随意到近乎随地大小便程度的胡乱渲泄做出的反应，但究其根本，则是来自现代汉诗的内在要求。

现代汉诗的发轫，可以追溯到近九十年前胡适的白话诗尝试，甚至更早时期一些诗人的设想和口号。作为尝试的白话诗后来有了诸多改观，又被称作新诗，渐渐自觉为用现代汉语写作的现代汉诗。这种新诗歌被一批受到西方文化影响的现代知识分子发明，其最初的立足点之一，是对中国古诗一般基础的反对。譬如它抵制古汉语，换用白话俗语和全新的现代汉语作为诗歌语言，因而报废了中国古典程式化的、格律严谨的诗式。所以，现代汉诗的写作，也跟上了岸的鲁宾逊似的，尽管贫乏，但却自由。背离了旧的诗歌大陆，现代汉诗是以所谓"自由诗"的样式开始其新生涯的，其情形，可以借用奥登在《论写作》里的一段话说明大概：

写"自由诗"就像荒岛上的鲁宾逊，必须自己煮食、洗衣、缝补。

偶尔在例外的情形之下，这种男子汉大丈夫的独立精神会产生与众不同

的杰作，可是大多数结果却是一团糟——床上的脏被单没有铺好，地板

没有打扫，满地是空瓶……

这使得许多人想到要给现代汉诗穿上一套制服，哪怕那其实是一副镣铐。这样，至少这位鲁宾逊在场面上不至于太过与众不同，会让人以为他一切有序，被照料或看管得很好，其实际生活的芜杂凌乱就算没有改正，也可以有所掩盖。近九十年的新诗歌历史上，就一再出现过寻求和规划新的统一诗式或现代格律的图谋和努力，然而，不幸（不妨说所幸），每一次都一败涂地。

这或许因为，背离旧诗歌大陆的现代汉诗尽管的确是一个鲁宾逊，但他的新领地却远远辽阔于他曾经以为的小小荒岛，就像现代汉诗的实际情况，这个鲁宾逊要做的，是从一个小小的荒岛那点面积开始拓展，直到把旧大陆改天换地翻为新大陆。在这么一个鲁宾逊的这种进程里，现代汉诗所用的语言值得打量。现代汉语作为不同于古汉语的另一种汉语，跟现代汉诗以反对古诗一般基础为立足点相一致，也跟古汉语呈一种反对的关系。古汉语是方言口语和外来语之外，现代汉语的又一大来源，但现代汉语对古汉语的承继，却多是以反向和对照的方式实现的。当古汉语已经充足圆满、固步不前、仅属于往昔，现代汉语却翻转过来，不要拘束、满含可能性、用未来追认着它的此刻。由这种语言成就的现代汉诗，自由度可谓相得益彰。当现代汉诗意识到自己的领地并非一座小小的荒岛，意识到自己是一位大陆上的鲁宾逊，其奋力迈开的步武、宽广的视野、深沉的思虑和归向远方的渴念，会更需要不拘诸如床上的被单、地上的空瓶这类小节的自由。现代汉诗拒斥那种制服般的格式和像镣铐一样给自己戴上的铁律，实在是本能和本性使然。

这却并没有使得现代汉诗相对容易，反而更多困难。现代汉诗跟任何语言任何样式的诗歌一样，试图远离散文，它的自由体和自由化不等于散文体和散文化，它诗歌的规定性恳求着现代汉语的节奏和音乐。现代汉诗与众不同的节奏和音乐是如此与众不同——它要使每一首诗是这首诗本身，每一首诗是由这首诗形成的那么一种诗——它最大限度地避免诗人声音的类似化和类型化。每写一首新诗就要走一程新路，来一次新历险，每一首新诗在语调、节拍、形式、结构、布局等方面，都是一次新的抵达。由于没有可以称之为"他律"的外在诗律，现代汉诗的写作更具挑战性和创造性，它需要诗的高度自律！——现代汉诗不仅是自由诗，也是自律诗，且主要是自律诗。现代汉诗这位鲁宾逊要有与众不同的杰作产生，就得与众不同地总是反躬自问和勤于收拾自己。这是否大陆上的鲁宾逊跟荒岛上的鲁宾逊的不同所在呢？

现代汉诗自律的可能性，由于诗人们渐渐成熟的对现代汉语的自觉和自主意识。这片大陆上的当代诗人已经为自己的语言卓有成效地去做的事情之一，就是缴械了文革语词暴力，消解了红色话语系统，颠覆了官方言说模式。汉语性或中文性，正是这种语言改正的内在依据。

就像现代汉诗是一种反对古诗的故意发明，现代汉语也是一种被有意识地自觉发明的语言，它既大量承继和借用了古汉语、方言口语和外来语，又近乎坚决地排斥着这三个方面的负面影响。现代汉语为反对古汉语而出生，其出身里却有着几乎全部的古汉语成份。然而，反叛的孩子终将父亲的骨血完全化为了自身的骨血，从父亲的容颜习性里挣脱出来，成为有着只属于自己的容颜习性和自我意识的另一个人。现代汉语也只能是相对于古汉语的另一种语言。这仿佛鲁宾逊，把来自旧大陆的那一套，在自己的领地里翻新为一个只属于鲁宾逊自我的国度。方言口语，跟古汉语之于现代汉语的情形正相似，只是关系更为直接和亲密，可说是现代汉语之母。但现代汉语这种被书写所总结和规范的成长中的语言，却毕竟不是方言口语了。中国当代诗人里某些热衷"口语化"写作的企图，近乎语言意识的"恋母情结"，其寄生感、依赖性和乱伦的可能，倒也并非不能转化为诗歌手段。现代汉语跟外来语的关系，则像是一种男女关系了。那除了是一种两情相悦，也还是一次次相互征服。现代汉语通过翻译得以成年，从翻译诗里，现代汉诗看见了自己的另一个自我，常常让有些人（从父母的角度？）对之产生无限焦虑、痛惜和恼怒，他们似乎以为，汉语为此损失了什么。可为什么并不对此作如是观？——那并非外来语对汉语的入侵，实为汉语出发去远征！再怎么着，翻译也是自汉语的楼台朝远方眺望……翻译给了现代汉语一种新的语言视野，为诗人提供了更多的语言想象和可能性。

在跟古汉语、方言口语和外来语的对话和对照中，现代汉语确立着自身。现代汉语之汉语性或中文性的依据，也要到这种对照和对话里寻找和发掘。当现代汉语被视为其自身，现代汉语的汉语性或中文性，也一定不在其自身之外。现代汉诗跟现代汉语的历史都极为短暂。它们差不多同时出生，而且在某种程度上，可说是相互为对方而生。现代汉语为现代汉诗提供了语言，现代汉诗歇力丰富着现代汉语。二者的另一共同点则是，现代汉语和现代汉诗都是在对未来的展望和想象里认定其自我的，它们也只有在未来的追认和回忆中真正成形和确立。无疑，现代汉语和现代汉诗正是出于现代性的必须而来到这块大陆上的，其自己为自己制定规范的现代性品质，正是题中应有之义。现代汉语的汉语性和中文性，也一样需要在现代性前提下考虑和体察。现代性内在于现代汉诗和作为其诗歌语言的现代汉语。

同样的，所谓现代汉诗的中国性，也一定具备着现代性品质，就像现代中国和当代中国的中国品质里，现代性如此这般鲜明触目。正是惯穿其中的现代性，使得现代汉诗的中国性也不能在其自身之外事先被定义，而惟有在发生和发展中呈示和显现，在未来之眼的回看里变得清晰和完整起来。这不免又让人想到了鲁滨逊——他的那个自我从他被抛的那一刻开始完全属于了自己，其自我的成长和成形，则跟他艰难踏上的那片未知的新岸密切相关。

作为一种写作的现实，当前的现代汉诗跟它身在其中的，且要在节奏音韵的字里行间充分呈示和幻化的当前中国相一致，都具有现代的、发展中的全部因素。现代汉诗这种现代的发展中诗歌，跟现实中国这个现代的发展中国家正相匹配，这或许正是现代汉诗之中国性的最大特点，这也是现代汉诗这一用现实中国的语言——现代汉语写作的诗歌，几乎不可能不具备现实的中国性的重要保证。

出于丰富、壮大和成熟自我的意愿，现代汉诗企图承继和发扬古老中国和古代汉诗的全部精华，正像为了同一目的，现代汉诗企图"拿来"域外文明及其诗歌的全部精华。应该注意到，现代汉诗承继、特别是发扬的企图里，正有着它反对甚至反动于旧中国和旧汉诗的出生和出身之因而必须与之争胜的信心。这使得现代汉诗在处理它跟古老中国的传统文明和古典诗歌的传统之美的关系时，无论如何都会将其自我和自主性放在首位。现代汉诗的中国性在这一侧面不会表现为它对古老中国和古典诗歌的盲目回归，而将表现为对它们有点儿戏剧化的辨析、解释、清算和重估。这依然取决于现代汉诗的语言和现实态度。

在现代汉诗的另一侧面，其中国性往往更引人注目。中国大陆当代诗歌跟政治的关系，几乎是譬如说谈论一个诗人的写作及其周边时回避不了的话题。这片大陆上的诗歌从来就是一种政治。遥远的不论，近代以来，国家命运跟诗的命运总是休戚相关，荣辱与共：公车上书、戊戌变法与诗界革命，辛亥革命、五四运动与新诗尝试，中华人民共和国的建立与红色诗歌的风行，文化大革命的发动与当代诗歌的发生⋯⋯诗歌主动地去做了政治气候的风向标和晴雨表，却也是被动地随政治语境的变动而改换自己的嗓音⋯⋯怎么看，诗歌都像是政治的附庸，这的确令人厌倦，对正在成熟起来，获得自主意识的当代诗人，则实在令他们感到厌恶。1980 年代的诗人们，无论诗歌青年运动中的诗人还是更注重诗的自律及生命和精神要素的诗人，都有意识地不让自己的诗歌写作关联政治，更不用说去呼应政治了。或返回自我，或远逸高翔，新的诗歌语言建立在外于政治的另一世界里。然而，外于政治依然是一种政治表态；并且，不止是个讽刺，1989 年那起骇人听闻的政治事件，竟成了对这种新语言和新诗歌的一项检验。

正当诗人们以为可以背向伪劣恶俗的政治而在诗歌写作里自成一统，达成美学自治的时候，六四事件又强行把诗歌纳入了政治的炼狱！在 1989 年，中国的政治和中国诗歌又一次合上了节拍：当政治生活来到一个冲突的顶点，诗歌也恰巧处在它周期性的转折点上。这使得 1980 年代张扬喧哗的中国当代诗歌版图变得不那么有动感了，变得简明和清净了。清醒过来的诗人们顺理成章地不再继续其梦中的事业了，因为，似乎，在无比丑陋的现实面前，至少诗人有理由怪罪诗歌——无论高贵和优雅的诗歌，"崇低"和"媚俗"的诗歌，语言实验室里的诗歌，宣扬和服务于随便哪一种意识形态的诗歌，反价值、反文化的诗歌，抒发古老情感、意欲回溯传统之源的诗歌⋯⋯它们为转型的时代和共同体存在的理由何在呢？而那些并没有淡出，继续写下去的诗人，实在是醒得更早，或始终保持清醒的诗人，他们打一开始就埋首专注于自己与众不同的个人化写作，并且"在坚定的个人写作里不把写作缩小为个人的"。他们知道，史蒂文斯所谓"诗是诗的主题"，意味着一首新诗，还得是在驳斥一般意义上的诗歌的基础上才告成立的诗，它是内倾的，不向诗歌之外寻求任何依靠，却要尽力让一切向心于诗。

1990 年代的诗人们从诗歌写作的炼金术里抬起头来重新打量眼前的现实，包括一向不愿意沾边的政治，既是"六四"震撼的直接反应，也是这块大陆上的当代诗歌写作行进到某一时刻的一种需要。并且，惟有出于诗歌写作本来的需要，这种打量和更深入的观察才会内化为一个诗人的经验和感想，才会带来诗歌写作的新意。其生长点，则刚好和只能是你先前的写作。这番打量并没有实质性地改变中国当代诗歌的语言追求和语言态度，只是，写作者的姿势有所不同了，或许写作者的姿势也并无不同，那位鲁宾逊仅仅改变了写作时身体的方向。于是，政治、现实、时代、日常生活里的杂质和历史图景里的乱象，这些朦胧诗之后的新诗人在其诗歌写作中有意避开，并不愿与之迎面相向的东西，再次需要诗人们透过诗歌将它们正视。要之，需要让诗歌跟它们建立一种不同于以往的看似反常，实则是更正常的关系。诗歌既不隔绝和回避它们，也不过于简单地介入它们——因为看似体现诗人主动性和承担意识的所谓"介入"，却常常令诗歌终于不过是譬如说政治事件里一个投反对票的小摆设，诗歌实际上弃其自主，不由自主地被非诗化，被消化了。现代汉诗就像现代汉语，不应该被容纳，而应该有一个可以容纳和消化杂质的健康的胃。基于此，1990 年代以来中国大陆的当代诗歌显得更为开阔、湍疾、相对和浑噩不洁那诗歌写作的漩涡中心，却留出了魅力无限的呼啸的空穴。真理和绝对悬而不论，诗歌写作不再急欲抵及和触摸它们——大陆上的鲁宾逊要让诗歌朝向无限，让世间万物在一首诗里翻江倒海……

显然，鲁滨孙的故事还得要讲完整。自某个群体的代言人返回个体自身依然不够，现代汉诗必须返回诗歌本身；返回诗歌本身也还不够，现代汉诗还得从它的汉语性、中国性和现代诗性出发，迈向追认和光大其过去和现在的那个未来。等到造好了大船，他终于要像另一个奥德修那样踏上返乡之旅，去找回和融入伟大和悠久。其途径并不确切惟一，其结局也不能预先设定，可以料到的，是他的命运里仍然少不了持续地漂泊。

陈东东

2005．12．上海

曹疏影

公海来信

（亲爱的，这是公海
我趴在灰蓝色的甲板上
风吹过深陷的膝窝
"谁都不属于"，我想
我摸自己的颧骨，摸到两块悬崖

买弄的民俗刚刚开始
我发现那些旅游拍照的人
是多么可恶，在沙滩上，纯洁的
晶体盐上。想到岛上的三千种植物
绝不雷同的叶腺，我就战栗
就更恨那些不知好的人
好像我从前不曾恨过他们

但我也不属于和他们相反的人
我游荡在公海。我不是谁的
那保存过我的一切的人
又改了主意——我发现寄居蟹
朝生晚死，白贝壳用一辈子
爱惜自己的珍珠，我又能爱惜什么
美酒一夜打翻，半滴，不留

这是公海，一个毫无规则的世界
阳光四处瞧着，汽油冲刷过的甲板
偶尔闪出小巧的彩虹，我趴在一处
安静的灰蓝色中，突然决定死心
记忆中的家，不过砌在砖头缝里
冬天一到，那楼就抖成根白骨。
事实上一年以前，我就开始频频梦想大海
那时，我还属于那种相反的人，抗着不顺从
抗着所有对峙的梦想

Cao Shuying

translations by Caroline Crumpacker and the author with Zhang Er

Letter from the Open Sea

(My dear, I'm lying
on a ship's blue deck
wind on my legs
touching the sharp cliffs of my cheekbones
and thinking I belong to no one.

The tourists begin their sad performance,
I hate the ones with cameras most of all.
The shining sand all nerves and motion,
I tremble at the life inside it,
despising the tourists for missing everything
yet wanting more.
As if for the first time, I despise them.

Not them, but not their enemy.
On the open sea, I belong to no one.
The one who cherished me changed her mind.
A soldier crab gives birth and then dies.
A white oyster guards a pearl
during her quick life. And what do I guard?
Good wine spilled out on a careless night, not a drop left . . .

The open sea has no limits.
The sun wanders freely over it.
The deck, just cleaned is soft with rainbows
and I am lying in its blue silence
and suddenly decide to give up hope.
Our home was the crack between bricks.
In winter it trembled like a frail bone.
A year ago I began dreaming of the ocean,
of defiance and escape, of fear and doubt.

现在，让她和他抗去吧
我到了公海，一个没有规则的
世界，谁都不是谁，谁都懒得
成为自己，一海的嗡嘤——
浪花上一片寂静）

亲爱的，我就是那个保存过你的人
现在，在砖头缝里给你写诗
未曾见过你信上的一切

粉蝶
　——纪念祖母

那个夏天落在一车阳光里
溅出沿途野菊，鼓着小腮帮
看我们远去

加大油门，没有谁
再提起她了，好风凭借碎石雨
我看见公路上游着骨灰的薄光

父亲抱着我的肩膀，指点我
辨认大豆的叶子，停车时
我摸到它们的眼泪，还很小

很硬，鼓在狭长的绿眼角里
成群的粉蝶拐弯抹角，也有一只
搂住草杆，尽量贴紧发抖的翅膀

哦，我认出了她的老年斑，这些
她咒骂过的斑点，我走近一步
她的脸就折叠着飞开了

父亲从玉米地里弯腰出来，已经
埋好了，他说，再过些日子

Now he and she have all of that.
I've come to the open sea, a world without limits
where no one is the one, and we are all too lazy
to come into ourselves. The ocean roars but there is silence
above the waves.)

My dear one, I cherished you.
I write this poem for you from the crack between bricks
and in response to all that I've only seen happen in your letter.

The White Butterfly
— for my grandmother

The summer emptied sunlight into our car.
Mother chrysanthemums lined the road,
puffing their cute red cheeks and blowing us along.

We drove quickly and no one spoke of her.
Gentle breezes and a spray of gravel.
A film of ash and bone along the highway.

Father touched my shoulders and
explained how to recognize soybean leaves
among the tall grasses. When we stopped the car,

I touched the tears still firm in their narrow green eyes.
Swarms of white butterflies circled above us.
One hugging a long green reed, gathered its translucent
    wings together.

Oh, I had recognized the age spots
she cursed so bitterly. When I came close to it
her face folded its translucent
features together and flew away.

会有粗根筑一座碉堡给她

回去的时候，也是野菊引路
一只兜风的金龟子在挡风玻璃上撞死
父亲抱着我，谁都不再提起她了

魔方

"我玩魔方呢！"
她拆开红色脚，
蓝色手，骨缝里的寒气
挤成一面黑

电视停电，她
没见过大海
布带鱼张望床头
爸妈垂着脑袋，算计着
一张床单
经得起多少次尿炕

合法中文，说一句
给一寸身高，她三十寸了
高糖低钙，钙
沉在脚脖子上，跑不动
游戏里，小学揪住她的辫子
她偷着在辫子外吃糖
糖也笑着，吃她，
从一粒小白牙开始，十三年后
吐出骨头

第二副身子，魔方做的
一天凸起一块，自己上色
六面都不和谐，六年
闷在土里煮，尾巴溜上云彩
大操场半空呆傻

Father walked out of a cornfield, "It is done."
he said, "Her grave will be a den of roots."

Going home, the mother chrysanthemums led us on,
and a beetle crashed into the windshield.
Father held me and neither of us spoke of her again.

The Magic Cube

"I'm playing the magic cube!"
She separates its red feet
from its blue hands.
Its chilly black skeleton
rising into a square black face.

Television. The power out.
Lack of travel. Lack of ocean.
A ribbon-fish doll stares at the bed.
Her mother and father, heads bent,
wondering if the sheets can stand another bed-wetting.

Standard Chinese. A sentence learned.
An inch gained. 4 feet tall.
Carbohydrate surplus. Calcium deficiency.
She can't run. Her ankles heavy.
The bullies pull her braids.
She fights back in secret with candy.
The smiling candy devours her.
Tooth by tooth, bone by bone.

Thirteen years later, another body
in the magic cube.
Squares the color of her days.
Six dissonant sides for her next six years
growing in the earth of her home, back to the sky.
The playground staring at her blankly.

"水！水！"她咬着土
爬出来，梦中浇水
把四肢粘成花园——前面的
冲前，后面的……

爸妈低头，在土里挖自己
一滩子孙泥，一滩
博士泥，其实什么都没有，其实
她用泥巴养目

红色脚，蓝色手，她抠净
嘴里的土，魔方厂破产
秋风刮倒一批春天
魔方碎成小日子，蹲在蛋糕里
搂着蜡烛睡觉。

我谈起——

我谈起那些浓橙色的黄昏——在我们
小小的金花园，你把我叫作
你的孩子。我忍不住去揪你的胡须
它们在春风里飘起小旗．时不时
还在我们过于繁茂的眼神里
添一个逗号。我躲过你的胡子
荡秋千——我谈起那些浓橙色的黄昏
——大人是孩子的玩具

现在我费力地谈起那些浓橙色的黄昏，甚至
还说起逆光的松花江，说起几年前
正在发育的小腿撑破鲜红的泳衣。你断断续续地
翻着书，希望在它自身的逻辑中
找到一页正常的清晨，好指给我看。
不用找了。我们不是正坐在黑夜吗
如果不够黑，就把头伸到水底
旋涡将指引我们，触碰那些疙疙瘩瘩的

"Water! Water!" she crawls out
of the earth, dirt around her mouth.
Dreaming of water on a garden
of arms and legs. Chest to the front, bottom to . . .

Her parents, heads bent,
clawing the earth.
Their pile of clay offspring.
Their pile of clay Ph.D.s.
None of it real.
Her spirit mired in the clay.

Red feet. Blue hands.
She digs herself out
with clay in her mouth.
The magic cube corporation dissolves.
An autumn wind blows away spring.
The magic cube scatters into small days
perched on birthday cakes
asleep with their candles.

Talking

I'm talking, again,
about our endless orange twilights —
loosing ourselves in our amber garden,
you calling me girl as I float into your beard.
Spring breezes punctuate the ravished language
in our eyes. I swim deeper in.
Rocking on the swings in the endless orange twilight.
A man becomes a girl's favorite toy.

Still I'm talking
about our endless orange twilights,
about sunset burning on the SongHua River,
my teenaged legs ripping a cherry red swimsuit.
Off and on. You leafing through a book

杂质，鱼食和白费的口水。

关于水，你知道的比我多。有的从天而降
有的在精致的茶杯里浸泡着南方。而我
只见过硬邦邦的灌木丛，没有朋友
粗糙地生在大坝上，只见过和耳朵
一起冻伤的脑壳．煮猪下水剩下的黑油。
你说粉嫩，我说倒了个儿的轮船
你说闻着挂花长大的黄鳝，我说漫街洪水中
逃荒的圆木盆——你说黄昏中我们做什么
我说那些浓橙色的黄昏

再一次，我谈起那些浓橙色的黄昏
（最后一次了，亲爱的）

拉线木偶

　1
她们一直跟着你，这么多年
在后面，飘于无形。
有一次我怀疑她们是女巫
花边裙悬地三寸，不见脚趾
后来，你跑到日记里
回了趟家，说在成都的大街上
看见几只小脚，没心没肺地
瞎溜达——逗点当年，真的
只是点缀么？

　2
有一次，我们情到深处
我瞧见有人在山那边眨眼
泪水在湖里闪光，你的后背
湿了，额头也飘起一场
发毛的小雨。一，二，三
一共三个．沉默地收着毛线——

for signs of dawn. To show me a theory of sunrise.
But isn't ours a darkness?
When it isn't dark enough, don't we stick our heads
deep under the cool water, into the whirlpools
of fishmeal and our wasted conversation.

You know the water.
Rain in your Southern city is tea steeped delicately in china cups.
But here, the shrubs are thirsty and friendless
along the white dams. Here is the dry cold and frostbitten
ears, the dark grease of pigs' guts left to rot in the sun.
You say pink and soft. I say steamships capsized.
You say sweet olive flavored eels.
I say wooden tubs evacuate in flood season.
You ask me what to do.
And I answer in our endless orange twilights.

Again, one last time, I'm talking
about our endless orange twilights.
(One last time, to you, love)

Marionettes

1.
For years they have followed you,
the three ephemeral moons behind your back.
I imagined they were witches, skirts
floating footless above the ground.
And when your diaries take you home,
you see their feet pausing along the streets
of Chengdu to display their useless beauty.

2.
Your back a thunderstorm,
Your eyes hidden behind mountains.
Tears shimmering a lake. Your forehead drizzling.
One two three. Three of them holding their breath

我想起你对待抽屉的习惯
总是塞进大半，却剩下一截
危险的尾巴——怎么？不舒服了，亲爱的？
为什么你的红毛衣越来越紧，为什么
你被裹得时时皱眉，露出
贼的面目？

3
是的，就在你背后——
她们同时升起三轮月亮，你眼皮下
坚定的影子就乱了，就害怕
还怕心里的嗡嗡声——，你买了好多橡皮
刷牙一样清除着多余的眼睛
和耳朵

　4
抱紧你，她们离我更近了
我可以足够精确地形容她们
——我说其中的一个最为亲切，每每
捧出水晶球般的食物，吹开热气
我看见一些路过的小餐馆
筷子委屈了，去敲对方的头
破烂的单身宿舍，亮着
危险的红灯，大白天拉上窗帘
谁的衣角丢了，挂在树枝上
哭呵，它光秃秃的——鱼刺
扎着小树叶的喉咙……还有一个
最美、长颈上的钢笔，全身写满
那喀索斯的小说——我知道
你仔细读过，字里行间到处是
湿淋淋的星斗，那些难为情的修辞
你一笑，它们就里出外进

　5
害怕我讲这些么？是的
她们就在你背后——你弯腰抱我

and pulling their strings closer and closer.
I remember the tails you left dangling
from dresser drawers, waiting to be pulled.

What's is it? Do you feel bad, darling?
Why is your red sweater so tight?
Why do you look so shifty?

3.
Three moons always there,
more faithful than your shadow.
You're scared, feeling them inside you.
You bought many erasers to rub out
their eyes and listening ears.

4.
When I hold you, they loom over me,
I see them perfectly. The plain one with a crystal ball
of steaming food. Through the steam
I see a roadstand, chopsticks clacking their heads together.
I see a girl's dorm and the cheap red lamp
threatening her curtains drawn against the sun.
I see the lost clothes belonging to . . . who?
Hanging ripped on the throat of a naked tree.
The most beautiful of the three has marks on her swan's neck.
The myth of Narcissus written all over her.
I know you've read her many times. Stars glow between the lines.
The embarrassing hyperbole of your smile.

5.
Do I scare you? Yes.
They are right behind you.
When you bend to embrace me,
three lights drop with you,
their faces shining fiercely.
When you dance with me,
they float beside us like heartbroken leaves.

她们就垂下五官端正的白炽灯
你摇着我跳舞，她们就飘起心酸的落叶
你更像她们的木偶——眼睛朝前
瞳孔却被拽了回去
——害怕我讲这些么，亲爱的
我们去照镜子……

You are their marionette, your eyes
drawn backwards even as you face me.
Do I scare you? Darling.
Now let's look in the mirror.

陈东东

点灯

把灯点到石头里去，让他们看看
海的姿态，让他们看看
古代的鱼
也应该让他们看看亮光
一盏高举在山上的灯

灯也该点到江水里去，让他们看看
活着的鱼，让他们看看
无声的海
也应该让他们看看落日
一只火鸟从树林腾起

点灯。当我用手去阻挡北风
当我站到了峡谷之间
我想他们会向我围拢
会来看我灯一样的
语言

外白渡桥
（《喜剧》第 5 章）

暧昧的建筑，凭空被造就
一座桥征服了断裂的梦
在两股浊流交汇的三角洲
在反向的漩涡般升起的城市
一座桥抖开钢铁的旧翅膀
要完成可疑和妄想的飞翔
它僵硬的姿势靠船头来

Chen Dongdong

translations by Joseph Donahue, Chen Dongbiao with Zhang Er

Light The Lamp

Shine the lamp into the stone.
Let them see the swirling print of the sea.
Let them see the primordial fish.
Let them see the light itself,
a lamp raised high on a mountain.

Shine the lamp into the river.
Let them see living fish. Let them see
More deeply into the silence of the water.
Also, show them what a sunset is like —
a firebird bursting from the forest.

While I fend off the north wind
with my hands, light the lamp.
While I stand between the canyons
let them crowd around me, let them see
my words are a lamp

Waibaidu Bridge

Held in air by emptiness
This bridge binds the severed dream
On the delta, where two currents enfold their froth
In a city spinning counterclockwise over the drain —
Old wings of steel and iron swing wide
The backbone straight, as if soaring off
Through the air were possible

— A hope only strengthened by
The passing ship with its own flurry of parts
But the sun like a flaming medallion throws shadows

抬高，它复杂的关节
支持着形象。而太阳却如同
滚烫的别针，把阴影文刺进
河流的皮肤。肮脏的
河流！里面是否有幻想的
鱼类？生殖之力被集中起来
鳞甲映射出时间的青光

霓虹用七彩维持着弧度
一对旧翅膀奋力在拍打
生锈的钢翼得病的肺叶
肺叶里贮存过怎样的烈火
如同袒露在风中的篇章
铁桥又会有怎样的疑问句
去贯串每一对死亡双行体

况且从云絮的俱乐部方向
从证券交易所打开的窗口
通过铁桥那弯曲的假诗意
那怪异的拱形和倾斜的透视
城市扩展它错误的胜景
漂浮的权力，循环的喷泉
热烈的少女和冷漠的

市政厅，以及折扇般
打开的乐园：这填实的涨滩
沧桑颠覆，跟阅历等高的
执拗的纪念碑如一截
脖梗（又一截脖梗，新的
倒高潮）——那空洞的头颅
甚至没有自虚无中长出

铁桥朝向宽一点的江面
江面给城市异质的繁忙
一艘红色巨轮在移动
在缓慢地膨胀，仿佛扩音器

That are words across the skin of the river
The quivering filth. Are there phantom
Fish within? Even here, births occur
The scales look slimy in the light of time

A neon light glows with seven colors
The old wings are waving as hard as they can
If the bridge were a bird it would have lung disease
What flame of what infection burns within its breathing
— Or perhaps the bridge is simply a question mark
As ancient, sacred texts blow away in a wind —
No one knows what to ask of death

From the clouds that look like exclusive clubs
From the open window of the stock exchange
Through elaborate analogies for the bridge
Its eerie ascent and unfolding view
The city lays out false and wonderful scenes
Floating power, circular fountains
Excitable girls, an indifferent

City Hall, and a folding-fan
Opens, and we see the shoals of paradise
Washed away. The only lasting monument
To the measure of our experience is
Our towering stubbornness. Each stiff-neck
Is higher up than the last. Even after decapitation
Our skulls are only empty, not even full of pure nothing

To one side of the bridge, the mirror of
The water widens, flows with the full sweep of city life
Meanwhile a large red cruise ship is approaching,
Looming, like a stack of amplifiers on a dark stage
Blotting out the notes of weaker musicians
— Cranking up the volume of an age
That just can't get any louder

压倒众乐队涣散的嘈杂
——把一个时代
放大到不能再放大的音量

殖民的次高音蔓延和稀释
海关把尖顶还给了伪古典
爱奥尼石柱间自行车滑出
——！自行车疾掠
逆于红色巨轮的方向
去攀爬提前到达的暝色
提前到达的世纪之暝色

是铁桥加强这突然的暝色
是铁桥的飞翔逼排和提升
当逆行的自行车此岸到
空中，当自行车陷阵于
放大的死寂，黑暗挤压进
打开的身体，黑暗塑造了
骑车人一颗孤悬的心

铁桥的旧翅膀奋力拍打
它要把飞翔延伸进夜
生锈的钢翼
　　　　　　　得病的肺叶
——是怎样的火焰以
华灯的方式大面积降临
比黑暗的统治还要彻底

比黑暗的统治还要彻底
灯光广泛地整形和易容
一种弧度得到了确证
一枚亡灵被重新锻炼
——在甚于白昼的刺痛的
视域，倒影是死的嘴脸
抛出的终得以收回

The arias of some alto dissolve into the air
Above the Customs House, with its tacky rooftop
And fake classical style as, between Ionic pillars,
A bicycle slips free. The bicycle sweeps fast
Away from the large red cruise ship
Uphill into a dusk arriving ahead of time

The dusk of the whole century arriving ahead of time
This sudden dark seems called to be
By the iron bridge, seems sharpened in
Our sight by the decree of the iron bridge
When, from this bank and into the air

The disappearing bicycle is lost in
The amplified deathly stillness
Breathing sucks darkness into the body
Darkness fills the heart of the cyclist
Suspended in his solitude

Up down the joints of the bridge strain
Iron wings have rusted that would fly away
Into the night, are creaking
                    diseased lungs
What splendid flame
— city lights falling across a large field —
Is more real than the reign of the dark
More real than the reign of the dark

Than the face of the dark to which the lights
Lend a kind of radiance, verified only
When a fleck of dead soul is burned anew
This hurts the eyes even more than daylight
Than day, the true face of death
All that is worthless is free to drown

The hinges of the bridge rise and fall
What flight there is tumbles onto the other bank
The bridge is the reach of the city into space

铁桥的旧翅膀奋力拍打
飞翔沉重地落到了彼岸
这探身出空间的城市触手
以鸟儿的失败连缀了世纪
去贯串每一条再生之路
但庞杂的架构令它多暧昧
妄想的力量，更托举起它

外滩

花园变迁。斑烂的虎皮被人造革
替换。它有如一座移动码头
别过看惯了江流的脸
水泥是想象的石头；而石头以植物自命
从马路一侧，它漂离堤坝到达另一侧

不变的或许是外白渡桥
是铁桥下那道分界水线
鸥鸟在边境拍打翅膀，想要弄清
这浑浊的阴影是来自吴淞口初升的
太阳，还是来自可能的鱼腹

城市三角洲迅速泛白
真正的石头长成了纪念塔。塔前
喷泉边，青铜塑像的四副面容
朝着四个确定的方向，罗盘在上空
像不明飞行物指示每一个方向之晕眩

于是一记钟点敲响。水光倒映
云霓聚合到海关金顶
从桥上下来的双层大巴士
避开瞬间夺目的暗夜
在银行大厦的玻璃光芒里缓缓刹住车

The centuries are linked by it's failure to soar
If only over the route of every rebirth . . .
Eerie span: so much iron held in the air
By the sheer force of our delirium.

The Bund[*]

The garden turns. (Flashing tiger skin
Had been replaced by naugehyde.) Like a floating pier
It turns away from a too familiar riverbank.
Now concrete seems to be rock; rock believes itself to be flora
Drifting beneath the dike, from one side of the street to the other.

Only the Waibaidu Bridge resists the change
Only the divided water below all that iron
And the gulls hovering in the air above the border
Posing a question: is this muddy shadow
From the sun rising at the Wusong Port,
Or from a dawn bright as the belly of a fish?

The city delta quickly turns white.
Actual rock rises up into the monumental tower.
Between the tower and the fountain, a bronze statue,
Four faces peering north, south, east and west, a compass in the air
Revealing, like a UFO, the dizziness of each direction.

On the hour, a bell. The bright water shines,
And the gold dome of the Customs Office soaked in mist.
The big double-decker bus coming down from the bridge
Turns away from the instant dazzle of a dark night,
Slows to a stop before the glassy splendor of a high-rise bank.

─────────────────────

[*] The colonial name of an embankment and port in Shanghai along Huangpu
River, where in the 1920s and 1930s overnight prosperity brought corruption and
what was seen as a decadent life style.

低岸

黑河黑到了顶点。罗盘迟疑中上升
被夜色继承的锥体暮星像一个
导航员，纠正指针的霓虹灯偏向
——它光芒锐利的语言又借助风
刺伤堤坝上阅读的瞳仁

书页翻过了缓慢的幽暝，现在正展示
沿河街景过量的那一章
从高于海拔和坝下街巷的涨潮水平面
从更高处——四川路桥巅的弧光灯晕圈
——城市的措词和建筑物滑落，堆向

两岸——因眼睛的迷惑而纷繁、神经质
有如缠绕的欧化句式，复杂的语法
沦陷了表达。在错乱中，一艘运粪船
驰出桥拱，它逼开的寂静和倒影水流
将席卷喧哗和一座炼狱朝河心回涌

观望则由于厌倦，更厌倦：观望即沦陷
视野在沥青坡道上倾斜，或者越过
渐凉的栏杆。而在栏杆和坡道尽头
仓库的教堂门廊之下，行人伫立，点烟
深吸，支气管呛进了黑河忧郁物

窗龛

现在只不过有一个窗龛
孤悬于假设的孔雀蓝天际
张嘴去衔住空无的楼头还难以
想象——还显露不了
建筑师骇人的风格之虎豹

42

Low Bank

The river is black. So black, the compass wavers.
And the cone-shaped evening star, a gift to the twilight,
is like a navigator correcting for the glowing directional arrow —
The piercing words of starlight, riding the wind once again,
wound the eyes, even of those reading along the dike.

Book pages turn over in the slow-moving gloom.
A chapter opens, a crowded street along the river.
From the flowing water, from the streets under the dike,
from a higher spot: the halo of lights atop the Szechwan Road Bridge.
Buildings and idioms slide down into a pile

along both banks. The pages are dense and many.
They seem written by a neurotic. The eyes panic in
the tangles of sentences. The Europeanized grammar
wrecks the expression. In the mayhem, a freight ship
hauling human waste slips out under the bridge.
Perhaps its closing wake will sweep away
the noise, the vulgarity, this whole purgatory,
in a rush back into the depth of the river.

For those out for a walk, it's crushing to
Have to look at. Especially when a gaze tends towards the asphalt hill
or drifts back across the now cool railing. And where
the railing and the slope end, by the warehouse
once a great cathedral, a pedestrian stops, lights up a cigar,
and sucks depression like a black river into his lungs.

At the Window

All that seems possible now is
A window and a lonely horizon as blue
as a peacock. In it's mouth a hollow pavilion.
It's hard to pick out, lacking, as it does,

但已经能推测：你透过窗龛
看见自己，笨拙地骑在
翼指龙背上，你企图冲锋般
隐没进映现大湖的玻璃镜？也许
只不过，你刚好坐到梳妆台边上
颈窝里倦曲着猫形睡意

那么又一次透过窗龛
你能够看见一堆锦绣，内衣裤
凌乱，一头母狮无聊地偃仰
如果幽深处门扉正掀动
显露更加幽深的后花园，你就能

预料，你就能虚拟：你怎样
从一座鱼形池塘的肤浅反光里
猜出最为幽深的映象———一个
窗龛如一个倒影，它的乌有
被孔雀蓝天际的不存在衬托
像幻想回忆录，正在被幻想

语言跟世界的较量不过是
跟自己较量——窗龛的超现实
现在也已经是你的现实。黄昏天
到来，移走下午茶。一群蝙蝠
返回梳妆镜晦黯的照耀。而

你，求证：建筑师野外作业的
身影，会拉长凝视的落日眼光
你是否看见你俯瞰着自己
——不再透过，但持久地探出
窗龛以外是词的蛮荒，夜之
狼群，要混同白日梦

The lions and tigers of
A dreadful architectural style.

At least, through the window, you
Can see yourself, clumsy, clinging to the back
Of a pteradactyl, soaring as you struggle to plunge
Into a glass mirror that reflects a big lake.
Or else, you just sit on the edge of a dresser
With a sleepy cat around your neck

As again, through the window —
A beautiful brocade in a heap, underwear
Flung around, a lioness wearily laying on her back.
If in the depths a door is opening
To a garden, more secluded, deep in the back,

You can either predict, or make things up:
The image on the glass of a shallow fish-shaped pond
Is the most serene and deepened visions —
But a window is the reverse of a reflection.
Its nothingness balances the emptiness
Of the peacock blue horizon
Like an imaginary memoir in the act of being imagined.

Language does not fight against the world,
Only itself. Your surreal niche by the window
Is all you can claim for real. Evening
Approaches. Take away the tea tray. Bats flicker
In the gloomy illumination of your dresser mirror.

You make out the silhouette of an architect
As he does his work. He will lengthen the light
Of sunset. Now do you see yourself overlooking yourself?
— Not just through, but stretched out for good.
Outside: a ferocious wilderness of words. The night
Sends wolves to mingle with your daydreams.

咏叹前的叙述调

码头高出岸线一小截
推自行车去赶渡船的邮递员
要稍稍拎一下生锈的把手
这表明春江听从了季节律令
浊流上涨，繁忙像汽笛
噪音解散着烟尘那滚滚的
黑制服编队。接着是轻微却已经
明显夸大的坡度，一直到江心
好让自行车性急如大猎犬
向下疾冲……邮递员跟上
一路小跑，他的形象
十年后又一次没入船舱油污的
晦暗，已变幻成一个
黝黑的支局长，跨坐着摩托
如骑上了常遭罚款的命运虎
过江是他的一次暂歇。渡轮贴上
对面码头橡皮胎护沿时一阵
轻颤。他赶紧又启动
他刚刚眯缝眼看到的那叶
柔软的船帆，也赶紧化作他塑料
头盔上摇摆的翅膀，追随疾驰
犹豫地掀动……景象在
加速度后面合拢，立即就成了
过去笼罩的石头废墟，而迎面
更朝他扑来的道路，则是他
十年前投递的挂号预约函

Recitative Before the Aria

The dock is higher than the shore
To catch the ferry, a mailman pushes his bicycle
He pulls up gently on the rusty handles
The river is in compliance with the spring
Currents swirl, dirty. In the commotion,
A boat whistle offers a break from soot billowing
In the shape of a black uniform. Next comes
A short steep drop towards the river.
The bicycle, like a dog on a hunt,
Lunges downhill. The mailman dashes
After, pulled along, whose image
After ten years once again disappears
Into a cabin's greasy gloom, where he turns
Into a dark-skinned Division Director
Straddling a motorbike, a tiger
Of destiny he rides and often gets fined.
Crossing this river, he can catch his breath.
Until the bow whacks the rubber bumper on the far shore.
The whole boat quivers. He's quick on the kick-start.
That leaf-soft sail visible, moments ago, through his half-closed eyes
Is in a flash the wings on his plastic helmet
Hesitant, trembling, speeding in pursuit . . .
Scenery blurs. He guns the bike.
His acceleration makes of all that flies by
The broken stones of the past.
And the road rushing before his face
Is a registered letter he delivered
Once, ten years ago

韩博

一个下午的自我修改

必须承受客观的落木
作为前提，森林公园再次迎来了
自娱的深秋
必须接纳，一片落木
在无边的呼啸中看到了来世

懒散的翻阅者
无意开启踌躇的落木
他期待一场更迟的到来
一次更加无助的疏离
芬芳尸体上的第一场雪

必须承受
势不可挡的到来，放弃表达
一座接纳无边落木的宫殿
包容了无边的死亡，秋天的
最后一片秩序

向树木的遭遇学习语言
我拣到了足够的，偏离的词
绿色的革命，清秀的落日
你必须学会接纳
大气中漫无目的的牺牲

革命音乐的叙事

带毒的字眼情意绵绵
又一个深秋，风吹雨打，主人公落了一地

Han Bo

translations by Jason Pym and Mark Wallace

An Afternoon of Self Assessment

One has to accept the fact that the leaves
Fall in a world you can't influence, the forest park
Again finds late autumn amusing itself.
One has to admit a falling leaf
Echoes its next life in the scream of its descent

The lazy browser
Doesn't want to notice the drifting leaf
He expects a later arrival
A more vulnerable alienation
The first snow covering fragrant corpses

One has to accept
The arrival that no power can stop, abandon explanation.
A palace of endless falling leaves
Contains a death one can't understand,
Autumn's last sequence.

In the trees' confrontation, one studies what it means to speak.
I've plucked enough deviating words,
The green health of revolutions, delicate setting suns.
One has to master acceptance
Of the purposeless sacrifice in the air

The Story of Revolution's Song

Constant poisoned words of official approval
Another late autumn, wind and rain,
the protagonists drift to the ground

把吟咏剥开
让青年虚弱，昏迷，梦见胜利
黄海上空的青年
只是在摸索
光

企望铸成喻世者
粉饰一帧早年的插图
青年心力交瘁
那警世书的
第一句

黄海之上，万米高空，斗争早已离题万里
机舱里，青年被交还子宫
中止了，杜撰的斗志
刹住了，降落带来阵阵委屈的啜泣

公共汽车·两姐妹

年长的一个，锯下
他的双腿。年幼的那个
把他装进麻袋
堆上阳台。看上去
他只是积雪中的一袋杂物

圆脸的一个，叉开双腿
像鸟儿张开翅膀。长脸的那个
栖落在座位上，左腿
压住右腿。她们的裙子冬夏两用
短得好似春光

年长的一个，捏着杯子
品味断腿中的收获
虽然不多，总算

Peel away the eulogies
Let youth be weak, in a stupor, dreaming of victory
Above the Yellow Sea
Youth merely fumbling
For the light

Longing to cast an image of the fabulist
Whitewash a picture of childhood
Youth is exhausted
The first sentence
In that book of didactic tales

Above the yellow sea, 10,000 meters in the air
The denunciation digressed long ago
Youth has been put back in the womb
Suspended in the passenger cabin
A contrived will to fight
Stopped short, the descent brings
the spasmodic sob of those who feel wronged

A Bus : Two Sisters

The older one, she sawed up
His legs. The younger
Stuffed him into a burlap bag
Piled on the porch. In the snow drift
He looked like a sack of odds and ends.

The round-faced one opened her legs
Like a bird spreading its wings. The long-faced one
Perched on the seat, left leg
Pressing down the right. Their all-season skirts
Hung short as the joys of spring.

The older one, pinching a wine glass,
Savors the harvest of severed legs
Though it's not much money all things considered.

能把酒杯斟满
还可以切上几片香肠和咸肉

圆脸的一个，打量着邻座
他可能是位谢顶的上帝，在后半夜
降临。他说，要有光，她就有了
假发、皮靴、手袋、香水、内衣
和尽情聊天的移动电话

年幼的那个，也学着
把自己斟满，好像一截雨水淋透的松木
躺在菊花衰败的锯木厂
她爱上了满口粗话的劳动模范
下班之前，他把奖金塞进袜子

长脸的那个，今天很累
车厢里没有她的上帝
她想休息，去买本杂志
再给妈妈打个电话，就说
一位副教授向我求婚，我很犹豫

年长的一个，只想多飞一会儿
蒸馏酒的翅膀
刚刚张开。年幼的那个
还想插上红酒的羽毛，逗留在
客人拥挤的低矮天空

圆脸的一个，是位贫困的
天使，出差人间的隆冬
也要赤裸双腿。长脸的那个
还要献出肚脐，为了观察和微笑
为了陈列福音的样品

年长的一个，听到车轮
在窗外，碾过新雪
就像……二十年前，那个

Still, now she can pour a full glass
And cut a few slices of sausage and bacon.

The round-faced one looks at the chair beside her.
Probably she'll get a balding god, arriving
In the deep night. He'll say "Let there be light" and there will:
A wig, underwear, perfume, a handbag and leather shoes,
And a cell phone she talks on as much as she wants.

The younger one is also learning
To pour herself full, like rain-drenched pine
Lying in a decaying saw-mill, surrounded by chrysanthemums.
She fell for a foul-mouthed employee-of-the-month.
After he gets off work, he hides his bonus in a sock.

The long-faced one, today she's tired
Her god isn't on the bus.
She wants to rest, buys a magazine,
Phones her mother again, says
An assistant professor proposed to me, I don't know what to do.

The long-faced one only wants to fly longer,
Wings of distilled liquor
Just spread. The younger one still wants
to make a gown of red wine, to loiter
where single guys crowd under darkening skies.

The round-faced one, an impoverished
Angel in mid-winter on a business trip to the world of men
Insists on baring her legs. The long-faced one
Wants to display her navel, wants to watch others and smile
As she shows off her bounty.

The older one hears tires,
Outside the window, crush the fresh snow
Just like . . . Twenty years ago, that night
When she only wanted to phone,
Only wanted a night when her waist wasn't cold.

只想打一个电话的夜晚
只想，不让肚脐着凉的夜晚

长脸的那个，似乎看到
北风挟着钢锯，为车窗
撒下一抹暗白的锯屑
公路起伏，生意清淡
晚景……不过就在杯中

年幼的那个，当然相信
上帝，以及貌似上帝，或与上帝
年纪相仿的夜半乘客
藏在袜底的奖金，逃不过
战胜了爱情的明眸

圆脸的一个，跨过杂物
的时候，差点摔倒，突然的刹车
接着是打滑，翻车，滚下公路
她坚持站着，想象着
一只鸟儿，怎样乔装成锯屑

未成年人禁止入内

拉着一只液态的手，游荡。
海水不知道我也是海水
它用裸体推着我的裸体
企图把我冲上海滩。

我从一个自己
游荡向另一个，我拉着
自己的手。我没有忘记液态的路
绕过暗礁，从上海，去内蒙古。

我在海滩上搁浅。海浪扑上来
扇我的耳光，就像要掐灭一只水底的

The long-faced one looks like she sees
The north wind grasping a hacksaw, scattering
Dirty-white sawdust beneath the window.
The road undulates, business is slack
In the twilight years . . . But there's comfort in wine.

The younger one of course believes
In her god and those who look like him,
Midnight passengers just his age.
Money in a sock will never escape
The bright eyes of one who has conquered love.

The round-faced one almost falls when she steps
over some junk in the aisle. A car suddenly brakes,
Then skids and overturns, rolls beside the road.
She stands persistently, imagining
A bird; how can it disguise itself as sawdust?

No Entry for Minors

Clasping a liquid hand, drifting.
The sea water doesn't know I'm sea water too
Its nakedness pushing my nakedness
Trying to wash me up on shore.

I drift from one self
Into another, I clasp
My own hand. I haven't forgotten the liquid path
That winds around a submerged reef
From Shanghai to Inner Mongolia.

I'm stranded on the beach. Waves break
Lapping at my face, as if to extinguish a candle
Beneath the water. The beach seems too young.
I remember an unmarked fork in the road.

Red tide. I hear a man and woman
Take off swimsuits in the rented tent,

蜡烛。这是一片猝不及防的
海滩，记忆中未曾标出的岔路。

赤潮。我听见，在租用的帐篷里
脱去泳装的男女，用眼神
交换观点。你更臃肿了。是啊
你也老了。年轻的时候也见不到赤潮。

你发现推土机了吗，还有民工
扛着铁锹，朝海滩上走来。
他们赶来清洁浴场？
你还是那么天真，仔细瞧瞧

他们在为铁锹安装胶卷
推土机每抓一把海藻，就把镜头
推向我们。别忘了还有头顶的风筝
它专门钉在天空上，一动不动。

从沙堆奔向海浪
赤裸的男孩，牵着风筝游荡。
他的话儿在海风中睡着了
像手中的风筝，骑在半空不上不下。

一篇观察作文绊倒了他
男孩摔了一跤，呛了几口海水。大海
这个题材太大，太庞杂，连塑料袋
被风吹起，也算个主题。

他的妈妈向我兜售玉米，怀里揣着一则
晚报的征文启事。她看不见我
但她坚持对我朗诵：起风了
是啊，风，有几个人能骑上风啊。

海风被车轮剪成碎片，一辆二八自行车
闯进作文的草稿。年轻的她抱住他

Imagine how they stare at each other
And notice they've each grown different.
You're fatter. Yes, and you're older.
When I was young, the tide was never red.

Did you see that bulldozer? And the laborers
Shouldering spades, walking up the beach?
Are they hurrying to clear the bathing area?
You're still so naive. Watch carefully —

They load their spades with film.
With every bulldozed pile of kelp, the camera lens
pushes closer toward us. Don't forget the kite above your head.
Completely motionless. It's nailed to the sky for a purpose.

Running toward the waves from the dunes,
A naked boy clasps the string of a drifting kite.
His manhood sleeps in the sea breeze
Like the kite in his hand, rides the air suspended.

A descriptive essay tripped him. The boy fell,
Choking on mouthfuls of seawater. The sea
Theme is too broad, too cumbersome, even a plastic bag
Blown by the wind becomes a motif.

His mother tried to sell me corn, in her pocket she held
An announcement from the evening paper
soliciting articles. She couldn't see me
But repeatedly said it was getting windy
Yes, the wind. Few people can ride it, you know.

The sea breeze was cut to shreds by the wheels, a bike with 28 inch tires
Charging into the essay's first draft. Youthful, she grasps
His young waist. Sitting behind him, she cries out
As he rushes into the sea, at his attentions
bestowed before the gathering darkness.

In the sea water, drifting, he clasps her hand.
He points to the kelp on his head. This part

年轻的腰，在后座尖叫，任凭他
冲进大海，任凭他事先准备好了夜幕。

海水中，他拉着她的手游荡。
他把头顶的海藻指给她看，这一段
可以写：游夜泳的人，几乎
不能探出头来呼吸。

沙子也不错，她还是把头探了出来
身体钻进另一个好题材。她事先准备的
是正午的背景：他的手指捧着沙子
模仿沙漏，向她的身上堆积最浪漫的事。

沙子拉着我的手，游荡
沙子不知道我不是沙子。但是，我
已经陷入了海滩的立意，被海风推着
拉着沙子的手，谋篇布局。

出去吧，别总呆在帐篷里，我想
下水，该洗个澡了。不，我要
把你埋起来，让沙子
掩盖你的隐私，然后一起去吃海鲜。

不，我不吃，去年，也是在这儿
我吃了生蚝，差点回不了家
这一带的海滩上，到处都是蜷曲的
海藻、橡胶、肥皂泡沫，还有那些墨绿的

永远也无法投胎的孩子！
妈妈，风筝栽下来啦！它已经
在天上站了很久，一定很累
就让它回到地上吧，我给它修一座城堡。

年轻的她帮他掘开一条年轻的
护城河。我溜过她冰凉的

I can describe: the night swimmers are barely able
To raise their heads to breathe.

The sand is also good. She raises her head and squeezes her body
into another bold motif. The first thing she prepares
Is the midday background: His fingers hold the sand,
the grains drain through, and he heaps upon her
these most romantic treasures.

The sand clasps my hand, drifting.
The sand doesn't know I'm not sand. I have already sunk
Into the concept of the beach. Pushed by the sea breeze
That clasps the hand of sand, I plot more of the piece.

Let's go out, don't stay in the tent all day, I want
To go in the water, we should wash. No, I want
To bury you, let the sand cover your intimate secrets
then go and eat seafood together.

No, I don't want to eat seafood. Last year I ate oysters
Right here. I almost couldn't get home.
Coils of rubber, kelp, soap bubbles
Cover this stretch of beach, along with greenish black stuff

From a child who will never be born.
Mother, the kite has come down! It's already
Been in the sky too long, it's certainly tired.
We should let it come to earth; I'll make a castle for it.

Youthful, she helps him dig a youthful
City moat. I have slid in the ice-cold gap
Between her toes, clasping sand, drifted in her
Palace chamber, sometimes open.
His youthful hand weaves

A wreath of kelp. He resolves to overcome the boy
Whose manhood drips, and in her name, construct
The grandest castle, moat and monument on the beach,
Including a mausoleum for this underwater emperor.

脚趾缝，拉着沙子，在她那时开时合的
宫殿间游荡。他年轻的手编织出

海藻的花环，他决心超过话儿滴水的
男孩，以她的名义，修建海滩上
最为宏大的城池和纪念碑，甚至包括
一座水下假想的陵寝。

海浪扑倒在我的背上，掰开
我拉着沙子的手。卖光了玉米的
妈妈，掰开男孩抓着沙子的手
她用报纸扇他的耳光：

涨潮啦，你还在贪玩！
人活一世，草木一秋
有几个人能有机会，恰好骑上
膨胀的大海，啊？

死神拉着孩子的手，游荡。
妈妈拉着男孩的手，向防鲨网
奋力游去。别怕，把身体当成一只风筝
细心观察自己的感受，当你下沉时。

拉着一只液态的手，风筝
向海底的我游荡。我骑在液态的
自行车上，绕过已经发生的事，为他送来
在海浪中坍塌的素材。

海底沉积着另一片海滩。不曾降生的人
在字里行间提到了来世：那是
一段幽闭的水路，岸上只有空气
浸泡着迟迟的时间，他并不知道

你也是她的他。他拉着她的手
和他摊开地图——你从未去过内蒙古

The waves lap at my back, pull away
My hand that clasps sand. The mother, who has sold
All her corn, grabs the boy's hand that clutches the sand.
She boxes his ears with the evening paper:

The tide is rising and you're still playing!
People only live once, the grass and trees die every fall.
Few get a chance, are lucky enough to ride
The swelling ocean, right?

Death clasps the hand of the child, drifting.
The mother clasps the boy's hand, straining to swim
Towards the shark nets. Don't be afraid, use your body as a kite.
When you sink, carefully watch your own feelings.

Clasping a liquid hand, the kite drifts
Towards me as I lie on the sea bed. I ride the liquid
Bicycle, skirting things that have already happened, bringing him
The source material collapsed in the waves.

On the sea bed, another beach accumulates. No man was ever born
Who mentioned his next life between the lines: that's
A dark stretch of waterway, and on the bank, only air
Soaks up the slow time. He doesn't know

That you are also her, and him. He clasps her hand
And spreads out a map — You've never been to Inner Mongolia.
The road sign dissolves at the fork in the road, your last drop
Of liquid inspiration hits the surface of the sea.

I turn towards a place it's not worth going.
The sea water discovers I'm also sea water
Its nakedness pushes me to digress. I am clasped
By a liquid hand, drifting.

路标在岔路溶化，你最后一滴
液态的灵感，跨过海面，滴进了另一滴。

我拐向一个不值一去的
地方。海水发现我也是海水
它用裸体推我离题。我
被一只液态的手拉着，游荡。

乡间腾空术

他们说，你接触了大地
也算是，临时地，摸到了事物的根

搂抱着鸡鸭猪狗，你摆脱空气
下沉到山区的土路

但是只有三天，万物的根继续向下
你追不上那些神经质的根须

空气纠缠你肿胀的脚，刚刚三天
背包里的石头又变成气球

他们说，最终，你背离了大地
仅仅三天，天空好像不是吸尘器

牡丹江

雪意出发，火车进站

导演同意如许开场
镜头梦见她骑着乌云
还乡，少小抚琴的手指
此刻，勒紧乌云项上的缰绳
乌云又被另一个镜头梦作

Dropped into Wilderness

They say, for a moment you've touched mother earth
For a moment touched the root of things

Embracing chicken, duck pig dog, you shrug off the air
That's sunk into the mountain track

It only lasts three days, the root of everything keeps going down
You can't catch up with the nervous shoots

Air tangles your swollen feet, three days all gone
The stones in your rucksack feel again like balloons

They say, in the end, you abandon mother earth
For three short days the sky wasn't a vacuum

Mudanjiang City

Snow began to fall, the train entered the station

The director agreed it should begin this way
The lens dreams that she rides a dark cloud
Back to her home town, her young musician's fingers
fastening reins on the cloud.
Another lens dreams that the dark cloud
Is steam, the drunk locomotive
Plunges the derailed rider into the harbor
In the steamy bath house; she dreams that the lens
Arranges a surprising abyss just for her

She awakes, discovers
The world enshrouded in steam

Cut to a scene of swimming in winter
The director hopes the river will show
In her dreams, then change into the corner of a bathhouse,

蒸汽，醉酒的火车头
冲入骑手脱轨的港湾
在蒸汽浴室，她梦见镜头
为她安排的竟是深渊

她醒了，她发现
世界上到处都是蒸汽

一个冬泳式的过渡
导演渴望，江水也能被她
梦见，化作浴池一隅
雪花也为蒸汽写意
镜头使她并紧两腿，她立在
跨江的公路桥上，看着
少小的她，跟着爸爸
跃入冰水里幽黑的清晨

北风吹送，丫头还乡

三天两宿，火车帮她
重新找回了黑夜，她枕着
雪地上空的黑暗
还到梦乡，她梦见葱白
而不是红肿的手指，萦绕在
键盘间吟弄，"直把香港作
南极，日日白夜无尽头"

……
白夜，那位诗人
她被唤醒，那些诗句

导演为她寄来一封
情书，她无法忆起
歪扭的字迹，出自哪一位
温水和泡沫环绕的诗人
她只能用手指回忆

The snowflakes just like steam.
The lens makes her stand up straight
On the road going over the river, watching
Her younger self as her father
Leaps into the dark morning, soaked in the icy water

The north wind blows, the girl returns home

Three days later, the train helps her
Find the night all over again, she rests her head
On the darkness above the snowy ground.
Back in dreamland, she dreams that her red fingers,
Delicate and no longer swollen, linger
On the piano keys, playing "Even Hong Kong
Can be like the South Pole, day after day
Of sunlit nights without end"

. . .

Sunlit nights, she is awoken by
The poet, those lines of poetry
The director sends her
A love letter, she has no way to recall
Whose crooked handwriting she's reading,
Which poet surrounded by warm water and foam
Sent it to her.
She can only use her fingers to remember
Their bodies, maybe
Now and then she lets the verse
Flow all the way through her

But maybe the letter was really a durian
That arrived with her on the same train,
Juice and smell dried out by the journey

那些器官，也许
偶尔一次，她允许诗句
流淌进自己的身体

也许，那不过是一只榴莲
与她同车到达，汁液
与气味，早已被旅途抽干

韩东

有关大雁塔

有关大雁塔
我们又能知道些什么？
有很多人从远方赶来
为了爬上去
做一次英雄
也有的还来做第二次
或者更多
那些不得意的人们
那些发福的人们
统统爬上去
做一次英雄
然后下来
走进这条大街
转眼不见了
也有有种的往下跳
在台阶上开一朵红花
那就真的成了英雄——
当代英雄

有关大雁塔
我们又能知道什么？
我们爬上去
看看四周的风景
然后再下来

你的手

你的手搭在我的身上
安心睡去
我因此而无法入睡

68

Han Dong

translations by Donald Revell and Zhang Er

About Da Yan Pagoda

About Da Yan Pagoda
What more to know?
The people come far
To climb it, to be
Heroes for once, or even a second time
Some of them, or perhaps more.
The unhappy ones, and also ones
Ample in the flesh of their leisure.
These, whole gangs of them, climb together,
Becoming heroes for once,
And then climb down,
Disappearing instantly almost
Into the streets and crowds below.
There are also those, a very few,
The seed people who, leaping from the stairs,
Burst into scarlet flowers.
These are the true heroes, yes,
Heroes for our time.

Of Da Yan Pagoda
What more to know?
We climb into the view,
Then hurry down.

Your Hand

With your long hand lain upon my body
You fell asleep easily,
And so I'm awake. Slowly,
The lightness of your hand

轻微的重量
逐渐变成铅

夜晚又很长
你的姿态毫不改变
这只手应该象征着爱情
也许还另有深意
我不敢推动它
或惊醒你
等到我习惯并且喜欢
你在梦中又突然把手抽回
并对一切无从知晓

跨过公路

公路上一只麻雀的尸体
麻雀活着就是为了被汽车轮子撞翻
在此之前它曾经飞翔
一阵疾风改变了方向
突然间一道耀眼的白光
麻雀以为进入了天堂
现在它就躺在公路中央
镶嵌在大地上
还是一副展翅欲飞的模样
三个猎人向这古老的图案致敬
跨过公路，走进茫茫草原

三月到四月

三月到四月
我记得你多次离开
船头离开了原来的水面
船尾压平涌起的浪
又激起另一些

Turns leaden.
The night lengthens.
Neither of us moves.
This is the ache of love, I suppose,
And much else into the bargain.

I dare not waken you, nor even
Push your hand aside
Until I get used to it, even fond of its weight.
Suddenly, some twist in a dream
Moves you off me,
And none of this matters.

Crossing the Highway

On the blacktop
      The body of a sparrow
            Crushed by a car

She had been flying
      When the wind sheared
            Forcing her down

There was a dazzle of white light
She thought it was Heaven

She lies on the highway
      A delicate inlay
            Her wings extended still

Three hunters walk out of the tall grass to cross the road
They look down at her a while, into the ancient pattern

Then disappear into the tall grass on the other side

五月，我的房屋
就要从水上漂走
像一根断木或新枝
我们中的一个将成为
另一个离去的标志

或许不动的是我
在听觉的时间中
我已固定了多年
岛上垂下折断的枝条
抓住你后又被水流带走

回想四月，我怎样沉浸于
绿色的水域，观察
某种发光物的游动
你的闪烁带给我熄灭后的黑暗
我已被水击伤

六月前面是更开阔的海洋
我只能从星辰的高度爱你
像月亮爱下面最小的船只
一去不返但始终是
海洋上的船只

潮湿

潮湿的夜在森林附近
我打开河蚌中的灯
打嗝的声音从听筒的一头传来
也是刚才电话发出的声音
水雾比烟更稳定
眼睛因此低垂
铁在生锈，木头在腐烂
肉被泡得发白
我甚至翻不动一页书

From March to April

I remember you left so many times
From March to April,
The prow of your boat lifting out of the water,
The stern pressing down,
So many waves in its wake.

And then in May
My house was adrift
Like a broken spar or a torn branch.
You and I took turns
Marking each's departure.

But maybe not. Maybe
If I listened to these years
I'd hear my roots gripping down into the island
And my branches sometimes catching you,
Then breaking away.

Remember April when I
Submerged in the green water,
Watching an efflorescence of horizon,
And your shine brought me a darkness brighter than that
When it was gone and I was drowning?

In front of June is the open water.
I can only love you from a star's height,
The way that moonlight loves the smallest boat,
The boat that never returns
But is always out there.

Damp

On a wet night near the woods
I strike a match and light a candle in a clamshell.
It burbles like a telephone.

海棉再也不能吸收
每只碗都满了
悲痛的时候从眉梢往下滴水
我的每片指甲都在出汗
消息像一只飞不动的鸟
翅膀一直触到淤泥
而灯光使我联想起某个部位的
普遍红肿

城墙上

起风的时候我们恰好在平台上
或者这城楼千年以前就建于风口
高空的这阵风围绕着廊柱
使你的肉体无法在领口躲藏

既孤独又愉快
像我用手按住的这张白纸
你抱着自己的胳膊，一个
容易感冒的孩子
最轻柔的风也是一次冒险

我就这样沿着台阶故意把你领上来
选择两把紧靠栏杆的靠椅
我使你有生病的可能、掉下去的危殆
操纵城砖、钓云和四个方向的风
如果你一直和我待到晚上
我还会为此放出布袋中的月亮

棉田上的云朵

我要这样一件衬衫
白色的棉布衬衫
最像衬衫的那种衬衫

Who's calling? It's not good news.
Fog is statelier than smoke. It moves slowly.
I lower my eyes:
Rusted iron, rotted wood,
Meat gone white with the damp.
My hand is too heavy to turn a page.
The kitchen sponge is sopping,
Every bowl of it overflows.
My eyebrows are sodden.
My nails sweat. It's sad.
The news is like a flightless bird
Dipped in mud.
That candle in the clamshell reminds me
Of an ordinary swell of me.

On the City Wall

When the wind comes up, we're on the platform of the wall
built in the wind's teeth a thousand years ago.
Gusts swirl in the colonnades and into our clothes.
There's no hiding for your flesh.

You're weak and you're lonely, but giddy as I am
When I'm writing.
You hold your arms tightly around yourself, a kid
easy to catch cold, even the softest wind is
a blushing adventure.

And so I clamber you up the cold stairs
And sit you down on the edge of the battlements
At the gusty corner where the danger is greatest.
I am the Lord of walls and winds.
Stay with me until night comes. I will show you
The moon in a cloth bag and let you hang it in the clouds.

我不说它是
衬衫中的衬衫
我以我的皮肤要
洗浴后一件干净的衬衫
必须是穿过多次的
从阳光下收回、折好
必须是那之前的漂洗
纺织、棉田和云朵

华灯初上

我滞留在四壁的阴影里不点灯
眼睛张开窗户张开。我吐出
对面大楼上的灯火，我叙述
灿烂火红的夜晚。你神奇深奥的喷火者
我是我的提着红色灭火器的虚无的消防队员

雨季

一所房子的四周在下雨
只有一面有窗，提供下雨的景象
主人犹如阴郁的司机
驾车驶过漫长的雨季
经过相同的房屋和侧面
时间的路标已模糊一片
前进，相对于明亮的雨丝和水滴
安全就像盲人眼中持久的白雾

一声巨响

一声巨响
我走出去查看
什么也没有看见

Cloud in a Field of Cotton

I want such a shirt
Cloth cotton white
And no mistake,
Though I do not mean
Something special.
For my skin's sake
I want a clean shirt after a bath,
White, well-worn
By the sunlight and brought in neatly,
Cleaned and rinsed beforehand
Homespun as a cloud in a field of cotton.

As the City Comes Alight

I stay in the darkening and keep it dark.
Eyes open, window opens. I spit fire into the lights
Of the high-rise across the way, one
By one. I am telling the story.
First the sky turned a brilliant red, and then the city caught fire.
You, the mysterious firebrand.
I, a fireman for myself in fact, carrying a red fire extinguisher.

Rainy Season

It rains around the house of three dead walls.
A single window shows the rain.
You'd think you were driving an old car
Through a cloudburst, passing
The same few streaming houses again and again.
The road signs of the season blur.
Water covers the window with a fine silk —
Something serene, like the white fog in a blind man's eye.

一小时后
我发现砧板
落在灶台上
砸碎了一只杯子

砧板丝纹不动
杯子的碎片也是
静静的

当初砧板挂在墙上
杯子在它的下面
也是静静的

爱情生活

有可能
就尽量做爱
不做爱
也要抱着
要互相说话
彼此看着
不能走神
你在想什么
我在想你
生气的时候
不拿正眼看你
也要拿白眼看你
不说话的时候
也要在心里骂你
要保持
清醒的状态
不要睡过去
睡觉是各自的事情
要抱着睡
握着睡

Noise

A crashing sound.
I walk outside, take
A look around — nothing.

After an hour
I go to the kitchen and find
The cutting board fallen to the counter
And shards of glass everywhere.

Everything still,
The cutting board, the shards of glass so still.
All's quiet.

An hour before, the cutting board hanging on its nail
And the water glass below it
Were quiet too.

Family Romance

When possible
Make love to your soul.
And when it is not possible,
Embrace,
Speak,
At the very least look at each other.
Stay focused.
Of whom are you thinking?
I am thinking of you.
Even angry,
When I cannot look you in the eye,
I am looking at you.
When I cannot bear to speak to you,
I curse you quietly in my heart.

在里面睡
至少也要
手拉着手
像在过一条
车流飞奔
凶险万状的
马路

I remain vigilant.
I am always watching.
There is no sleep
Apart from you.
We must embrace in our sleep,
Cling fast in sleep,
Fuse and flow in sleep,
Or at the very least
Join hands and leap
Into the traffic of ten thousand dangers,
The swarming souls.

胡续冬

水边书

这股水的源头不得而知，如同
它沁入我脾脏之后的去向。
那几只山间尤物的飞行路线
篡改了美的等高线：我深知
这种长有蝴蝶翅膀的蜻蜓
会怎样曼妙地撩拨空气的喉结
令峡谷喊出紧张的冷，即使
水已经被记忆的水泵
从岩缝抽到逼仄的泪腺；
我深知在水中养伤的一只波光之雁
会怎样惊起，留下一大片
粼粼的痛。
　　　　　　所以我
干脆一头扎进水中，笨拙地
游着全部的凛冽。先是
象水蚤一样在卵石间黑暗着、
卑微着，接着有鱼把气泡
吐到你寄存在我肌肤中的
一个晨光明媚的呵欠里：我开始
有了一个远方的鳔。这样
你一伤心它就会收缩，使我
不得不翻起羞涩的白肚。
　　　　　　　　　但
更多的时候它只会象一朵睡莲
在我的肋骨之间随波摆动，或者
象一盏燃在水中的孔明灯
指引我冉冉的轻。当我轻得
足以浮出水面的时候，
我发现那些蜻蜓已变成了
状如睡眠的几片云，而我

Hu Xudong

translations by Ying Qin, Daniel Comiskey and Maged Zaher

From the Water's Edge

There's no telling where this stream of water begins or where
it winds up after it seeps into my spleen.
The flight paths of those delicate mountain nymphs
have warped the contour lines of beauty: I know deep down
how those dragonflies with butterfly wings
can tantalize, so elegantly, the Adam's apple of the air,
forcing the canyons to cry out in nervous chills, even though
memory's pump has drawn water
from cliff crevices to the narrows of the tear ducts,
and deep down I know how the wild goose in the glistening light of ripples,
nursing a wound in the water, will bolt when startled to cast off
a vast sheet of shimmering pain.
                    So to cut
to the quick, I plunge into the water headfirst
and flounder around in the harsh cold of it all. First,
like a dragonfly nymph, I keep to the shadows and stay humble
among the pebbles. Then, as a fish blows bubbles into
a yawn, which you deposited under my skin, as bright and bewitching as
        daybreak,
I begin to form a faraway air bladder that will
contract whenever you're sad, leaving me
no choice but to roll over and show the white belly of bashfulness.
                    And yet,
most of the time it will just be like a water lily
swaying with the waves between my ribs, or
like a Kongming lantern* lit on the water's surface,

---

*Kongming lantern: Invented by Zhuge Liang, or Kongming, a strategist of the
Three Kingdoms Period (220-280 A.D.), this lantern was made of lightweight
materials, which allowed it to rise up like a hot-air balloon when lit.

则是它们躺在水面上发出的
冰凉的鼾声：几乎听不见。
                         你呢？
你挂在我睫毛上了吗？你的"不"字
还能委身于一串鸟鸣撒到这
满山的傍晚吗？风从水上
吹出了一只夕阳，它象红狐一样
闪到了树林中。此时我才看见：
上游的瀑布流得皎洁明亮，
象你从我体内夺目而出
                         的模样。

月坛北街观雪

雪下得不算大，但足以覆盖
我们精益求精的抬杠。你脸上的
公务员阴云迅速消退，浮现出
小学时代的纯朴乡村。我也一样，
像好斗的鸡公突然被扔到一个
遍地食欲的打谷场。满满一嗉囊的
幸福时光！我们手拉手
                         出门去看雪。
附近的小公园此时看上去
还算清秀，白生生地
空着。平时这里散布着
神情怪异的男人，他们交换着
切口和爱，交换着使小树林
阴森起来的肉体。我们曾在一个下雨天
闯进过这里，他们之中最亲热的两个
仇恨地看着我们：我们是他们的
仇恨。
         但现在是下雪天，
同情的雪遮蔽了他们的器官
只剩下寂静的冷，和我们寂静的
再次闯入。你猫着腰

guiding my slowly drifting lightness. When I'm light
enough to break the surface,
I find those dragonflies have turned into
cloud fragments in the shape of sleep itself, while I've
become their wintry snoring, barely audible as they lie
upon the water's surface.
                                    And where are you?
Are you dangling from my eyelashes? Can your word "No"
still entrust itself to a string of bird songs and be spread
through this dusk covering the mountains? The wind blows
a setting sun from out upon the water and, like a red fox,
it dodges into the grove. Only then do I see it:
the waterfall upstream shines bright, flows clear,
just the way you look when you rush out, shimmering
from inside this body of mine.

                    –Y.Q. and D.C.

Watching Snow, North Street of Moon Temple

Nobody could call this snowfall heavy, but there's plenty to cover
the bickering we two strive to perfect. On your face,
the clouds of a municipal clerk quickly depart, revealing
the rustic villages of the elementary school days. And me,
I'm like a fighting cock suddenly tossed onto
a threshing floor, knee deep in appetite, my bird belly filled
with the best of times! We two, hand in hand,
                            head out to watch the snow.
The little park nearby now looks passably delicate,
remains deserted, fair
and tender. Usually, scattered here and there,
are men with weird expressions — they exchange
secret codes and lust, and barter with bodies that make
the grove gloomy and cold. Once, on a rainy day, when we
blundered into this place, the two most intimate of them
stared us down with hatred — we'd become
their hatred.

在干枯的迎春藤之间穿行，你的头发
碰掉的冬青浆果落在雪里
就象我落在你不经意的言辞里。
我追赶着你。追到的
却是墙根下
　　　　　一只肥胖的灰喜鹊。
你第一次清晰地看到
灰喜鹊的脚印：那么大，
像黑板上忘光了的一堆
数学运算符号。也有小一点的，
像我们在中学课堂上传纸条时
写的暗号：那是麻雀的脚印。
你骄傲地用植物的语言
宣布你的新发现：不同于
灰喜鹊的互生脚印，麻雀的脚印
是对生的。
　　　　　"那是因为它们用双脚
一齐蹦。"说完你也开始蹦，
从我们早恋的树枝上，蹦回
我们的中年门槛。这门槛
现在是小公园里的一张
积满落雪的椅子。我们一同
坐了上去，而后站起来，像
海豚一样地扭身。
　　　　　"哈哈，
你的屁股印没有我坐的圆！"
你笑着。我看见你的眼睛里
有一口井，而我的眼睛正在
这口井的井底，悠着，井口上是
飘飞的雪花
　　　　　没有封冻。

But now it's a snow day,
and the snow cloaks their organs in sympathy.
Only the tranquil coldness remains, and our tranquil intrusion
again. Arching your back like a cat,
you scurry through the withered vines of winter jasmine, and the holly
    berries,
bumped by your hair, fall into the snow —
just like me, falling into those carefree words of yours.
I am chasing you. Yet the one I catch up with,
at the foot of a wall,
        is a plump, gray magpie.
And you see clearly, for the very first time,
the footprints of the gray magpie: so huge,
like a bunch of arithmetic symbols on the blackboard,
utterly forgotten. Also, there are smaller ones,
like the codes we used when we passed secret messages on paper scraps
in middle school classes — those are the footprints of sparrows.
In the language of botany,
you proudly declare your new discovery: unlike
the alternate tracks of the gray magpie, the footprints of the sparrow
are opposite in alignment.
        "That's because they hop with both feet
together." After stating this, you start hopping too,
hopping from the branches of our puppy love
to the doorsill of middle age. That doorway
is now a snow-covered bench
in the little park. We sit down together,
only to spring up, spinning around
like dolphins at play.
        "Aha!
My ass-print is rounder than yours!"
You're smiling. In your eyes I see
a well, with my eyes deep down
at the bottom, gently floating. Above, the mouth of the well —
snowflakes drifting in flight —
        not sealed, not frozen.

    –Y.Q. and D.C.

风之乳
　　——为姜涛而作

起床后，三个人先后走到
宿舍楼之间的风口。
个子高的心病初愈，脸上
还留有一两只水母大小的
愁，左右漂浮。短头发的
刚刚在梦中丢下斧头，
被他剁碎的辅音
在乌鸦肚子里继续聒噪。
黑脸胖子几乎是
滚过来的，口臭的陀螺
在半空中转啊，转。

不一会儿，风就来了。
单腿蹦着，脚尖在树梢
踩下重重的一颤。只有
他们三个知道风受了伤：
可以趁机啜饮
　　　　　　　风之乳。

他们吹了声口哨截住了
风。短头发的一个喷嚏
抖落风身上的沙尘，个子高的
立刻出手，狠狠地揪住
风最柔软的部分，狠狠地
挤。胖子从耳朵里掏出
一个塑料袋，接得
出奇地满，像烦躁的气球。

他们喝光了风乳里面的
大海、钢、元音和闪光的
电子邮件。直到散伙
他们谁也没问对方

Milk of the Wind

— for Jiang Tao

After getting up, three guys walked - one at a time -
To the windy passage between the dormitory buildings.
The tall one had just recovered from a broken heart, on his cheeks
Still floating the melancholy, each the size of a jellyfish.
The short-haired one
Had just dropped an axe in his dream.
And the consonants he chopped
Continued their clamoring in some crow's belly.
The dark-skinned fat one, practically
Rolled over here, his bad breath like a top:
Spinning, spinning in midair.

Moments later, the wind came
Hopping on one leg, its tiptoe stepped
Heavily on the treetop. Only
These three knew that it was wounded
And they could seize the opportunity to suck
                              the milk of the wind.

They whistled and stopped
The wind. The short-haired one, with a sneeze,
Shook the sand and dust off the wind's body. The tall one
Acted immediately, grabbing
The softest parts of the wind, and ruthlessly
Squeezed it. The fat one fished out a plastic bag
From his ear and filled it
Tremendously like an agitated balloon.

From the milk of the wind, they drank up
The sea, the actinium, the vowels, and the shining
Emails. And until they broke apart
None of them asked the others
Who they were, and how they knew that
The wind was wounded last night.

—Y.Q. and M.Z.

是谁，是怎样得知
风在昨晚的伤势。

成人玩具店

她是他的硅胶孔，他是她的
兰色振动器。拆迁、半价，
白天的喇叭包围他们，女店员
表情生动，讲解顾客心中的鬼。

他们被关在橱窗里。面对
肮脏的玻璃，男女顾客分拣
目光的软硬。他们则安静地
注视着对方原料里的安静。

长夜漫漫。偶尔会有一两个
坚定的鬼留下来，在黑暗中
挑拨他们不插电的羞。即便
如此，也不妨碍他们用渴望

接通电源，穿过脆弱的玻璃，
在一起剧烈振动。她是他
揪心的紧，他是她不顾一切的
快。他们是局部，是局部的爱。

夏天令他们有了温度和永远：
他们在商店倒闭之前火热地
隐身。女店员草草记下一笔：
"女 A、男 B 两款样品遗失。"

虎蚕

我记得八岁的时候，为了给偷偷养在课桌里的虎蚕
找柞树叶，我逃课，钻进学校后面的深山里。

Adult Toy Store

She's his silica gel hole, he's her
blue vibrator. The dismantling of the store and the half-price sale —
the loudspeakers surround them during the day, the female shop attendant
with lively facial expressions sheds light on furtive ghosts in the hearts of
      shoppers.

He and she, imprisoned in the shop windows. Facing
the dirty glass, male and female shoppers sort through and select
the softness and hardness of gazing. He and she, also gazing, but only in
      silence
at the silence in each other's raw materials.

The night endures, without end. Once in a while, one or two
persistent ghosts linger in the darkness,
toying with the unplugged shame of those two. Even
so, that doesn't stop them from plugging into the power
of desire and, across the fragile glass,
vibrating together violently. She's his
heart-wrenching tightness, he's her reckless
high speed. They're each a piece, a part of love.

The summer brought them warmth and eternity:
before the store goes out of business, they fervently
hide themselves away. The female shop attendant noted carelessly:
"Female A, Male B — two display models missing."

–Y.Q. and D.C.

Tiger Silkworms

When I was eight, in order to find leaves of toothed-oak
For the tiger silkworms kept secretly in my desk
I skipped class, and inched my way
Into the deep mountains behind the school.
On my way back, crossing a dried-up ditch, my step was not wide enough

91

在回来的路上，在跨过一条干枯的壕沟的时候，
我步幅不够大，摔到了沟底。

沟沿撞得我的心口生疼。至少有两分钟，
我呼不出气，也吸不进。外面的气在我努力睁大的眼睛前面，
像花岗岩一样坚硬，像云母一样反射着下午三点
毒辣的阳光。里面的气，肥大，冰冷，像死鱼，噎在
我细小的喉咙里。从书包里散落一地的柞树叶连带长满尖刺的柞树枝
在一瞬间散发出新鲜的被采摘的气味，而后，就闻不到了。
至少有两分钟，我脑子里全是妈妈未曾生下来的弟弟。
我哭，但哭不出声音。弟弟和我都没有声音。

当死鱼游进了阳光，我爬起来，回到教室。肮脏的、不健康的小脸上
泪水的纹路倔强地向胸口伸展，但，没有人注意，包括
让我罚站的老师。甚至连我都没有注意到，
有什么东西顺着这该死的纹路
三下两下，钻进了我心里。

长大后，我常在夜深人静的时候钻进失眠的深山里。
那里地形复杂，有一个溶洞直通心脏，但掩埋在
参天的冷杉林中。终于有一次，在病房里，我找到了
洞的入口，走了进去。我发现心脏里
长着一颗巨大的柞树，树上，爬满了黑白相间的
虎蚕，它们正在吐丝，每根虎蚕的肚子里都有一个
下午三点的南方的太阳，吐出来的丝结成了一大片感激的阳光。

祖先
（为月半节祭祖而作）

我的祖先曾经变成一只蜻蜓
飞到我的蚊帐里，看我背书。
我咿咿哇哇，它的翅膀劈劈啪啪。
我得到母亲的忠告，没有把它
捉住，扯成碎片去喂门口的
蚂蚁宝宝。祖先在我一觉睡醒之后

I felt into its bottom, and bumped against the edge.
My chest hurt. For at least two minutes,
I couldn't breathe in or out. I struggled to keep my eyes open, and saw
The air outside of me as hard as granite, and like mica
It was reflecting the vicious sunlight of
Three o'clock in the afternoon.
The air inside of me, fat and cold like dead fish, chocked
In my tiny throat. The leaves of toothed-oak fell out of my school bag
All over the ground, and the thorn-covered twigs
Released instantaneously a fresh, newly-plucked scent.
After that, I could smell nothing.
For at least two minutes, my mind was filled
With the thought of my yet born brother.
I cried, but couldn't make a sound. Neither my brother nor I had a voice.

When the dead fish swam into the sunlight
I got up, returned to my classroom. On my dirty, pale face
Vines of tears stretching stubbornly toward my chest.
Yet, no one noticed, even the teacher
Who made me stand in class to punish me. Even I didn't notice,
That something, following these damned vines,
Had swiftly inched its way into my heart.

After I grew older, whenever the night was deep and quiet
I often inched my way into the deep mountains of insomnia.
The landscape was complicated, with a cave leading directly to my heart
Yet it was buried under a fir grove reaching to the sky. Finally
Once, in a hospital's ward I found
The entrance of the cave, and walked in. I found that
A huge toothed-oak had grown in my heart.
Black and white checkered tiger silkworms
Crawled all over it, spinning silk, inside each of them
There was a southern sun of three o'clock in the afternoon
Their silk formed a vast sheet of grateful sunshine.

—Y.Q. and M.Z.

神奇地离开了密封的蚊帐，留给我一对
考场上的蜻蜓眼睛和抄袭的好运。

我见过我的么爸不顾奶奶的提醒，
用火钳夹死了一根在堂屋里
善意盘桓的菜花蛇，数小时之后，
我的堂妹就被滚热的开水
烫伤了后背。堂妹尖叫着，
惊恐的嘴里吐出绝望的蛇信子。
如今，她已经出落得丰满俏丽，
但背上，仍留着祖先蜕下的蛇皮。

今天，气温高达 41 度，我光着屁股，
在宿舍收拾行李。从一本满是灰尘的
旧书里，突然跳出了一只蚂蚱：
尖头，赭石色，典型的南方山地品种。
我实在是无法想象一把四川盆地的骨灰
如何在北京组合成这怀旧的活物。
我打开窗，祖先轻轻一跃，在空中
消失，似在教我避闪汗水中的小生计。

Ancestors
(For the Mid-Month Memorial Ceremony)

My ancestors were once transformed into one dragonfly
And flew into my mosquito net, in order to watch me
Recite a lesson from memory.
I was "yi yi wa wa," its wings were "pi pi pa pa."
I followed my mom's advice, not to catch it or
Tear it into small pieces to feed it to the baby ants
In the doorway. Later, I woke up
My ancestors had miraculously left the tightly closed net
Left me both good luck and a pair of
Dragonfly eyes to help me cheat in my exams.

I once saw that my youngest uncle disregarded grandma's warning,
Using a pair of fire-tongs, to kill a well-meaning rape-flower snake
Lingering in the living room. Several hours later,
My younger cousin was scalded by boiling water
On her back. While she was screaming,
The snake's tongue was desperately sticking out of her horrified mouth.
Nowadays, she's grown well shaped and pretty.
Yet on her back, the shed snakeskin of ancestors is still there.

Today, the temperature was as high as 41 degree C, naked,
I was packing in my dormitory. A grasshopper
Suddenly jumped out from a dust covered old book:
Head pointed, ocher colored, a typical breed of the southern hills.
Honestly, I can't imagine how those bone ashes from the Si Chuan Basin
Have transformed into such nostalgic living creatures in Beijing.
I opened the window, and my ancestors made a gentle jump, disappeared
In midair, as if to teach me to dodge the trivialities in heavy sweats.

–Y.Q. and M.Z.

黄灿然

给妻子

亲爱的，生活不怎么好，
但也不会更糟。
结婚六年，孩子五岁，
你还保持单纯，对爱情抱有幻想，
这是你的幸福；
我呢，还继续写诗，并且越写越玄，
你知道也不容易。
我们谈了恋爱，做了夫妻，
有了家，生了孩子，
两地分居，通信，打长途电话，
然后团圆了，高兴了，不满了，
笑了，哭了，吵了，好了。
我知道生活并不太糟，
可也不期望会更好，大概就是这样。
日复一日，年复一年，
我们都会改变，但相去不会太远，
生活就是这样，大概就是这样，
只要你还保持单纯，对爱情抱有幻想，
我呢，还继续写诗，并且越写越玄。

女儿

我的小冤家，小喜鹊，小闹钟，
她的灵魂到处飞扬，幻想的翅膀高于蓝天，
她说："爸爸，"眼里闪烁迷人的光辉，
然后就不说话了，继续在床上蹦跳，
仿佛蹦跳才是生命的责任，藐视我坐着的笨样。
她又说："爸爸，"这回嘴边露出一丝儿微笑，
然后又不说话了，继续唱她自编的歌儿，
灵魂飞上了天，我敢肯定。

96

Huang Canran

Idiomatic English Versions by Meredith Quartermain with the author
other translations by Jane Lai and Ha Jin

To My Wife

My dear, life is not quite good,
but it will not get worse either.
After six years of marriage, with our child five years old,
still you preserve purity and have an illusion of love;
this is your blessing
and I, I still write poems that, over time, become mystic;
you know that's not easy either.
We fell in love, became man and wife,
had a home, had a child,
then lived in two places, wrote letters, made long-distance calls,
then reunited, satisfied, disappointed,
laughed a lot, wept too, quarreled and reconciled.
I know that life is not too bad
and don't expect it to get better — probably that' s how it should be.
Day after day, year after year,
we will change, but will not change a lot,
this is what life is, and probably that's how it should be,
as long as you still preserve purity, and have an illusion of love,
and I, I still write poems that, over time, become mystic.

–M.Q.

我的小捣蛋，小淘气，小冒失鬼，
她的灵魂真不在身上，像一个风筝拼命飞升，
我得每时每刻抓住那条想挣脱的线，
让她知道地球在这儿，爸爸在这儿。
她说："爸爸，"声音也是梦一般的，
然后又不说话了，继续在床上蹦蹦跳跳，
仿佛爸爸是她自己的脑袋，
隔一会儿就要摸摸还在不在，
或者像一杯水，渴了喝它一口又放回原处。
"爸爸，"这回她悄悄给我一个吻，
并且知道我会感到幸福——她目光比我还敏捷——
"爸爸，"她说，"咱们去公园玩好吗？"
迷人的光辉，甜蜜的微笑，梦一般的声音，
灵魂终于降落在身上，但立即又要起飞，
"好啊，"我说，我怎么好意思拒绝呢，
我这个幸福的爸爸。

黑暗中的少女

一张瓜子脸。生辉的额、乌亮的发
使她周围的黑暗失色，她在黑暗中
整理垃圾，坚定、从容、健康，
眼里透出微光，隐藏着生活的信仰。

她的母亲，一脸忧邑，显然受过磨难
并且还在受着煎熬，也许丈夫是个赌棍
或者酒徒，或者得了肺痨死去了，
也许他在尘土里从不知道自己有个女儿。

每天凌晨时分我下班回家，穿过小巷，
远远看见她在黑暗中跟母亲一起
默默整理一袋袋垃圾，我没敢多看她一眼，
唯恐碰上那微光，会怀疑起自己的信仰。

My Daughter

My little rival, little magpie, little alarm clock,[*]
her soul is flying around, high in the sky on amazing wings.
'Father,' she says, her eyes glistening and radiant,
then she stops short, keeps jumping on the bed,
as if jumping is life's real duty, defying my stupid sitting.
And she says again, 'Father,' this time a faint smile
in the corners of her mouth,
then she stops short again, goes on singing her self-made songs —
her soul soaring up to the sky, I believe.
My little troublemaker, little mischief, little harum-scarum,
her soul is indeed not with her, like a kite struggling to fly higher.
All the time I have to catch hold of the thread that's billowing away,
to remind her that the earth is here, father is here.
And she says, 'Father,' even her voice is dreamlike,
then she stops short again, keeps jumping and jumping on the bed,
as if father is her head —
she'll touch it once in a while to make sure it's still there,
or like a glass of water, she'll drink a mouthful
when she's thirsty and then put it down.
'Father,' this time she steals a kiss from me,
to make me happy — her glance is quicker than mine —
'Father,' she says, 'let's go play in the park, okay?'
Radiant, sweet, dreamlike,
the soul returns at last, just in time to take off again.
'Okay,' I say. How do I have the nerve to refuse,
when indeed I am such a happy father?

–M.Q.

---

[*] In Chinese, *magpie* contains the root words *happy bird*; and *alarm clock* is formed from the words connoting *noisy clock*.

家

家是选择性的，
你不站在这一边，
便要站在单身那一边，
没有回旋的余地
并且犹豫的时间
也没有多少年。

我站在租来的家的阳台，
手扶着剥落的石灰，指尖
触到一根腐烂到腰身的
青草，是青草：它的下半身
还是那么年轻，用
腐烂的顶端做它的头。

女儿最像一株植物，
长得比植物还快，
才刚刚毛茸茸的，
突然间变成了嫩枝：
我几乎没有注意到
她抽芽吐叶的日子。

妻子像夏天，像雨伞，
像一只蜂后，但她采蜜
——从我枯瘦的胸膛。
她心里有一根弦，要我
时不时拨弄，但不能
太响、太尖、太刺耳。

我在几寸光阴里
装满抱负，
像货船上的水手
平稳又不安，靠想像

The Girl in the Darkness

An egg-shaped face.
Her shiny forehead and glossy hair dispel
some of the darkness, in which she' s sorting trash.
She looks steady, healthy, at ease,
her eyes giving a faint light shading
her faith in life.

Her mother wears a sad face
and has obviously suffered, still miserable.
Perhaps her father is a gambler or drunkard
or died of TB long ago.
Perhaps he, underground now,
doesn't know he has a daughter.
Every morning I leave work for home in the small hours.
When going through that alley, I will see her,
together with her mother, sorting
and bagging trash in the darkness and silence.
I dare not glance at her twice, afraid
to meet that faint light and doubt my faith.

–H.J.

Home

Home is alternative,
either you stand on this side
or on that side of being single,
between them there is no room for maneuver,
and the years for hesitation
are also very few.

I stand on the balcony of my rented home
with my hand on the peeling whitewash,
my fingertip touches a stalk of grass
rotten to its waist.

过日子，而想像
确实可以提供风暴：

这露台，未尝不是船舷。

你没错，但你错了

由于他五年来
每天从铜锣湾坐巴士到中环上班，
下班后又从中环坐巴士回铜锣湾，
在车上翻来覆去看报纸，
两天换一套衣服，
一星期换三对皮鞋，
两个月理一次头发，
五年来表情没怎么变，
体态也没怎么变，
年龄从二十八增至三十三，
看上去也没怎样变，
窗外的街景看上去也差不多，
除了偶尔不同，例如
爆水管，挖暗沟，修马路，
一些"工程在进行中"的告示，
一些"大减价"的横幅，
一些"要求"和"抗议"的政党标语，
一些在塞车时才留意到的店铺、招牌、橱窗，
一些肇事者和受害人已不在现场的交通事故，
你就以为他平平庸庸，
过着呆板而安稳的生活，
以为他用重复的日子浪费日子，
以为你比他幸运，毕竟你爱过恨过，
大起大落过，死里逃生过
——你没错，但你错了：
这五年来，他恋爱，
结婚，有一个儿子，
现在好不容易离了婚，

Yes, it's green: its lower half
is still so young.

My daughter's like a plant,
but grows faster,
downy she was,
when suddenly she turned a tender twig,
I barely noticed
her sprouting days.

My wife is like summer, like an umbrella,
like a queen bee, though she collects nectar
from my skinny chest.
There's a string in her heart, which demands
that I pluck it from time to time, but not be
too loud, too sharp, too piercing.

I load a few inches of time
with ambitions
like a sailor on a freighter,
feeling at once steady and turbulent,
living off imagination,
and imagination does provide storms.

–M.Q.

You're Right But You're Wrong

Since for five years, every day
he takes a bus to work from Causeway Bay to Central,
and returns from work from Central to Causeway Bay,
riffling through his paper on the bus,
changes his clothes every two days,
three times a week his shoes,
cuts his hair every two months,
has not changed his expression for five years,
nor his build
though now aged thirty-three instead of twenty-eight,

你那些幸运的经历他全都经历过，
而他经历过的，正等待你去重复。

翻译

新闻翻译员朱伯添
正在翻译有关北约空袭
科索沃和塞尔维亚的新闻，
其中一段列出几个
被轰炸的科索沃城镇，包括：
普里什蒂纳，普里兹伦，
Vucitrn，Gnjilane，
Djakovica 和佩奇。
Vucitrn 以前没碰见过，
《外国地名词典》也查不到。
他想，后面那几个城镇都是新名字，
反正读者也不知道什么是什么，
不如删掉算了，简略为
"普里什蒂纳、普里兹伦等城镇"，
上司也肯定不会在乎；但是，
他想到自己的责任，不应偷工减料，
便查更厚的《世界地名翻译手册》，
是武契特恩。Gnjilane
以前也没碰见过，查《世界地名翻译手册》，
是格尼拉内。Djakovica
以前也没碰见过，查《世界地名翻译手册》
查不到，他想，更薄的《外国地名词典》
查到的机会更少；他知道 kovica
可译为"科维察"，但是 Dja 如何发音
他没有把握，很多阿拉伯
或穆斯林国家的地名以 Dja 开头，
都译成"贾"，但他不敢贸然采用；
他反复细看，终于找到阿尔巴尼亚
也有一个以 Dja 开头的地名，
也译成"贾"，科索沃居民主要是阿裔，

he looks pretty much the same
even the street scene outside the window is much the same
but for some exceptions, like
burst pipes, drain repairs, roadwork,
some sign declaring "work in progress,"
banners announcing "final sale, "
political placards with slogans that "protest" and "demand,"
shops and their displays noticed only during traffic jams,
traffic accidents after both culprit and victim have gone,
you would think him ordinary,
living a routine boring life,
wasting his days through daily repetition,
and that you are luckier than him, after all you have loved and hated,
gone through life's ups and downs, escaped death's jaws,
— you're right, but you are wrong:
in these five years, he has loved,
got married, had a son,
and after much trouble got divorced,
your lucky experience he's had it all,
and what he's been through, awaits you yet.

–J.L.

Translation

News translator Zhu Botian
was translating the news of NATO
bombing Kosovo and Serbia,
in which there was a list
of bombarded Kosovo towns, including
Pristina, Prizren,
Wuteqien, Genilanei,
Jiakeweica and Pec.
He'd never heard of Wuteqien,
nor did it appear in the *Dictionary of Foreign Geographic Names*.
Since these towns had strange names
which readers didn't know,

译成"贾"错不了，于是他把 Djakovica
译成贾科维察。为了更肯定
他又顺手查一下那本《外国地名词典》
说不定凑巧可以查到。果然很凑巧！
果然查到！果然是贾科维察！但是，
想到这些城镇可有可无，
上司和读者都不会在乎，
他又把它们删掉，只留下
科索沃首府（加上这个
背景说明，以方便读者）
普里什蒂纳和普里兹伦。
但是，他又想到忠实性，
尤其是想到这些地名下
有几个平民被炸死，
有几十个人被炸伤，
有更多房屋被炸毁。
所以他又按了一下鼠标，
把删掉的地名恢复过来，
加上原来的，完完整整读成：
科索沃首府普里什蒂纳、普里兹伦、
武契特恩、格尼拉内、贾科维察和佩奇。
他很清楚，上司可能会不耐烦，
把他恢复的又再删掉，说不定
连普里兹伦也删掉，只剩下
"科索沃首府普里什蒂纳等城镇"，
或更干脆一点，简略为科索沃
——科索沃谁都知道。

夏雨

夏雨，你总让我写不够，
我刚完成一首诗，一团灰云
又迅速从对面大厦顶掠过。
这会儿我出门之前
看见客厅满是阳光，就猜

he thought, why not delete them and put
'Pristina, Prizren and other towns'?
He was sure his boss wouldn't care; but,
considering his duty, he thought, this jerrybuilding's no good,
so he checked the voluminous *Geographic Dictionary of the World*,
and found that Wuteqien was Vucitrn and Genilanei was Gnjilane.
For Jiakeweica he found no equivalent,
and he guessed that the chance was slight
of finding it in the smaller *Foreign* dictionary.
He understood that *-keweica* could be translated as *-kovica*,
but was not sure about *Jia*, though he knew it formed the beginning
of many place names in Arabic and Muslim countries,
and could be translated *Dja*.
At last he found in the *World* dictionary
an Albanian name which began with *Jia*,
and was translated *Dja*,
and since most Kosovo residents
were Albanian, he was certain that *Dja* was right,
so he translated *Jiakeweica* as *Djakovica*. To confirm this,
he picked up the *Foreign* dictionary, hoping
that by a fluke he'd find a full equivalent. He really was lucky!
He found one! It really was *Djakovica*! But,
considering these towns were insignificant,
and his boss and readers wouldn't care,
he again deleted them, leaving only
'Pristina, the capital of Kosovo [this explanation
was necessary for the convenience of readers],
and Prizren.' But
again he thought of faithfulness,
above all he realized that in these places
civilians had been killed,
dozens of others wounded,
and still more houses destroyed.
He clicked the mouse again,
to replace the deleted names,
so the whole passage read,
'Pristina, the capital of Kosovo, and Prizren,
Wucitrn, Gnjilane, Djakovica and Pec.'

你大概在另一个地区忙碌，
当我来到楼下，
地面已满是水泡，
好像下足了半个小时；
那会儿我走进湾仔地铁站
还阳光普照（但我承认，
你已给足提示：闷得很），
而当我从测鱼涌地铁站出来，
你已倾巢而出，满街是水，
雨伞像蘑菇，一顶顶，
在我周围开放！
你一叹息，我们就赶紧
收衣服；你一变脸，
我们心就暗；你一甩身走了，
我们还在窗前探头。

删改

新闻翻译员朱伯添
经验越来越丰富，知识面
越来越广，对世界的了解
也越来越深；不仅如此，
他发现他对国际局势
已形成自己的看法，
而且可怕地准确，例如
日本经济长期低迷、
亚洲金融危机、
香港楼市暴跌，
都在他意料之中；
再如"九一一"恐怖袭击，
也在他意料之中，只是
规模和方式难以置信；
当小布什竞选总统，他的经验、
知识面和了解开始
化为一种不祥的预感；

He knew well that his boss might be impatient
and might delete what he'd undone,
perhaps even sweep away 'Prizren,' leaving only
'Pristina, the capital of Kosovo, and other towns,'
or sweep away the towns altogether and put 'Kosovo'—
everyone knew Kosovo.

–M.Q.

Summer Rain

Summer rain, I never write enough of you:
I just finish a poem, when another group of gray clouds
swiftly rushes over the opposite highrise.
Before I went out,
seeing my living room still full of sunshine,
I guessed you were probably busy in another region,
but when I came down to the street,
the ground was already full of bubbling puddles,
as if it had been downpouring for half an hour.
When I went into Wanchai subway station,
the sun was still shining everywhere (though I admit
you had dropped me a hint: it was sultry),
and when I emerged from Quarry Bay station,
you were turning out in full strength, water everywhere!
Umbrellas mushrooming all around me!
You sigh and we rush
to bring in the laundry; you change face
and our hearts turn dark; you storm away
and still we're popping our heads
out of windows.

–M.Q.

当小布什组阁，拉姆斯菲尔德、
沃尔福威茨、赖斯露面，
当弗莱舍在白宫新闻发布会上亮相，
他更加不安，当美国拒绝
《京都议定书》和退出
美俄反弹道导弹条约，
他开始感到恐怖：
他原来还打算尝试写文章，
分析和评论国际局势，
但他发现他已不是在观察
而是带着那不祥的预感
陷入对局势的极度关注中，
他看到局势发展的脉络，
但内心的恐怖
使他视野中的画面
缺乏足够的清晰度，
他无法描述它，
他无法表达它！
美国入侵伊拉克，只是他脑中
那个恐怖画面的一个小亮点，
犹如巴格达夜空里的炮火，
而他看到的，是白天里的废墟，
世界的废墟！
他在翻译中恪守并达致的
准确度和清晰度
也开始动摇，
他不得不作一些删改，
例如将"与伊拉克的战争"
改成"对伊拉克发动战争"
或"对伊拉克动武"，
将"为解除萨达姆的武装
而展开的与伊拉克的战争"
删成"攻打伊拉克"，
他没有违背忠实性，
而是忠实于真实性，
毕竟，当那幅恐怖的画面

Revising

News translator Zhu Botian
was much more experienced now, his range of knowledge
much broader, his understanding of the world
much deeper; furthermore,
he found that he had formed
his own views on international affairs,
which proved to be terribly correct, such as
the long-term depression of the Japanese economy,
the Asian financial crisis
and the meltdown of the Hong Kong property market —
all happened as he had expected.
The '9/11' terrorist attacks
also did not surprise him
except for the scale and the method.
When Bush Junior ran for President,
Botian's experience, knowledge and understanding
became an ominous presentiment;
and when Bush Junior formed his cabinet,
and Rumsfeld, Wolfowitz and Rice showed up,
with Fleischer at White House news conferences,
Botian's unease began to grow;
when the United States withdrew from the Kyoto Protocol
and the US-Russian Anti-Ballistic Missile Treaty,
a sense of terror began to grip him:
initially he had planned to write articles
to analyze and comment on the international situation,
but he found that he was no longer observing.
Instead, he saw with that ominous presentiment
the developing pattern in the situation.
A sense of terror prevented him
from seeing clearly enough the picture in his mind,
he could not describe it,
he could not express it!
The American invasion of Iraq
was merely a bright dot in the picture,
like the artillery fires in the night sky of Baghdad,

掠过他脑际，
忠实性无非是镜头中
巴格达夜空里烟花似的炮火，
而真实性是白天里
赤裸裸的废墟。

呼喊

新闻翻译员朱伯添
对国际时事了如指掌，
对本地新闻不感兴趣，
他不知道十多年来
任何一个香港小姐的名字，
也搞不清楚回归六年来
吵吵嚷嚷，究竟发生过什么事，
每次他收到选举宣传品
就顺手扔进垃圾箱，
民主党和民建联
他似乎知道哪个是哪个，
自由党是什么
他就完全没有概念；
　　　　直到"二十三条"
这奇怪的名字出现
他才感到不妙，
但哪怕是这个时候
他也仍然记不全
那个叶什么局长的名字，
只是她那副嘴脸
像来自动物农庄，
令他感到不适；
接着非典型肺炎爆发，
他才每天买几份报纸，
急着看疫情发展，
奇怪为什么不封锁威尔斯医院，
奇怪为什么不炒掉杨永强，

while what he saw was the ruins of the day,
the ruins of the world!
The principle of accuracy and impartiality
in translation, to which he firmly held,
also began to shake,
and he felt obligated to do some revising,
such as replacing *the war with Iraq*
with *the war launched against Iraq*
or *the use of force against Iraq*,
or changing *the war launched on Iraq*
to help disarm Saddam Hussein
to *the war attacking Iraq*.
He didn't betray his principles;
he was faithful to the truth:
when the picture of terror
ran through his mind,
faithfulness was nothing but the artillery fires,
which were like fireworks, in the night sky of Baghdad,
while truth was the ruins of the day,
which were naked.

–M.Q.

Outcry*

News translator Zhu Botian
knew international events like the palm of his hand,
but had no interest in local news;

---

*On July 1, 2003, the sixth anniversary of Hong Kong's handover to China, 500,000 Hong Kongers took to the streets to express their discontent with the government. The scale of this mass demonstration, second only to the 'June 4' mass demonstration in which one million Hong Kong people participated, surprised everyone — the government, the opposition parties, even the demonstrators and organizers themselves. The reasons behind it are many, but mainly the government's plan to force enactment of Article 23 and the government's incompetence, especially in its handling of SARS which led to 299 deaths. This was not only the highest number but also the highest death rate in any of the SARS infected regions.

奇怪为什么不使用中药，
奇怪一些普通常识
竟把政府给难住了，
等到非典被赶走，
已不见三百条人命；
这之后他保持了
读本地新闻的习惯，
这可不得了！他发现
整个社会像一堆垃圾，
而官员们还不断乱扔；
二十三条又抛出来，
七月一日就快逼近，
他要参加游行！
他连"六四"也站在路旁，
但这回他一定要破例——
可糟糕，那天他得上班，
也请不到假，上不了街！
他想来想去，决定派儿子
做他的代表，儿子十五岁，
虎背熊腰，前一阵子
还跟着他追看非典新闻，
但他得跟儿子详细解释
什么叫二十三条，
保证他不会被父亲误导，
让他明白这对父亲重要，
对儿子更重要；
　　七月一日下午，
他照样四点半起床，
儿子已经去了维园，
妻子照样把他的晚餐装进饭盒，
他照样在楼下搭巴士，
天空晴朗，阳光猛烈，
巴士经过北角，擦过维园，
透过寂静的玻璃窗，他看见
繁枝茂叶掩映下的维园
人头攒动，标语牌林立，

114

he could not name any Miss Hong Kong over the past decade,
nor did he know, six years since the handover,
what had really happened, what people had been wrangling about;
every time he received election propaganda,
he just threw it in the dustbin without opening it.
It seemed he could tell the DAB party
from the Democratic Party.
As to what the Liberal Party was,
he really had no idea.[*]

    It was not until the strange name
'Article 23'[†] appeared
that he sensed something was going wrong,
yet even at this time he could not remember
the full name of Secretary Ip What,[‡]
except that her look,
from an animal farm,
made him feel uncomfortable.
Then came the outbreak of SARS,
which prompted him to buy several newspapers everyday.

---

[*]DAB party: a pro-government party whose chairman Tsang Yok Sing resigned after insisting that most of the participants were being used or misled. Democratic Party: main opposition party. Liberal Party: a somewhat centrist party that represents businessmen.

[†]As part of Hong Kong's constitution, Article 23 gives government and police a wide range of powers. The article states, among other things, that any branch organization that is part of an organization banned by the Mainland Chinese government based on state security grounds can also be banned in Hong Kong and that the police can enter residential buildings and arrest people without court warrants and evidence. After the '7/1' demonstration, Article 23 was postponed.

[‡]Secretary Ip What: Secretary for Security, Regina Ip Lau Suk-yee who was prime promoter of Article 23. Earlier, Ip had criticized Hong Kong's journalists for their coverage of students arrested during unauthorized protests, likening the media to Napoleon, the pig in George Orwell's *Animal Farm*. Her remarks were often very controversial, and the arrogant attitude that she often adopted during the promotion of Article 23 prompted her detractors to resort to even attacking her bushy hairstyle, nicknaming her 'Broomhead.' Before and even after the '7/1' demonstration, she insisted that people were misled. Soon after '7/1', Ip resigned from her post.

巴士经过告士打道， 他看见
告士打道和百德新街一带
人山人海，黑压压一大片，
他看不见却好像看见
儿子就在人头里标语下，
他听不到却分明听到
此起彼伏的呼喊
他再细听，那呼喊
来自他内心深处，恍若
来自海底，挣扎着要冒出
阳光猛烈的水面，汇入
玻璃窗外的人头和标语，汇入
人头里标语下
他儿子那尖锐的
呼喊……

回到山上来

当阳光从不远处的山顶
悄悄下移，他站在山腰
一块生着小草的石块上
俯望笼罩在一片尘雾下的
城市高楼群，微笑着说
从空气清新的山上看下面
就像一个上了年纪，渐渐达观的人
——他这样的人——
回想早年混乱的生活；
他说如今心境平和，尤其是
每天与树木和花鸟为伴
身体也变得舒畅多了，
尤其是沉闷时，想到明天
一大早又可以回到这山上来
就感到一阵莫名的喜悦
——此刻他脸上的喜悦：
两排整洁的牙齿，红里透亮的皮肤，

With great anxiety, he followed the epidemic,
and just could not understand
why they didn't close Prince of Wales Hospital,*
why they didn't fire EK Yeoh,[†]
why they didn't use Chinese medicine,[‡]
why the government was so senseless
to common sense. SARS receded
leaving three hundred deaths.
After that, he kept the habit
of reading local news.
He made a spectacular discovery:
society as a whole was like a rubbish heap;
still the officials kept increasing it;
and now the issue of 'Article 23' re-emerged.
July 1 was drawing near,
he wanted to join the protest!
He was an onlooker even on June 4,

---

*Prince of Wales Hospital: where the outbreak of SARS in Hong Kong started. It was long after the outbreak, with many hospital workers infected, that the hospital closed its emergency room (in fact by then workers were in short supply and no citizen ventured to go there). The hospital was never completely closed. According to later testimony, in the very early stages of the outbreak, some front-line doctors in the hospital had suggested that some parts of the hospital's services be closed, but their recommendations were rejected by the Hospital Authority that runs Hong Kong's hospital system.

[†]EK Yeoh: Secretary for Health and Welfare, who often took measures only long after the media focused on specific problems. Although he was widely criticized, he refused to resign. One year after this poem was written, and co-incidentally when the translation of this poem was just completed, on July 7, 2004, two days after the Legislative Council SARS inquiry report which put the blame on him, and when local newspapers stated 'Calls grow for Yeoh to go' and 'Yeoh must go, say Sars Victims," Yeoh resigned at last.

[‡]Chinese medicine: this is widely used in Guangzhou and other SARS infected regions in China, where the death rate is very low, and was very effective in fighting the SARS virus. However, the hospital system in Hong Kong insisted on not using Chinese medicine.

让我想起待会儿要照临的阳光，
而如果是在尘雾下的街道上，
在水果档前，在茶餐厅里，
我会想起善。

but this time he was determined to march.
Alas, he could not take that day off,
could not go to the street!
After thinking it over, he decided to send his son
as his representative. His son was fifteen,
strong as a tiger — not long ago
they'd followed the SARS news together.
But first of all he explained to his son —
so as not to 'mislead' him —
what 'Article 23' was —
that Article 23 was even more important to him
than to his father.
       The afternoon of July 1 he woke at 4:30,
his son had already gone to Victoria Park.*
As usual his wife put his evening meal in a food box.
As usual he took a bus at a nearby bus stop.
The sky was clear, the sun was fierce,
the bus passed North Point, then Victoria Park.
Through silent windowpanes,
he saw trees in the park overwhelmed
by a sea of human heads and placards.
At Gloucester Road and Paterson Street
huge throngs of people crowded in dark masses.
He could not see but seemed to see
his son among those heads under those placards.
He could not hear but seemed to hear
an outcry, now rising, now falling:
      an outcry
deep within his heart, a cry
from the bottom of the ocean,
rising to the sun-fierce surface
of heads and placards outside the windowpanes —
and among those heads under those placards,

---

*Victoria Park, is where mass demonstrations in Hong Kong often take place. It's often a starting point of a demonstration which ends at Government headquarters.

sharp and shaking, his son's
outcry . . .

–M.Q.

Come Back to the Mountain

As sunlight is gliding over from the nearby summit,
he stands halfway up the mountain, on a stone
topped with young grass, gazing down
at the swarm of the city' s buildings veiled in smog,
and says with a smile that from this slope where
the air is fresh, the sight below makes
one feel like an aged man growing wise and tolerant
-he's such a man-
who recalls the chaos of his early years;
that he too is calm now, the daily company of trees,
flowers and birds puts him at ease,
especially, if gloomy, he will remember that
early next morning he' ll be here again,
how suddenly he feels a peculiar joy
— the same joy on his face:
his two rows of neat teeth and ruddy skin
remind me of the sunlight about to arrive,
and if I am on a street under smog,
or in front of a fruit stand, or in a cafe,
I cannot but think of good.

–H.J.

姜涛

情人节

整整一天都空着，倒扣在厨房里
经历了姨妈们的挑剔
而暖空气的确吹自无底洞
让小舌迎风招展，红肿如求知欲
但是没有女大学生来辅导
只好沿蚂蚁的智商去吃牛肉面

肉香弥漫在巷子里
惹得蠢人也意想天开，轮翻揭开
身体的盖子，看到杂草、齿痕和土坎
那些似乎都是热情生活
最后的落脚点。（只是有点痒，象是
被一只自白派的蚊子叮过）

多亏还有事可做，谢绝
梦想和书籍的邀请，并计划
将空空的一天当作三部曲
先排练其中的头两部：扮演红脸的少年
加大球鞋的尺码；挖空
指甲里的矿山；一日写下一篇

养猪日记。回头却远远望见
天空里嵌着一蔚蓝的衣橱
明白了为何洗好的衬衫上
常粘着隔代人的鸟屎
因而不能无忧无虑，弹起冬不拉
博取女房东的欢心

但三十而立，总还要出门
出租车义薄云天
羊角风吹得槽牙乱颤。

Jiang Tao

translations by Chris Dusterhoff and Li Chun with Zhang Er

St. Valentine's Day

The whole day was vacant, and you handstanded in the kitchen
Putting up with the carping of your aunts
The warm air undoubtedly blew from the abyss
Leaving your small tongue waving in the wind, scarlet and swelled
    like your thirst for knowledge
But no female student came for tutoring
So you had to follow the intelligence of ants and had beef noodles

The street was soaked in the aroma of beef
Which forced even the foolish to daydream, and in turn to open
Their lids, only to see some weeds, teeth-marks and ridges
Which seemed to be the final shelter
For their enthusiastic life (only a little bit itchy, as if
Having been bitten by a Confessionalist mosquito)

Luckily, you still had something to do: refusing
The invitation of dreams and books, and planning
To make the vacant day into a trilogy
Of which the first two chapters were to be rehearsed:
    you would act as a red-faced lad
Enlarging the size of your sneakers, carving out
The mines in your fingernails, and writing

In your journal on pig-raising. Looking back from a distance,
You saw a blue wardrobe embedded in the sky
Thus you understood why the newly-washed shirts
Were always stained with the excrement of birds from the last generation

没瞧见城市的底盘正倒悬着
露出了女司机们乌黑的排气管。
（整个场面稍显尴尬，却引人遐想）

使得男司机欲罢不能：
当众吞下方向盘，吐出分飞燕。
多少人已经老了，悄悄拔掉了
雄心的三向插头，从皮大衣下
端出鸟语花香的生产线
只有你还一声不吭，为双腿安装

变速的机关，一路经过
小桃林、区政府和清水湾
为的是让独身生活追上闪电。
但它跑得太快，满头婆娑的电力，
以至于丢掉了假牙、户口和前妻
成为大厅里的不速之客。

接下来的一部，显然仍不够色情
因为不肯在电脑城里媾合于一只超频蝴蝶
只好原路返回
冒单身省亲的危险，置身于
一场孝心风暴，听病榻尽头的母亲
解释婚姻的先验性

"家庭理财，一把好手，能掐会算
把冷却的午餐分给后代
督促过剩的钙质提早形成智力的蜂巢
容纳水和蜜，光与线——
继而批判文明和吃相，一双乖儿女
会圆睁美丽的豹子眼"

没有人阻碍你抛弃马铃薯般的过期女友
但你不能将她们的哭泣当作绷带
缠在白云的骨折处。
"无边无尽的语境啊，正被云的手腕讲述"

Therefore, you could not be as carefree as to play Dongbula[*]
To please your landlady

Nevertheless, since *a 30 year old man should stand on his own feet*
        leaving home was inevitable
The cab *howled loud to the sky*
An up-whirling wind blew so fiercely as to shake the molars in all directions
You missed the spectacle of the upside-down oilpan of the city
Which revealed the blackish exhaust pipes of the women drivers
(The whole scene seemed a little awkward, but called for daydreaming)

The male driver could not help rubbernecking
Swallowing the steering wheel in public, thereafter he *spat out a pair of
        swallows*
So many people had turned aged, and silently pulled out
Their three-prong plugs, and from underneath their fur coats
Took out with both hands the product line of warbles and floral scents
Only you kept silent, and fixed both of your legs

To a manual transmission, made your way
By a small peach grove, the district government and the Clear Water Bay
So that your bachelor life could catch up with the lightning.
But it ran so fast that its head was in a whirl of electric power,
And it lost its false teeth, registered residency and ex-wife
And thus was reduced to an uninvited guest in the lobby.

The next chapter was apparently not pornographic enough.
Unwilling to have intercourse with a loitering butterfly in the computer plaza,
You had to take the same way back
At the risk of coming home alone, placing yourself
In a storm of filial piety, listening to you mother, at one end of the sickbed,
Explain the apriority of matrimony

"Household financing, an able hand, good at counting,
Dealing out the chilled lunches among your children,

---

[*]Dongbula: a popular Kazak string-and-pluck musical instrument

其实你太过自责，她们都是过来人，
即使经历的是美食节

腰身也不会过分地丰盈。
一份耕耘一份收获，劈砍牛肉的斧子
已被小牛当作另类的榜样
你也不必打扮成忏悔的负心汉
捆住两只牛蹄，
主动到人堆里去自首

因为整整一天都空着，和纯净水桶一道
等待着被流动小贩拎走。
而最后一部还是留至午夜，以满足
陌生女郎的导演欲
屠刀停在娥眉上，主持着诗歌热线：
首先要温柔地褪去、褪去她

周身的辣椒、蒜瓣、以及
清山翠谷的脚尖
随后的礼节，当然是躬身退让
在早春的卧床上，尽量前仆后继
推起刨花一样的海浪
并为纸的舌头涂满花生酱

慢跑者

终于等到了这一天，到邮局领取退休金
可以早睡早起，完全听凭内心的安排
六月的天空象一道斜杠插入，删除床板尽头
肉感的悬崖，溅起一片燕语莺声
以及昨夜房事中过于粗暴的口令

缺乏目的，做起来却格外认真
白网球鞋底密封了洪水，沿筋腱向脚踝
输送足够的回力，一步步检讨大地

126

Using the extra calcium to form a honeycomb of intelligence
Which accommodates water and honey, light and string —
And afterwards criticizing civilization and their table manners, a pair of lovely
    children
Will open wide their pretty eyes like a leopard"

No one would stop you from abandoning your girlfriends, outdated as
    potatoes
But you could not take their sobs as bandages
And wrap them around the fractured part of the white clouds
"Alas! The immense context is being related by the writs of the clouds"
In fact, you had been self-condemned, and they were experienced women
Even if what they had experienced were gourmet food festivals.

Their waists were not too plump.
So much work, so many rewards. The ax for beef-chopping
Was modeled by the calves on its heterodoxy
It was not necessary for you to pretend to be a repentant betrayer,
Bundling together two cow hooves
And confessing to the crowd on your own volition

Because the whole day was vacant, and with the mineral water barrels,
You were waiting to be carried away by the street peddlers.
But the last chapter should be postponed till midnight, so to fulfill
A strange woman's desire to be a director.
With a whittle remaining on her delicate eyebrows, she hosted a poetry
    hotline:
First you should tenderly undress, undress her

From her whole body the hot peppers, garlic cloves, and
The tiptoes of green mountain and valleys
The following etiquette, of course, was to bow and concede
And on an early spring bed, try as hard as possible
To push out ocean waves like wood shavings
And apply peanut butter to the tongue of paper

只有老套经验不足为凭，他决定尝试
新的路线，前提当然是：身披朝霞的工程师
还能爬上少妇茁壮的高压塔

"多吃大豆，少吃猪肉，每天用日记
清洗肠胃" 还要剥开个性
露出人格，"看看它还能否嘶嘶作响，
象充电灯里骄傲的旧电池"
所以，他跑得很慢，知道在赛跑中
即使甩掉了兔子，还会被数不清的霉运追赶

可行之计在于为体魄画上节奏的晨妆
肚子向前冲，让时光也卷了刃
但小区规划模仿迷宫，考验喜鹊的近视眼
于是，他跑得更慢，简直就是蹑手蹑脚
生怕踩碎地上的新壳（它们沾着晨光的油脂
刚刚由上学的小孩子们褪下）

他跑过邮电局，又经过家具店
其间被一辆红夏丽阻隔，他采取的是
忍让的美德，蜷起周身蔬菜一样的浪花
努力缩成一个点，露水中一个衰变的核
防备绊脚石，也防备雷霆
从嘴巴里滚出，变成肤浅的脏话

惊扰一片树叶上梦游的民工
而马路尽头，正慢性哮喘般喷薄出城市
朦胧的轮廓，清风徐徐吹来
沿途按摩广告牌发达的器官
这使他多少有点兴奋，想到时代的进步
与退步，想到成队的牛羊

已安静地走入了冰箱，而胖子作为经典
正出入于每一个花萼般具体的角落。
"我们的推论丝丝入扣，象柏油里掺进了
白糖，终于在尽头尝到了甜头！"

The Jogger

Ultimately came the day when I withdrew my retirement pension from the
Post Office
And thereafter I could go to bed earlier and get up earlier, all being up to my
choice
The June sky penetrated like a leaning bar which, at the end of the bed
The edge of the fleshy cliff, erased all the obscene words burst out,
All the overly rough, demanding words used during sex the night before

Without any real purpose, yet all was performed with extreme
conscientiousness,
The soles of the white tennis shoes held the blood, down from the tendon
They transmitted counter-force to the ankle, and step by step, investigated the
earth.
Following old experiences proved to be inadequate, so he decided to try
New routes. The precondition was, of course, the software engineer, wrapped
in sunlight,
Could still reach the top of a young lady's high-tension tower

"Science Men suggest you take more soybeans, and less pork, and use your
diary
To rinse your stomach everyday." Also, shed your individuality
And unveil your personality, "to see if it sizzles
Like an arrogant old battery in the rechargeable light"
Thus he ran very slowly, aware that in a foot race,
Even if you left the rabbit behind, numerous misfortunes would still chase
you

The feasible solution was to create a physique in the early morning with
certain rhythms
The belly flashed forward, blunting the blade of time.
But the layout of the suburb was that of a labyrinth, puzzling the nearsighted
magpie
Whereupon, he ran even more slowly, and almost crept
For fear that he would tread upon the newly-shed shells (from those
schoolward kids moments ago)

慢跑者意识到心脏长出多余的云朵
灵魂反而减轻了负担

他跑上了河堤，双腿禁不住打晃
看到排污河闪闪发亮地伸向供热厂
一轮红日刺入双眼，在那里
明媚之中，无人互道早安
只有体操代替口语，为下一代辩护

诗生活

我几乎在所有能找到的东西上写诗
牙刷、雨具、屋顶的壁虎、床下的乒乓球
我甚至也在女友的肚子上写诗
当然，写的都是蠢话和废话
说大师的肚子也被浮云广播过
剩下的小辈，高矮胖瘦的
亦步亦趋，走过了 90 年代。

夜里失眠时，也会暗自琢磨
写过的东西都哪去了，变成印刷的楷体小鸟飞走了？
还是转化成持续的不平衡挤压在脑后
坚持自我教育吧：写过的才是经验过的；
而夏天的窗子四面开着，枝叶纷披着
一叶叶，反叛的也就是被教唆的

除此之外，我还四处打探，在春光的自习室里
朋友们互掏耳朵，自打耳光，说老婆
以交往中的猜想与反驳为乐
难道这些，都是喜剧的一部分
要由暑期讲学的神来安排。
谁都不信，少年意气，也懒得去说

只有野蛮女友敢于提问
抱怨我想诗的时候多想她的时候少

He ran by the Post Office and then by a furniture store
Where he was cut-off by a red Xiali car. He then adopted
The Virtue of Tolerance, curling up the vegetable-like surges all through his
    body,
Trying hard to withdraw to a condensed point, like a disintegrating nucleus,
Precautious against any stumbling blocks to Virtue, as well as the wrath
Which may burst from his mouth, in the form of superficial curses

Which may disturb a migrant worker somnambulating on a pile of leaves
Where, at the end of the road, the city rose wheezing like a chronic asthmatic
In a blurred silhouette. A fresh wind breezed through
Massaging its way up the full-fledged organs of those billboards,
Causing him to reflect upon the advancement of time
As well as its setbacks, and upon the flocks and herds

Which moved into the fridge silently; iconic
The obese were squatting every corner, concrete as flowers.
"Our reasoning is free of flaws, in the way that asphalt is mixed
With some sugar, thus we finally taste the sweetness at the end of it!"
The jogger realized that extra clouds had grown out from his heart
Nevertheless his soul was relieved

He jogged up the riverbank, and his legs could not stop trembling
As the drainage ditch shimmered toward the power plant
And the red sun impinged upon his eyes.
In the radiant and enchanting sunlight, there was no exchange of "good
    morning."
Words were making way for physical jerks, defending the next generation

Poetic Life

I write down poems on whatever I can find:
Toothbrushes, rain gear, geckoes on the roof, and Ping-Pong balls under the
    bed
Even the belly of my sweetheart.
Certainly, all my poems are no more than some foolish words or rubbish
Saying that even the belly of the MASTER has been broadcast by drifting clouds

我只能从吃剩的鱼头上，暂时转移笔触
讲解不幸的七种含义
摸着她身上的锁骨和假山，聊胜于无

我的巴格达

我的巴格达，她在熟睡
下班后她就一直要求睡眠
是我，牵着天边的苍狗
迟迟不肯应允。

现在，橘红的街灯
终于说服了我，不再固执地
轻信原则，要随遇而安
不妨和熟悉的一切耍手段

瓦砾、泥浆、防空的树梢
——还有一切的峰颠
偶有轿车驶过，那也是偷情的妻子
耽搁了归家的时间。

而我的巴格达，她早已熟睡
枕在大山的臂弯里，她的眉毛
起伏着，屋檐起伏着
让云里的轰炸手，睁开独眼

瞄准的，原来只是一座空城。
那些无法搬空，无法解释的
依旧被青壮民工暴露的
其实，都是她的鼾声

在青春的地沟里滚动的浊流
睡吧，电话线已拔掉
当武器的告别，在远方
支配了新一代的如梦令、夜读抄

And that the mediocre poets, tall or short, plump or thin,
All followed his step, and thus muddled through the decade of the 1990s.

When sleepless at night, I always ponder privately
Where my works have gone, flying away like birds of printed script
Or returning as incessant misbalance pressed upon my brain?
So, I turn back to self-education: what has been written is what has been lived
But the summer windows on all sides remain open, the leaves having
    wrapped the trees
One leaf at a time: the antagonist is no other than the provoked.

Apart from this, I have been wandering around in the introspective room of
    springtime
My friends are cleaning each other's ears, slapping their own faces, and
    talking about their wives
Taking pleasure in the Conjectures and Refutations in their relationships

All these, ultimately, are components of a comedy
Subject to the whims of the God who is to lecture during summer semester
No one believes in the vigor of adolescence, or bothers to mention it

Only my sassy girlfriend dares to question
And to complain that I spend more time thinking about poetry than about
    her
Thus I have to temporarily divert my attention from the uneaten fish head
To the interpretation of the Seven Types of Misfortune,
Touching the clavicle and rockworks of her body —
I feel it's better than owning nothing

My Baghdad

My Baghdad, she is sound asleep
After work, she has been asking for a good sleep
It's I, leading a dog-shaped cloud from the horizon,
Who am reluctant to consent

我的巴格达，就座落在京郊
有两个晚上，我让电视
彻夜开着，好让卧室的尽头
更象是一个人的街垒

Now, the orange-colored streetlights
Eventually persuade me to be stubborn no longer
In my delusion of principles, but adaptive to my circumstances,
I might as well play tricks on whatever's familiar :

Tile fragments, slurries, and air-defense tree tops
as well as the pinnacle of everything
Occasionally, there passes by a car, in which is no other than an adulterous
    wife
Who has delayed returning home

Whereas my Baghdad has been in sound sleep for a long time
Pillowing her head in the arms of mountains, and her eyebrows
Arch and wave, as do the eaves
Which impels the bomber hidden in the clouds to open his only eye

What he aims at is virtually an empty city.
Those unmovable, those uninterpretable
And those revealed by industrious migrant workers,
In fact, are all her snores

As well as the muddy flows roaring in the ditch of adolescence
Ah, sleep, please. The phone line has been unplugged
When A Farewell to Arms, in certain remote areas,
Gets full control of the new generation's Dream Song and Night Reading
    Notes*

My Baghdad sits in the outskirts of urban Beijing.
Twice, at night, I have kept the TV set
Turned on till daybreak, so as to
Make the end of my bedroom look more like a barricade

---

  *Dream Song is a formulation in classical Chinese poetry; Night Reading Notes
is a genre in classic Chinese prose.

蓝蓝

萤火虫

我的眼睛保住了多少
　　萤火虫小小的光芒！
那些秋天的夜晚
萤火虫保住了多少
　　星空、天籁、稻田的芳香！

清凉的风吹进树阴
轻轻抱起活过的恋人
山楂树低垂的果实下
　　那互相靠近的肩膀

绿荧荧的小虫游丝一样织进
　　山林、村落、溪水的流淌
爱啊，温柔的亲娘
保住了多少往事和叹息
众多细小的生命
保全了我幸福而忧伤的一生……

在我的村庄

在我的村庄，日子过得很快
一群鸟刚飞走
另一群又飞来
风告诉头巾：
夏天就要来了。

夏天就要来了。晌午
两只鹌鹑追逐着
钻入草棵
看麦娘草在田头

Lan Lan

translations by Judith Roche and Huang Canran

Fireflies

My eyes have kept alive how many
    tiny twinklings of fireflies.
In those autumn nights
fireflies have reflected how many
    starry skies, night sounds and the scent of rice paddies.
Cool wind wafts into the shadowy trees,
gently embraces the ghosts of lovers who once loved
under the low-hanging fruits of hawthorn trees,
    their shoulders nestling together.
Green-glowing threads of light, the fireflies
    weave together mountain trees, villages, and flowing river.
Oh love, gentle mother,
you keep alive how many memories,
numerous tiny lives,
on the edge of my own life of joy and suffering.

In My Village

In my village time goes fast.
One flock of birds has just flown away
When another arrives.
The wind whispers to my scarf:
Summer is coming.
Summer is coming.
Midday, two quails chase each other
into a thicket of weeds.

守望五月孕穗的小麦
如果有谁停下来看看这些
那就是对我的疼爱

在我的村庄
烛光会为夜歌留着窗户
你可以去
因那昏暗里蔷薇的香气
因那河水
在月光下一整夜
淙潺不息

现实

没有白天，没有黑夜。
没有善。也没有恶。
一群人在受苦。
仅此而已。

没有绝对的词。
这些风吹散的薄纸的灰烬。

一群人在受苦。
就是这些。

永不休耕的土地里
只有一个女人挎着光辉的篮子
默默播撒种籽。

I watch mother-of-wheat grass[.]
bolting wild already in May.
If anyone else stops to see what I see
I will accept that as a way of loving me,
in my village
where candlelight shows the way
for night song that wafts through the window.
You can go there,
for the scent of roses in the twilight,
for the river that flows endlessly in moonlight.

Reality

No day, no night.
No good or evil.
People are suffering.
That's all.
No absolute word.
Ashes of thin papers are scattered by wind.
People are suffering.
Nothing more.
In the field that never lies fallow,
A woman with a basket
Is sowing seeds, speechless.

Nothingness

Nothingness, the great song of Being.
Ten thousand things arise from it to sing joyously —
how splendid the slow rising sun!

    [.]Shortawn foxtail is the English/American common name of Aalopecurus aequalis, the "mother-of-wheat grass" referred to in the poem. I kept the literal translation of the Chinese common name because it is more beautiful. –J.R.

虚无

虚无，最大的在之歌。

从它而来的万物在欢唱——
冉冉升起的朝阳多么辉煌！

孩子们伸手就会摸到苹果
圆满彤红地挂在碧绿的树上。

还有爱情——嘴唇渴望着嘴唇
灰烬中闪着一点发烫的火光。

白发苍苍的老人渡过童年
在积木搭成的乐园旁。

是的，一切都将归于虚无
而在之美梦与它一样久长。

弃儿

一个弃儿的身上有着如此多的疼痛
那遗弃他的东西借他的生命而活的长久

在一具肉体上留下偏头疼、胃溃疡
留下时间的结石和抑郁症

一个弃儿的身上有着如此多的伤疤
那些利刃、短锉奇怪地失去了后代

在下雪的深夜他把这一切紧紧抱在怀中
默默地念着一个唯一亲爱的名字

仿佛在他双唇间的闭合里跳动着一张
开始弯曲的人类的人的命运心电图——

Children can stretch out their hands and touch apples,
full and round and red, hanging on dark-green trees.
And love is lips longing for lips,
a burning spark lighting the darkness.
Old people, grey-haired, living a childhood
beside a paradise built of toy bricks.
True, everything will return to Nothingness
But the beautiful dream of Being is equally long and lasting.

Abandoned Child

An abandoned child is so full of pain.
Whatever abandoned him lives so long
by making use of his life.
In his body it leaves a migraine, a gastric ulcer,
a stone of time and despair.
An abandoned child holds so many scars,
but those sharp knives and rough files have softened,
losing their posterity.
Snowy nights he holds it all tightly in his arms,
repeating the only dear name silently,
As if in the thin line between his lips there throbs
an electrocardiogram of the fate of humanity,
which is beginning to zigzag.

Shock

You are asleep,
Dreaming of running.
Stars are in the sky and the sea tide is rising.
There is only this one thing —
You are dreaming of running.
Perhaps this is true,
as I watch your quivering eyelashes.
Your hand tells me I am becoming
Woman.

惊

你睡着。
做梦　奔跑
星星在天空而大海在涨潮

所有的只是一件事
你做梦　奔跑
也许这是真的
我注视着你微微颤动的睫毛

你的手告诉我我正在成为的东西：
女人。
不是花
也不是匿名的诗篇
——这也是真的？
当你帮助一个女人分娩自己
我从前居然不知道
她从未出生
如此漫长地等待你今夜的口令——

黄昏之忆

但那一刻，我是幸福
我是黄昏及所有
当那一刻你的拥抱
比上帝更近

我们无权相爱？
——但爱允许
太阳西沉，星宿渐亮
年轻的女工走在回家的路上。
你的呼吸和指尖的停顿
——但爱允许。

Not flower
Not anonymous poem.
— Is this also true?
You are helping a woman give birth to herself,
who didn't know until now
that she hadn't yet been born.
She has been waiting a long time
for this moment.

Memory of Dusk

At that moment I am happy.
I embody dusk and what it has held
at that moment when your embrace
    is closer than God.
We don't have the right to love?
    — but love allows itself.
The sun sinks in the west, stars are brightening,
young women are on their way home from work.
The moment holds its breath and becomes your fingertips.
    — and love allows itself.

Children's Day

My daughters, dressed in bright flowery costumes
Danced their laughter, wriggling like slender bean sprouts
As they peered into each other's rouge-smeared face.
Crowds of children joined them, squealing and shouting their glee,
A flock of honeybees,
Precious tiny lives.
    — I wanted no more from life.
Yet even I
    managed to have
A little bit more from that moment:
Tears of joy
And gratitude
And praise.

儿童节

我的女儿们换好了花衣裳。
她们互相看着抹胭脂的小脸
哈哈大笑。扭着嫩豆芽般的小腰。

更多孩子叫嚷着，他们围过来
一群快乐的蜜蜂
甜而小的生命。

——我不再要什么。
甚至
我也能
多出一点——在那一瞬间
——幸福的泪水。
——和感激。
——和赞美……

发现
　　——给我的孪生女儿

孩子在夜半醒来。
她只会爬，用一只小手
摸摸我的脸。
默默地她看着我，真乖。

我抱起她，为了
不惊醒另一个婴孩
——开门，走上阳台。

黑暗中，她睁大眼睛
久久望着一个方向
循着她惊奇的目光
我看到了伟大夜空中

Discovery

> — To my twin daughters

The child woke in the night.
Just beginning to crawl, her tiny hand
touched my face. Soundlessly, she looked at me.
    Beloved.
Mindful of her sleeping sister,
I wrapped her in my arms, silently
opened the door and slipped onto the balcony.
With wide and wondering eyes, she looked deep into the night,
and following her awed gaze I saw
in the great dark sky
    a star's
        shimmer.

How Long You Haven't Seen the Night Sky

Star. One. Another
It waits for your eyes every night.
A while ago you wrote in lamplight:
The sky is full of stars . . .
You blush. You were lying.
This one waits for you in the night wind,
Singing its bright star song.

He Who Possesses Very Little

The katydid and the cricket,
a green-clothed singer and a black-robed priest,
in a clump of pea vines one summer night,
whispering, murmuring,
"The silent," — the listener turns his head to hear —
"spring water has gently filled
    the deep pit of my sorrowful fate."

一颗星的
微明——

多久没有看夜空了

星星。一颗。还有一颗。
每夜它等你。
等你看它一小会儿。

那时，你在灯下写：
满天的星光……
你脸红。你说谎话。

它在夜风中等你。
静静唱着灿烂的歌。

拥有很少东西的人

螽斯和蟋蟀
绿衣歌手和黑袍牧师
在夏夜的豌豆丛中
耳语。小声呢哝

"这些——，"一个人侧耳谛听
"宁静的泉水多么温柔地填平了
我那悲惨命运的深坑——"

睡梦，睡梦……

我松开的手把你握紧
关上门以便你的穿越。

Sleeping Dream

My loosening hand tries to grip you tightly,
I shut the door to keep you here.
There is silence in my body,
you have already owned.
I fear . . . in each other's eyes,
changing shape, becoming smaller.

Untitled

I don't love coat: I love body.
Or, if the cotton shoulder pad is soul,
    I love that.
A calm at the heart of my desire,
I want both light and flame.
My love is humble and proud,
But here I am, wordless,
Enmeshed in your clothes
    And body.

我身体里的寂静
你早已得到。

我恐惧……在彼此的凝视里
变形　缩小。

无题

我不爱外衣而爱肉体。
或者：我爱灵魂的棉布肩窝。
宁静于心脏突突的跳动。

二者我都要：光芒和火焰。
我的爱既温顺又傲慢。

但在这里：言词逃遁了，沿着
外衣和肉体。

吕德安

父亲和我

父亲和我
我们并肩走着
秋雨稍歇
和前一阵雨
像隔了多年时光

我们走在雨和雨的间歇里
肩头清晰地靠在一起
却没有一句要说的话

我们刚从屋子里出来
所以没有一句要说的话
这是长久生活在一起
造成的
滴水的声音像折下的一支细枝条

像过冬的梅花
父亲的头发已经全白
但这近乎于一种灵魂
会使人不禁肃然起敬

依然是熟悉的街道
熟悉的人要举手致意
父亲和我都怀着难言的恩情
安详地走着

风景

经过多年的失望，
我终于搬走了窗口，

Lü De-An

translations by Ying Qin and Bill Ransom

Silhouettes

Father and I
Saunter side by side.
The autumn rain hesitates
In this cavernous lull after
The last outburst of rain.

We amble the intervals
Between rain and rain
Shoulder to shoulder, distinct
Clear, not a word to say.

We just walked out from the house
So there's not a word left to say
After our long life together.
Water drops like the snap
Of a brittle willow twig.

Like plum blossoms through winter
Father's hair is already all white
Halo of a kind soul, respectable.

Still this is the familiar street
All familiar people should wave their regards
Father and I both walk peacefully
In an unutterable loving-kindness.

但仔细一想，事实上
搬走的只是它的框架。

黑洞洞的，世界仍在原处，
可我毕竟已经离开，
在它的远方行走，
背负它的窗子框架。

天边飞过相似的候鸟，
想象当年的我也一样，
重复地走过这个或那个远方，
背负的是自己的窗子框架。

深夜

深夜。我梦见你居高临下。
海面上，一只海鸟正在低飞，
两岸是高高的建筑物。
我看见你朝着鸟的方向挥手，
似乎想让它知道你在这里：哪里？
我们曾经睡在其中的第十八层楼。
我看见你，瞳孔里面海在缩小，
一只鸟飞翔，像一只鸟的全景。
我感到你孤独，紧紧地抱住你，
感到你柔软的身体有一种晕眩的重量
在一次次的鸟瞰中下坠，下坠，
而最后一次却是在我的体内——
我们做爱，那也是我想告诉你，
我在这里，而那只鸟继续飞翔
也不过是睡觉前出来飞一飞
抑或想借助我们房间的光
去追随黑暗的鱼群，而在海面上
我们的光线摇曳直到海底……

Scenery

After many years of disappointment,
I finally removed the window,
But after a second thought, actually
What I took along was just its frame.

Well-bottom dark, the world is still
where it is after I turn away
To walk in its distant places,
Treasuring this window frame.

Those familiar migratory birds fly the edge of the sky.
Imagine that I was all the same then,
Walking repeatedly past this or that remote place,
Carrying my particular scenery on my back.

Deep Night

Deep in the night, I dream of you overlooking the depths
From the heights. Above the ocean, a seabird swoops low,
Tall, tall buildings crowd both shores.
You wave toward the bird,
As if letting it know that you are here: where?
We used to sleep on the 18th floor. The sea shrinks now
In your pupil. That bird flies, like a panorama of a bird.
I feel your loneliness, hold you tight,
Feel the fainting heaviness of your soft body
Falling, falling, when looking a bird's-eye view,
However, this last fall is inside my body —
We make love, that is also my wanting to let you know,
I am here, the continued flight of the bird
Is nothing but its taking a fly before sleep
Maybe it wants, with the help of the light from our room,
To follow those dark shoals of fish, while on the surface
Our light flickers, all the way through, to the bottom of the sea.

傍晚降雨

一整天都在炎热中逃避
直到傍晚，传来阵阵雷声
接着起风下雨，直到雨
真实地落进山谷，让几乎枯竭的
溪水充盈，形成了所谓的山洪
我们才意识到一点儿现实
直到有人在某处弯道上喊叫，隐隐
约约，而另一处曝晒了三天
用来扎扫帚的茅草花穗，再叫人来
把它尽数搬移却已经来不及

可事实上，此时附近并无一个
确实存在的人，而
这场而来时也似乎仅仅是为了
驱赶一只小鸟，好让它早早归巢；
而某种黑暗让洪水提早来到，是因为
雨似乎仍在一个模糊的现实的呼喊之外
是啊，我们以为雨不会落下，
这个世界也不会发生什么意外
以及那些白色的石头，它们永远
拒绝降临。在它们的祈祷声中——
我们还发现自己原是一些时远时近的事物：
我们曾经那么原始和容易受惊

曼凯托（长诗选章）

　1
曼凯托，一天雪下多了，这镇上的雪
仿佛小小的地方教堂，把节日的晚钟鼓响

已堆积到第二个台阶。但没有人
没有人站出来说这是季节反常

Evening Rain

Thunder dodges the scorching day until evening,
when wind whips real rain across our valley, swelling
Our parched little stream into mountain flood.
We wake to a bit of reality when someone yells
On some winding path, indistinctly and faintly,
While somewhere else, exposed to the sun for three days
The spikes of thatch grass, ready to be brooms, are lost.
No one really exists nearby at that moment
Onset of this rain seems simply
To drive a chickadee early to its nest.
Some kind of darkness drives the flood because
The rain still thunders outside a blurred, realistic wail.
Yes, we thought the rain would never fall,
Our people would never have accidents
And those white stones, they would forever
Refuse doom. In the murmuring sound of their prayers
We find ourselves to be just some objects — now near, now far:
We used to be so primitive, so easily startled.

Mankato (excepts)[*]

1

Mankato, too much snow for one day, the snow in this town
Like the tiny local church ringing the festival bell late,

Already drifted up to the second step. But no one,
No one steps up to declare this abnormal for the season.

---

*"Mankato" is a town named after the Lakota Sioux word "Makato," meaning
"Blue Earth."

"想想现在也该是冬天了，厚厚一层雪
必须把它们照例铲开，堆放两旁"

然而没有人在听，只是孙泰
在自言自语，在继续推开盘子——

事情总得有人去做——大家并不在乎
这句老话，是一种推辞还是表态

只是孙泰红肿的眼睛，在雪地上
看到一对斗殴的天使

翅膀完好无损，并有一阵微风
吹醒了他，在那温暖僻静的梦乡

   2
每天，总有一些人提早醒来
而成为我们出门时遇见的人

总有人在提早开始一天，然而
用不了多久，他们又要睡去

每天，当孙泰扫完门前雪
日子好像又回到了昨天

哟，我是说我不能理解
当孙泰活着的时候，他又是

怎样活下来的。在花园的后架旁
他奇迹般地赶上我父亲

喊着要到远方养蜂，已经
有了合伙人，可是没等父亲回答

他已踏上了海浪，月光下
撒出鱼网，像一个健忘的人

Think about it: It's about winter, this thick layer of snow
Should be shoveled and piled up on both sides, as usual."

However, no one listens except for Sun Tai.
Murmuring, pushing one's plate away —

Someone ought to do something — people didn't care
About this old saying, whether declination or statement.

Only the red and swollen eyes of Sun Tai
See a pair of angels fighting on the snow-covered ground

Wings intact, and a gentle breeze
Wakes him from the warm and secluded land of dream.

2

Every day, some people wake up early
And become those we meet when we step outdoors.

Always some people start the day early, then
Soon crawl back to sleep again.

Every day, Sun Tai finishes shoveling the snow from the doorway
And the day seems to turn back to yesterday.

Hey, I mean that I don't understand
When Sun Tai was alive, how he

Made his living. By the trellises in back of the garden
Like magic, he catches up with my father

Shouts his plans to go to faraway places for beekeeping, how he's
already found a partner, but before Father can reply

He's already stepping out onto the waves, in the moonlight
Casting his fishing nets just like a forgetful person.

一个爱开玩笑的人，从他的故事
跳开，从这座永恒的房子中走开

3
当孙泰把船从树影下移开
雪地上就有一个不大不小的船印

现在，我们把他的躯体翻个身
希望底下压着一封信。没有

或许信已经融化，利用
这场错误的雪。文字模糊了

或许根本没有文字。孙泰
自然把握不了这种美。他不会自杀

这第一场雪，当孙泰把船
推入水中他震惊于仿佛听见

处女的呻吟，仿佛在房间里
所感到的巨大空虚和委屈

一个大海的孩子，当他来到海边
他就注定要被一个拒绝回家的声音

永远地带走

6
继续下雪，地面又增厚半尺
或者说为了实现完美，雪按照

往年的惯例继续制造它的镜子
而等天气再冷一阵，所有的

过道，窗口，广场，凡是露天的地方
都将成为它装扮的好去处

A man who loved joking, he jumped away
From his own story, walked away from this eternal house.

3

Sun Tai moved the boat from the shadows of the trees
And left on the snow an impression of the boat, not too big, not too small.

Now, we turn his body over
Hoping to find a letter underneath. No.

Maybe the letter melted, making use of
This snowfall by mistake. Words all blurred

Maybe no words at all. Sun Tai obviously
Couldn't master this kind of beauty. He couldn't have committed suicide

This first snow of the year, when Sun Tai pushed
That boat into the water, he was shocked to hear

Something like a virgin moaning, as if
The vast emptiness and grievances felt in a room.

A son of the sea, when he came to shore
He was doomed to be taken away forever

By a voice that refused to go back home.

6

Snow keeps falling, the ground thickens another half foot
Or we could say that to achieve perfection, the snow

Keeps working on making its mirror as in past years.
When it becomes colder, all the

在这里，惟有乌鸦是真实的
在雪地上，它们的黑色瞳仁

在世界的白色眼圈里闪动，飞跃
冲撞，燃烧，沉寂，复活

在这里，惟一执著而天真的
也是这些乌鸦

它们落下又落下
这一只和更黑的一只

7

近来，每当我写一首诗，就像乌鸦
在雪地上涂改，涂改一首老掉牙的歌

比起抒情的天空，我目前更倾向于
陈述性的天空，啊，乌鸦的聒噪

比起写诗，我现在更喜欢写信
有时间有地点，人人读得懂

可是近来到底发生过什么——
一个星期除了雪花纷纷扬扬

仍像第一场雪，望不到它的尽头
除了乌鸦像白色坟地上的黑色火焰

充满了厌倦，而送信人已推迟
三天，今后会更久

啊，上帝，什么时候才能
让我们之间的通信稳定下来

Alleyways, windows, town squares, all places in the open
Make good locations to dress itself up.

Here, only the crows are real
In the snowfield, their black pupils

Flicker in the white eye sockets of the world, flying and leaping
Rushing and colliding, burning, quieting down as if dead, reviving.

Here, the only persistent and naïve
Are also crows

Who descend and descend again
This one and an even darker one.

7

Recently, every time I write a poem, it's like the crows'
Scribbling and correcting on snow, obliterating an old, toothless song.

Compared to the lyrical sky, now I prefer more
The declarative sky. Ah, the clamor of crows

Compared to poetry, now I like writing letters more
With a time and a place, everyone can understand.

But what exactly happened recently —
Besides snowflakes drifting, profuse and disordered, all week long?

Still, like the first snow of the year, its ending point is beyond sight
Except the crows, black flames in the white cemetery.

Filled with boredom, with the mailman late for three days
And longer waits expected in the future

Ah, God, when
Will the correspondence between us smooth out?

10

有一次，也是仅有的一次，我坐下
写诗，正巧孙泰推门进来

"怎样写诗？"他问"是否跟捕鱼一样"
但愿如此，我心想

后来的一天，我走向他的船，毕竟
他同意多一点见识对我有好处

在海上，一只乌贼弥留水中
晶莹透亮，犹如空气

又犹如乡村里小小的
飘泊的教堂，安静而忧郁

我请求孙泰慢点收网，而当我回头
只见水中黑烟弥漫，一片惊慌

乌贼逃走了，像一个犹大
诗也一样，诗背叛你

利用灵魂的浑浊

11

有些日子，孙泰的房子会
不知不觉地增高一层

"你怎么会这一手？"我路过
并顺手抛给他一块砖头

一个砌砖者俯身在云端
在金字塔似的房子上方

立梁那天，我抽出一天
帮助他拉住一根粗绳

10

Once, and only once, when I sat down
To write poems, Sun Tai opened the door and walked in.

"How to write a poem?" he asked. "Is it the same as fishing?"
I wish it were so, I thought.

Later one day I walked toward his boat, after all
He agreed that I should gain more experience.

At sea, a cuttlefish languished in the water
Glittering and transparent, like the air

Also like the tiny drifting church in the village
Quiet and dejected.

I asked Sun Tai to hold off pulling the net, then looked back
Only to see panic and black smoke fill the water.

The squid fled like a Judas.
Poems are the same, poems betray you

Taking advantage of the muddiness of the soul.

11

Some days, Sun Tai's house would
Gain an extra floor before we knew it.

"How come you have this skill?" Passing by,
I toss a brick up to him.

High in the clouds, a bricklayer bends over
Atop the pyramid-like house.

想象当年的十字架撑起
一个天庭也不过如此

"只剩下屋顶了"，我说：
"是否让我明天再来"

一个健忘的人，一个爱开玩笑的人
如今他身后留下了我们

和这片空空的，绝望的空间

18
我已离不开大海，
也不能想象，当我从山上的家

沿着台阶下来，
大海有一天突然不在了

昨天，我看见对面山上
的红色寺庙，一个泥瓦匠

从屋顶滚入地狱
一地面上栽下一朵大红花：为了什么

为了改造成一所普通学校
为了雨会漏下来，为了

驱散一阵云和有人用当天
的报纸包紧一头鱼。并且

重重地放在我们的穷桌子上
说这是蓄意已久的

19
同样地，假设一个早晨，我们
可以下降到海底，像潜入教堂

On the day to set the roof beam in place, I spend one day
Helping him to hold onto a thick rope

Imagining that in the past, nothing more than this
would shore up Heaven with the Cross.

"Only the roof is left now," I say,
"Do you want me back tomorrow?"

A forgetful man, a man who loved joking
Now he leaves behind him, us

And this empty, hopeless space.

18

I can hardly do without the sea,
Cannot imagine either that one day when we descend the stairs

From my house on the hill
The sea would be suddenly missing.

Yesterday, I saw on the hill opposite my place
The red temple. A tiler

Rolled down the roof and fell into Hell.
A big red flower was planted on the ground: what for?

For an ordinary school needs to be remade out of the temple
For rain could drip through, for

Scattering a burst of clouds, and someone
Wrapping a fish in the day's news, and also

Slamming it down on our poverty-stricken table
Saying that this had been long-contemplated.

但不需要那些说教的空气，我们
自由呼吸，周围是海星千年沉寂的光芒

我们将作为发现者重新找到孙泰
一个复合的灵魂，他几乎不认识我们

他说我们头顶上面另有一个世界
而我们从未在那里生活过

他的话语是泡沫。而我们试图理解他
至少我们一起上升，直到在天文学的

意义中上升到新的一天，那里星球是星球
真实而粗糙，像天狼星那样的星

只会像狼一样在脸上泛着灰烬的光
而孙泰读得懂这些神秘的熄灭了的语言

20
想想吧，那一天我们是怎样
推开人墙去辨认孙泰——

这个曾经吩咐我们等待的人
这个日夜行走在海面上

却不谙水性的人，他的姿势
已被摆放端正，已从一片烂木板

移到桌上，类似一个结论：
哦，上帝昨天造出一个孙泰

今天又在我们膝盖上放下另一个他
而对世界这些只是简单的事情

孙泰甚至还是微笑的，像他的童年
一个孩子，有着海螺般的听觉

19

Similarly, suppose one morning we
Descend to the bottom of the sea, like sneaking into church

But without the sermonic air, we
Breathe freely, surrounded by the light of sea stars, deadly quiet for a
    thousand years.

We, as discoverers, will find Sun Tai again
A composite soul, he hardly knows us

Says that there's another world above our heads
Yet we never lived there.

His words are foam. But we try to understand him
At least we ascend together, until we reach

A new day in astronomy, where stars are stars
Real and rough, stars like Sirius

Can merely let the ashen glow float on his face like a wolf
Yet Sun Tai reads these mysterious languages, long died out.

20

Think about how, on that day, we
Push through the pack of people to identify Sun Tai —

This man who once told us to wait
This man who rode the ocean surface day and night

Yet who never knew how to swim. His posture is
Arranged upright, in regular style, after being removed from a piece of
    broken wood

他摸上去甚至还是完整的，海水
的皮肤留下一层薄薄的盐

　　26
一场小而激动的雨，当它
把晶体的卵排在玻璃窗上

又在意义中隐藏起自己，我们
看到了一个斑斑点点的世界

雨的完美，使我们想起雨的缺陷
现在雨就下在它自己的缺陷里

在玻璃后面，而就像隔壁那个
跛脚裁缝，正在把雨点

歪歪斜斜地缝过春天
春天中的平凡的一天

这场小雨。还使我想起儿时
灯光下摆着那些蚕，小小的嘴

吐着一丝丝光，织出一个个
小而又小的天堂，它们的白色身体

也因此更加透明，托在掌上
直到变成蛾，再一下子释放了自己

　　28
想想我们开拓这个池塘
将给今后的日子带来什么好处

父亲和孙泰，当他们站在后院
一洼积水给了他们丰富的想象

168

Onto the table, as if a conclusion:
Oh, God created a Sun Tai yesterday

And today put at our knees another him
Yet to this world, these are merely, simply, things.

Sun Tai still smiles, as if in his childhood
A child who had conch-like hearing

He even feels whole, his skin of seawater leaves a thin layer of salt.

26

When a small burst of excited rain
Lays its crystal eggs on the glass window

And hides itself up in significance and meaning, we
See a world full of spots and stains.

The very flawlessness of the rain reminds us of the flaws of the rain
Now this rain falls into its own flaws.

Behind the glass, the rain is like that
Lame tailor next door, sewing crooked and

Awkward raindrops into the spring
An ordinary day in spring.

This small burst of rain also brings back my childhood
Those silkworms laid out under the lamplight, tiny mouths

Spinning threads of light, weaving heavens
One and another, small and smaller, their white bodies

draining to translucent. I cupped them in my palms
Till they turned into moths, then released themselves all of a sudden.

后来雨水的泛滥又成全他们——
想想他们挖土，把土运到别处

把水留下来，为什么不呢
我们有的是土地，况且

这里的冬天比夏天长——
想想下雪，结冰，当我们醒来

夕阳池面上，有小孩三五成群
朝着无穷的惯性的夜滑去，回来时

都已是大人，身后带来更多的孩子
更多的光，而父亲和孙泰

就是在这样的光中继续挖掘
直到碰上树根和骨头才挺起身缓口气——

世界并没有改变多少

28
Think that by digging this pond
How we'd benefit in the days to come.

Father and Sun Tai stood in the backyard
That water in the small depression fed them rich imagination.

Later the flooding rain helped them to achieve their goal —
To think that they dug the dirt out, carried all the dirt to another place

And retained the water, why not?
We had plenty of land, besides

Winter here was much longer than summer —
Imagine snow, the pond icing over, and when we wake

On the surface of the pond, under the setting sun, kids in threes and fives
Skate toward the infinite night of inertia, and when coming back

Already grownups bring more kids with them
More light, while father and Sun Tai

Continue digging in their enlightenment
Not straightening up to take a break until hitting tree roots
         and bones.

The world never changes much at all.

马兰

荷花少女

一把空虚的木椅
一位怀抱荷花的少女
在上面坐着坐着,
一支受伤的雁子飞过山岗
一位老人在湖边预言洪水的爆发
少女看见
人们随流而下

少女坐着坐着,不动
这姿态如同我们的遗忘是一种姿态
少女从水中而来
水越来越辽阔无边
水朝着陆地不屈地绽放
面积一次次地重复
世界越来越是一面镜子是一个平面
植物和动物再难区别和联系
包括荷花和少女

一把空虚的木椅依附着
荷花少女,荷花少女在
水下的世界,她走不出水
世界属于水了,陆地在水下
空虚的木椅是陆地的证据是一种生活

荷花少女
水上的悲剧属于异性

Ma Lan

translations by Martine Bellen and Charles A. Laughlin

Lotus Blossom Girl

A meditation bench, empty.
Girl embosoms a lotus blossom,
Sits on the bench.
A lone goose flies wounded over the mountain ridge.
Old man by a lake prophesies the flood.
A girl sees
People floating on the current.

The girl sits perfectly still.
Her posture reflects forgetfulness.
The girl swells out from water.
Water overflows without border.
A gushing cascade floods the land,
Its area increases exponentially.
The world's realm, increasingly a mirror, a level surface.
Discrete plants and animals are hard to distinguish.
Even lotus and girl fuse.

A wooden bench, empty, cleaves to
Lotus girl, the lotus girl
Is in the world under water, she cannot surface.
The world belongs to water, and the land is beneath.
The empty bench is proof of it, a way of living.

Lotus girl,
Tragedy of the flood belongs to men, not women.

坐在哪里

坐在一块冰上
下面是水

坐在他的家里
左右是花纸纷飞的岁月
摸了几本在地上走动的书
他们越走越瘦成群集队
上面灰尘满脸

坐在他的家外
抬头是蓝天白云
他在我身后指点我
你的美丽已是呛人的泪水

坐在自己的心里
很长的时间
坐成包裹像堆草本植物

坐在一根木头上
刻舟求剑
然后再回到冰上
下面是滚动的河流

下雨

下一场雨吧，我在他的嘴唇上
我很弹性，你看我的手指
弹琴的手。

让这位男人讲话，他要到哪里去
我可以离开他的嘴唇
我知道他会走得很快
可怎么样才能从左心室走到右心室

Where to Sit

I sit on a block of ice,
Water beneath me.

I sit in his house.
To the left and right are years carried by the wind like confetti.
I touch some books that are crawling across the floor.
They grow thinner as they trek, form groups,
Collect dust.

I sit outside his house,
Raise my eyes and see the blue sky, white clouds.
He is behind me, criticizing,
"Your beauty has become tears that choke."

I sit in my own mind,
Remain there for so long
I become a package, a bundle of herbs.

I sit on a wooden fence,
"Mark the boat to find a sunken sword"*
And then return to sit on the block of ice,
The current flowing beneath me.

It Is Raining

Let it rain. I relax on his lips.
I am flexible — look at my fingers,
They are nimble enough to play music.

---

*This idiom originates from an ancient story of an idiot who drops his sword from a boat, and to recover it, he marks the spot on the boat from which the sword fell, anchors the boat, and dives in (of course he does not find the sword). The story has been interpreted philosophically as a critique of the tendency to apply fixed standards to changing phenomena.

时间太小，我所看望的字体
也瘦可见骨
很久前我在路上，哭诉比较有力
现在下一场雨吧，抑制我
包庇我。

我的衣裳放在手上，和我
有浓雾般的距离

秋语

我感到一点饿，可我不知
该不该吃东西。已经立秋了
已经在深夜
或许只是乾燥的信息
玻璃杯破碎的那股意志和忧伤
或者象多余的选择一样不可思议
正是这个时候，我推窗而立
窗帘擦身而过，放肆又从容
秋天是有风的
眼到之处是半遮半掩的衣饰
眉来眼去的收割，庄稼
自己种下的庄稼呵庄稼
感动白色出没
太多的迷失，一种液体分界线
夏娃吃的是芒果还是苹果
水果不能互相替代
水果使女人的嘴最先成熟
可我饿了呀，当怀旧的时候
我身披一块碎花桌布
让餐巾纸裸体陈列
我在想，望梅止渴、画饼充饥
在收获的季节
这没有什么不方便
我一动不动全身就充满了泪水

Let this man utter his intended destination.
I depart from his lips.
I know he will set off quickly,
But how to get from the left to right ventricle?

Not enough time to spend with the sick font I am visiting
Who is skin and bone.
Long ago I was on the road. Tearful reproaches are relatively potent.
Let it rain, now! Restrain,
Protect me.

Though the clothes I wear touch my body, a thick mist
Separates me from the fabric.

Autumn Words

I feel a little hungry, but don't know
If I should eat something. Tonight autumn has already begun.
Perhaps, for you, this is dry information —
Volition and grief of a shattered drinking glass —
Maybe it's as inconceivable as options to spare.
Just now, I draw open the window and stand before it.
The curtain grazes me, wanton and blithe.
Autumn bears wind,
Adornments half-hidden, partly concealed, from the eye,
Eyeing each other as we reap crops,
The crops we sowed alone, the wind-blown crops,
Arousing crops, flitting into view
Having lost one's way with a fluid border.
Did Eve eat mango or an apple?
Fruit does not transfer,
Fruit makes women's lips ripen.
But I get hungry, when I'm loitering in the past.
I drape a floral tablecloth around my body,
Paper napkins line up to conceal my breasts,
I think: gazing at plums quenches thirst, sketching small cakes satisfies
    hunger.
In this harvest season nothing's inconvenient.

可泪水又被谁握在手中或者
仍躺在我的嘴里

事件

　事件（一）

没有听见一声猫叫
春天就开始了

比如，北京的风沙很大
满街的塑料袋全盘钻进了风中
我们外地人不懂这力量从何而来

我们看不见天，只能对视
或者看塑料袋，想象那无非是
一生的幸福在风沙之上，渐行渐远

一个以诗歌为名的聚会在酒吧
我们买了一朵玫瑰
一朵玫瑰等于一百朵玫瑰
我们坐着，听胡吗个唱
"我怎么会有感情呢？"

仍然没听见猫叫，在春天
猫不叫春，红杏却要出墙

　事件（二）

一只漏网的鱼跟踪着我
我不知道是什么意思
可能她被时间冲散
时间从背后而来，把眼睛推出眼眶
落在手心，奔忙不停

Before I know it, my body's covered in tears,
My tears have fallen into another's hand, or
They lie in wait in my mouth.

Events

Event I

Without even a cat's meow,
Spring has begun.

For example, the harsh Beijing dust storms.
Plastic bags on the street are stuffed into winds.
As outsiders we do not understand the source of this power.

We cannot see the sky, only each other
And the whirling bags, we imagine as
Life's joys that ride the dust, grow distant, taken by the wind.

There is a poetry-theme party at the karaoke bar.
I bought a rose —
One rose equals a hundred.
We sit and listen to Hu Ma-ge sing:
"How could I have feelings?"

Still, no cat meows this spring,
No yowling, though the red apricot has grown beyond the wall.*

Event II

A fish that eluded the net has been following me.
I don't know what that means.

---

*A common image in old Chinese romantic literature signifying pre-marital or extra-marital liaisons.

疾病一直跟踪我
我也不知道是什么意思
难道只能走向医院，抱着治愈的希望
从麻醉开始

还有一只服药的蝴蝶包裹我
我就跑进白天，低头
感受光阴滑入头发
一顶草帽浮在河里
这是儿时全部的梦想
随灰尘而舞，直到天黑

　　事件（三）

我离你很近
手心和手背的距离
我这么想念着你
香气都能伤人，这时

一只鸟
落在我的左肩
我的右翼从此失去平衡
今晚还能睡在哪里？

这个冬天
想比鸟飞得更远
我的爱人，这让我一病不起

我把自己推到世界之外
这是一种可能性
我模仿消亡，以自己之手
我的爱人，雪继续下着
叫我如何面对洪水
这个冬天
鸟又落在我的右肩

Maybe she was strewn by the flow of time.
Time comes from behind, pushes my eyes out their sockets.
They drop into my hands, dash about nonstop.

Illness has always followed me.
I don't know what that means, either.
Do I have to visit hospitals forever with the hope one day I'll be cured?
From the painkiller the doctor begins.

There is also a butterfly taking medicine that wraps around me.
I run into the day, my head lowered,
And feel the light and dark, months and years, melt into my hair.
A straw hat floats down the river,
Which is the dream of my childhood,
Dancing with dust until sunset.

Event III

I am close to you,
As distant as my palm to the back of the hand.
I miss you so much,
Even perfume can injure, now.

A bird
Falls on my left shoulder,
My right wing loses its balance.
Where can I sleep tonight?

This winter
Wants to fly farther than a bird.
My love, I'm so sick I cannot rise.

I thrust myself out of the world —
That is a possibility.
To imitate vanishing, I disappear my hands.
My love, the snow continues to fall,
Tell me how to face the floods.

我要么接受，要么拒绝

事件（四）

我面向你走，保持平仄
迈了左脚再出右脚，交叉而行

你种了一棵树在我的后背
　我的脖上套着一条围巾，那是蛇
遗忘了脱皮的细节
还有沉船，从童年
破门而入，看见我变成一堆衣服
挂在地上

我们把门从里面打开
一件又一件地清洗工具
需要五分钟，然后睡觉
无所谓四季轮转

那天用完了我的一生
也没能把衣服重新穿上

对话

那是个古国
有许多人头在飞
还有一颗挂在我的头上，永垂不朽

那是个市场
吃喝玩乐，打情骂俏
我的情敌就在我体内，昼伏夜行

那是场电影
你和他们杀戮
你保护了改行的牙医，假牙真做

This winter
A bird falls on my right shoulder.

I can accept, or reject.

Event IV

I walk toward you minding my pings and zes.*
As I stride with my left foot and extend my right, they cross.

You planted a tree on my back.
That is a snake. It forgot precisely how to molt.
Sinking boats since childhood —
I unlock the door and enter: I have molted into a pile of clothes,
Which hangs on the floor.

We open the door from inside,
Wash our tools one by one.
We need five minutes, then must sleep
Heedless of the cycle of seasons.

That day I used up my life
And was not able to put on my clothes again.

Dialogue

Over there is an ancient land.
Many heads are flying,
One of them hangs on mine, suspended in perpetuity.

---

*Literarily pings and zes refer to the strict prosodic requirements of traditional
Chinese poetry whereby the words chosen for a given line have to constitute a
sequence of tones that correspond to a standard pattern.

我手拿玫瑰花
在情人节
像高举一把白菜
挑战地球的引力
似乎苹果要掉下来
告诉我们从来没有一无所有

这么一个女人

我觉得，有一个女人在遥远的天国
她吃饭睡觉感冒伤风，还嫁了人
她把皮鞋擦得察言观色，把私生活夸张到直经水平
这样的女人最可能是白里透红的美女
我想象，美女，有一个女人是美女时
我的皮鞋是不是增加了宽度、高度
可我每天主要的工作是帮人测量距离
距离与距离的关系比我与女人的关系更有尺寸感
可我感受到时差，从出来的那天开始
那天冒着被抽象的危险，谁说危险是女人难产的前沿
难产过的女人都很逻辑，尤其是黄里透黑的准美女
我准美丽的女人呵，我认为
二十岁她将死于革命，三十岁死于非法同居，决不可能
四十岁死于车祸，死在路上的是我们时代的诗人
诗人，我又亲又爱的诗人，我还是你的宝贝吗？
我不是你的宝贝那我坐在谁的宝座上如此疯狂温柔！
温柔如雪的呵，我发现我真是宁为瓦全不为玉碎了
可疑的生活，虚拟的出售生活，我或者女人？
两者必有其一。我且痛且疼的女人，想隔岸观火为我
送终吗？我承认你应该得到满足，千里之行始于手下。
水流过来又流回去，很格律似的运动着，可我的一九九八年呢！
我种九百九十种玫瑰的女子，我发现风吹才能草动
而且谁也没有重叠我的手艺。在厨房卧薪尝胆你想着我的时候
我早就走了，我们住在不同的城堡，都有一双眼睛隔墙警惕我们
还说我们拥有伯乐。我告诉你吧我在路途中不停地转换方向想
寻找一个出口。火车那么容易穿插而过，

184

There's a market:
Eat, drink, and be merry; brawl over love and beauty.
My amorous rival lives inside my body, hiding by day, budding at night.

That, there, is a film.
You and the actors engage in a massacre.
You protect the pretend dentist, and dentures he inserts are taken for real.

I hold a rose in my hands
On Valentine's Day
As if bearing aloft some cabbage leaves
To challenge earth's gravity.
It seems the apple will fall,
An indicator there's never been utter nothingness.

A Woman Like This

Once upon a time there was a woman from a distant land.
She ate, slept, caught cold, even married.
She shined her shoes with eyes wide open, focusing on their colors, noting
     their moods, talked big about her private life.
This woman was most probably a beauty, red showing through white.*
I imagine she's spectacular; but simply because a woman's beautiful
Are her shoes wider, larger than mine?
My primary job is to help others gauge distance.
The distance between one person and the next, calculated by feet and inches,
     is more measurable than the distance between this woman and me.
I've been sluggish since the day I was made,
The day I first risked danger of abstraction; who says fear is the harbinger of
     a troubled pregnancy?
Women who have had difficulty birthing remain logical, especially those
     quasi-beauties who show black through yellow.

---

*"Showing through white" is a common expression describing beautiful skin; Lan plays on this later in the poem with "black showing through yellow," describing ugliness.

我在邃道里看到无数的鱼群从我头上游戏、欢喜，
这是命名的过程吗，我闻鸡起舞的同乡。这样的女人可能走多远，
虽说她成长为已婚者，激起公愤
这样的女人只能买公债还私债，两败俱伤

Oh, beautiful woman,

At twenty you will die of revolution, at thirty: illegal cohabitation,

At forty: an auto accident. The man who died on the road is the poet of our
generation.

Poet, oh fond and cherished poet, am I still your princess?

If I'm not, then on whose throne do I reign? crazy and tender as I am?

Tender as snow, I'd rather be a humble tile than precious jade hammered
into shards.

Dubious life, virtual life's sold — the woman or me?

One or the other. Woman plagued with painful wounds, will you, gazing at
the fire from across the shore,

Pay me your last respects? I want you to be satisfied; the thousand-mile
journey begins on the tip of your typing fingers.

The waters flow back and forth in decipherable patterns, but what's to come
of me this year!

I, a woman who plants nine hundred-ninety kinds of roses,* know that
grasses bend only when wind blows,

That no one can duplicate my craft; I know when you are in the kitchen

thinking of me and tasting bile, tempering your resolve.[†]

I have long since departed. We live in distinct castles, anonymous eyes
watching out for us over ramparts.

We both have good judges of talent behind us.[‡] I'm constantly changing
direction, searching

For an exit. The trains pass quickly

Through the tunnel

I see countless schools of fish swimming above my head, joyous.

---

*This line is from a popular song, the kind often sung in karaokes in China.

[†]Literally translates as "sleeping on brushwood and tasting gall." The dictionary
explains, "The state of Yue was defeated by the state of Wu [during the Spring and
Autumn Period of the Eastern Zhou dynasty, 777-475 BC], and Gou Jian, King of
Yue resolved to take revenge. He would taste a gall bladder and rest on brushwood
before eating and sleeping to remind himself of the humiliation he had experienced.
After a long period, he finally defeated the Wu."

[‡]Literally "Bo Le," a name of a legendary connoisseur of horses in ancient times.
His name is synonymous with "a good judge of talent."

Is this the process of naming, my prized, inspiring hometown friend?* How
    far can this kind of woman walk?
Though it is said she has married, eliciting outrage,
This kind of woman must resort to buying public bonds to repay private
    debts, both sides wounded, defeated.

---

*Another venerable idiom, literally "arising for sword practice at cock's crow."
The dictionary explains, "In the Eastern Jin dynasty, Zu Ti and Liu Kun were good
friends and often encouraged each other, and both rose at cock's crow to play with
their swords.

莫非

深蓝

天空，有你纸一样撕开的词语
天空，有我没见过的那种深蓝
就这样抱着。落叶落在地上
还是抱着轻呵，不太圆的月亮

升上了峰顶。来自谷底的波涛
让你梦时游动。黄栌冷寂的
夜晚，让诗人引火烧身。满山
溢香的节日，带着过往的云烟

眼看到了话说从前的年龄。是
什么，就是什么。什么不是
就什么不是。当我相信你也
相信的时候，树与树如此孤单

选自组诗《秋怀九章》

今晚

今晚，一定是你。密不透风的树林
落叶不断。今晚生死两头的线索
被拉扯。不答应的女人越看越美
甚至你无动于衷的样子也叫我

活该如此。月光避开所有的窗户
在你的时间里，拧紧果实的发条
我的疼痛，就在你心脏的附近
无人走过的树林全是你的声音
今晚，这世上只配给你我两个人
天是黑的，天是空的

Mo Fei

translations by Charles Borkhuis, Cheng Wei, Ying Qin and Zhang Er

Deep Blue

There, in the sky I saw your words torn apart like papers.
There, in the sky I saw a sort of deep blue I had never seen before.
Thus, in each other's arms we remained. Leaves were hurling down to the
    ground,
So light in my arms, the not so-round moon rose behind the peaks.

In your dreams you were swimming in the waves, rolling up from the depth
    of the valley.
The cold, silent night of the smoke tree woods made the poet draw fire
    against himself.
Full of the fragrance of the mountains, the festival
Brought with it the clouds and smoke of the past days.

Now we have come to the age to talk of things past. What is
Is what is. What is not is not.
When I begin to believe what you believe,
The trees become so isolated from one another.

                    –C.B. and C.W.

Tonight

Tonight, it has to be you. In the thick woods that can't be penetrated by
    wind,
Leaves are falling ceaselessly. Tonight both ends of the thread of life and
    death
Are pulled tight. Your refusal only increases your beauty.
Even your coldest look makes me feel I get what I deserve.

今晚，两个人加在一起的理由
足够你我不分左右，相依为命

选自组诗《秋怀九章》

时间之门（长诗选章）

0

时间，凭空而来。算尽机关依旧
不能打开人类的头脑。转换时间的
句法，依旧不能说出我对你的梦想
是一阵大风，走远了过去的河流
是一片汪洋抱着新旧交替的门柱
而我抱着你，怀念我们当初的时间

2

我要说我是幸福的，然而我不能
幸福的根源在哪儿，不能告诉你
是因为相信的人已经死去。不信的人
还没有到来，灵魂的嫌疑犯
知道痛苦将伴随我们一生。不问
何时何地，唯有痛苦不会麻痹我们

是一场经过化妆的游行，让一座城楼
虚设在灯火中。是一个女人的王冠
让一个弑君者在刀锋上擦着冷汗
谁把世界的奥秘当成儿戏，谁就是
儿戏中的道具。板着面孔的道具
让死亡渗出了油漆的光泽和裂痕

是倒置的镜子，被推到时间的尽头
是朝下的火焰和石碑，在智者的路上
是挂不住语言的事物，难以向你诉说
是你身边不在意的爱情，不可能久留

The moonlight avoids all the windows.
In your time, my pain is like a fruit with a tightly-wound, clockwork spring
Aching somewhere near your heart.
The woods, which no one passes, are filled with your voice.

Tonight, the world is only for us two.
The sky is black and empty.
Tonight, the reason that adds two people together
Is insufficient for us to distinguish left from right or be dependent upon each
    other.

                    –C.B. and C.W.

The Gate of Time (exerpts)

0

Time . . . released from the void, resorted to endless scheming
But still couldn't bless the human mind. I transformed
The syntax of time but still couldn't reveal my dreams about you.
It was a gust of strong wind that estranged the rivers of the past.
It is a vast ocean that guards the threshold of transition from old to new.
I, however, am holding you in my arms, cherishing the memory of our first
    days.

2

I want to say that I am supremely blessed, yet I cannot.
From where the origin of the blessing derives, I cannot say.
It is because the believers are already gone. The nonbelievers
Are yet to come. Suspected souls
Know that pain and suffering accompany us through life. No matter
When and where, but pain and suffering will not paralyze us.

It is a wedding under heavy makeup that adorns the gate tower of a city
In nominal lights and lanterns. It is the crown of a woman that
Makes a warrior wipe cold sweat against the blade of his sword.

是污点，除了血，无法清洗。除了
牺牲，赎不回诗人搭上一生的桌子

就是那张桌子，把一个人载入大海
掏空的抽屉，不能增加或减轻
一本书的份量。所有平静下来的
事情，随着一本书的翻动化为乌有
是浸透黑暗的一本书，将漂泊的智者
搜罗殆尽。最终的目击者又聋又瞎

里外都是一本书：没有文字可以记录
没有语言可以说出。如果没有你
没有春天，没有爱恨交加的
雷雨之夜，没有死者从标题上脱身
如果没有墓地中央的青草，没有
四周玉米宽大的叶子缠绕在记忆中

谁能听从命运的指派，在我们前后
出生入死？在我们前后扛着梯子
被一阵风架高，被一阵大风吹落
谁能在我们前后，看着满街的泥水
让灯光明灭无常，让一棵丁香
从遮掩窗口的高度上，轻声讲述

爱情的消亡。让一个诗人匆匆醒来
写下在早晨断了念的篇章，写下
四月里比星光更明媚的词句
写下来得及写下的一切。从短暂的
时间的门槛上，跨过去便跨过去
不可能再回头。回头再不可能

看见你的形容。你的四月被子留住
无眠的长夜，把昔日生活的花朵
打开。你却在长夜的拐角处折回
桃树密集的枝条。抽出来的时间

Whoever takes the secret of the world as a child's game,
Shall be a prop in the games of children, shall straight-faced,
Squeeze death like lacquer from a cracked surface.

It is the mirror placed upside-down that gets pushed to the end of time.
It is the descending flames and steles that fill the path of the sage.
It is the things that escape language that you can hardly be told.
It is the unmindful love closest to you that is impossible to hold on to.
It is the stain, rinsed and cleansed by nothing but blood,
Nothing but sacrifice that redeems the table, which has cost the lifetime of
    a poet.

It is that very table that carries one into the ocean.
The emptied drawers, cannot increase or decrease
The weight of a book. All things calm down,
But a book's turning leaves vanquish all into nothingness.
It is a book soaked with darkness that hunts up all the drifting sages
To near extinction. The final witness is both blind and deaf.

It is a book inside and out that cannot be recorded by words,
That can be told only by nothing. If it were not for you,
Not for the spring, not for the nights of thunderstorms
When love and hatred entwine, not for the escape of the dead from the
    headlines,
Not for the verdant grass at the center of graveyards,
Not for the broad husks of corn all around and their entanglement in
    memory,

Who would be able to obey the designation of fate and brave the untold
    dangers
Before and after us? Who would carry ladders in front and behind us,
Lifted up and blown off course by gusts of strong wind?
Who would watch whole streets full of sliding mud,
Let the lights go bright and dim capriciously, let a lilac bush
From the height of hiding the window, narrate softly?

让疼痛继续着，直到白昼的边缘
滑进不容揣测的躯壳，大千世界

让一两个托词举过了头。多么困惑
青春的富有者，却不能更早地享用
迟暮者享用的，是不在的大好时光
从硬币的两面开始的剥削，留下粉末
是一场赌博中难料的局面：输与赢
谁的手更有把握，谁的把握更有力量

刀锋的另一侧，是先知的一个眼神
洞开万物的灵魂。是未来的图景
在过去的一幅山水画中，透着亮光
宿命者春天的妄想，被一群乌鸦
纠集在枝叶繁荣的树冠上。此刻
谁是幸福的人，谁就知道幸福的本义

不仅枯干而且晦涩。幸福永远
在别的地方出没：是寄存的包裹
是一次旅行不小心丢失的手提箱
是老掉牙的一张合影。除了偶尔的
回忆，涌上我们心头的只有泪水
只有泪水中清晰可见的身世与苍桑

灯火连绵，夜深人静。一个诗人
赶在一场大雨之前，让一层纸
叠起的城堡，比大理石更牢靠
多年以后，一本拆散的书在尘埃中
理出头绪，在我还不懂的地方停顿
并为你留下空无一物的世界

南窗

永远的南窗，抱走积雪不留痕迹
太阳牵着卑微的一群，跃出河谷

The dying out of love: Let a poet wake up hurriedly
And write down passages left from the middle of morning's thought, write
   down
The words and sentences of April, more radiant and enchanting than
   starlight,
Write down everything that can be written down when there's still time.
From the transient threshold of time, a step over is simply a step over;
There's no return.

Return? Your countenance may never be seen again. This April
Of yours has been retained; long, sleepless nights
Open the flowers of the past. You, however,
At the turning corners of those long nights,
Break the thick branches of peach trees and bring them back. In time spared,
Let the pain continue, till the verge of daylight
Slips into the body's shell, which tolerates no conjecture; let the boundless
   universe

Lift above the head by one or two excuses. How confusing
That those rich in youth, however, cannot enjoy sooner
What the senescent ones knew — those magnificent times long past.
Exploitation, starting from both sides of a coin, leave powders behind.
In the unpredictable situation during a gambling game — to win or lose —
He whose hands represent more assurance is the more powerful.

On the other side of the sword, it is an expression in the eyes of a prophet
That enlightens the souls of all earthly things. It is the prospects of the future
In a traditional mountains-and-rivers painting , transparent to light —
The vain hopes of fatalists in spring, mustered and tangled by a flock of crows
In the luxuriant canopies of the trees. At this moment
Whoever is rejoiced and blessed, shall know the original meaning of bliss,

Is not only dead and dry, but also dark and obscure. Bliss always
Seeks out the land of somewhere else: it is a checked package;
It is the suitcase accidentally lost on a journey;
It is an old, toothless group photo. Except for occasional recollections,
there are only tears welling up in our hearts,
Only the experiences and vicissitudes of life seen distinctly and clearly
   through the tears.

失明的少年照例弹唱最后一曲
北风吃光了青草，天空嘘掉了寒星

这夜晚的话语，被悔恨用过的话语
放进了你都知道的诗篇。那不能
带来温暖的诗篇，垫高了唯一的
靠背：你坐下但不是为了休息

笔尖捅破了纸页。一股强劲的风
吹进了藏不住的书房，让诗人心跳
写字台也是诗人的悬崖：向上向下
是一架梯子，把你搂在它的怀里

选自组诗《快雪十八章》

记忆

快刀也老了。理不顺头绪的事情
缠着你。铁青的大苹果在碰撞
树叶在一棵树上争吵。一千枚
树叶，从一棵树上卸掉生锈的铠甲

装满发条的冬天，在雪原上走动
那曾经幸福的时光，只能叫你心痛
那早已过期的热水管，彻夜滴淌
敲敲打打的工具总也找不准地点

记忆，是一条长满蘑菇的密秘通道
记忆，是一把刻在抽屉外面的钥匙
想念的女人，不满一封信的篇幅
想念的书，被藏到无言的深处

选自组诗《快雪十八章》

The reach of lights and lanterns continues deep into nights quiet and still.
A poet, rushing before a heavy rain bursts forth, forcefully folds a piece of
　　paper
Into a castle, mightier than marble.
Many years later, a ripped and scattered book lying in dust
Gathers up and manages to sort out all threads of thought, pauses at places
that I still don't understand,
And leaves you the world void of even a single thing.

　　　　　–C.B. and Y.Q.

The South Window

The eternal south window carried the snow away without a trace.
Out of the river valley the dawn leads a crowd of lowly people by the hand.
And the boy who lost his eyesight is, as usual, playing and singing the last
　　melody.
The north wind devoured the green grasses, and the sky blew away cold stars.

Tonight's words, words that I regret having used
Have been put into the poems you knew, poems
That can bring no warmth. Raise up the solitary chair:
You sit down there, not for the purpose of taking a rest.

The pen point has pricked the paper and a strong wind
Rushes into the study, making the poet's heart beat fast.
For a poet the writing desk is also a cliff: the way up and down
Is a ladder, holding you tightly in its arms.

　　　　　–C.B. and C.W.

Memory

The sharp blade is old now. All the things that haunt you
Can't be put in order. The big livid apples are colliding with each other,
And in a tree the leaves are quarreling. A thousand leaves
Are unloaded from a tree like rusted armor.

半山坡

那键盘不是钢琴的
尽管它们发亮，规矩

又像字母表一样随意
把世界安置在小小的机关里

上帝说要有光
于是眼前一片漆黑

铁器时代的一块石头
在人类的半山坡上滚动

想起了十个以内的数字
十个以内手指的分量

为了一个简单的问题
我们花掉的心血是多么冤枉

选自组诗《清凉山》

石梯

一阵雨，一阵停
路上的尘土打扫干净

世界那么小
你又那么远

石梯仿佛湿漉漉的绳索
上去的人摇摇晃晃

就在身边走着
就在天边走着

Equipped with clockwork springs, the winter moves in the snowfield,
And the happy days of the past only make you hurt.
The hot water pipe drips all night.
Tapping here and there, the tool can't locate the leak.

Memory is a secret channel full of mushrooms.
Memory is a key engraved outside a desk drawer.
What the woman I miss said to me is shorter than a letter.
The book I miss was hidden in some speechless depths.

–C.B. and C.W.

Hillside

The keyboard is not that of a piano
Though it shines and is tidy.

It is casually arranged like an alphabet,
Putting the whole world in its tiny gearbox.

God said *let there be light*,
And a black lacquer appeared in the eye.

A stone from the Iron Age
Is rolling down the hillside of humanity,

Remembering numbers within ten
And the weight of ten fingers.

How worthless to spend
So much energy on such a simple question.

–C.B. and Z.E.

风信子捎来的风
长满了飞不动的羽毛

万物的季节多么不同
方死方生全凭一点运气

选自组诗《清凉山》

叫喜鹊不许叫

我要你每分钟都嫁给我。每一刻
都做我的新娘。这样的每一天

唯有你在我身边不走，才会到来
如果你答应了，我就可以永生

每天都忘在了心里，忘了也在
每天都想着，想起来就想死

世界不是我的，对你肯定就是
是你的世界在我这儿，什么都有

我要你每一天都无法离去。从此
让一个人放心的话别的人不会说

这样的夜晚我知道。知道并不好
这样的人仿佛闭上眼才能撞得上

每条街匆匆而过。每棵大树
纷纷扬扬，你看什么不是什么

每天不过是一天。因不变的心
每天都变了，让我恍如隔世

Stone Steps

The rain stops, and then returns,
Wiping away all dust from the road.

The world is so small
And you are so remote from me.

The stone steps are like a wet rope
Along which the climbers swing.

You walk by my side
As if you were walking beyond the edge of the sky.

The wind brought along by the hyacinth
Is full of plumes that are too heavy to fly.

So different are the seasons from all things on earth.
Upon whose luck their life and death totally depend.

–C.B. and Z.E.

Don't Let the Magpie Sing

I want you to marry me every minute. Be my bride
Every minute and each day will come if only

You stay by my side, and do not walk away.
If you do this, I will live eternally.

Every day I let you slip from my mind, but that can't stop me.
Every day I think of you, and whenever I think of you, I want to die.

The world is not mine; surely it is yours.
Is your world here by my side? Then it has all.

从今天起，我想每天都抱你回家
叫喜鹊不许叫，叫花儿满天飞

选自组诗《仿佛篇》

小闹钟

要听你心里说什么，其实不太难
在呼吸之间你有一阵轻微的歌唱

小闹钟滴滴嗒嗒。多少没用的水
抽干了灵光的夜晚。多少年过去

生与死总要见面，讲些个废话
让沉默咽下的烈酒，醉成烂泥

我的人一副好眼光，绕也绕不开
蚂蚁搬家的树叶，落花杂乱的小径

苦日子熬到头，我的人怎么办
若大一片树林，盛不下一个果盘

太阳在火上熄灭。星星在树上
丁丁当当。仿佛我的人还在梦中

分不清是谁，叫不来我的名字
好像天亮之前天亮了。一场雪

又白又细，里里外外都是爪印
一场雪让整个心思无处躲藏

要知道你在想什么，我问自己
就知道，想一想你就会跑过来

选自组诗《仿佛篇》

Every day I will make it hard for you to leave me. And from now on,
The words that calm a lover will never be said by another.

I know such kind of nights, and it is not good to know about them.
As if such a lover can only be met when you shut your eyes.

Every street passes swiftly as you walk by. Every tree
Blows and sheds. What you see is not what is.

Every day is only a day because the fixed heart changes daily,
Making me feel that a day is long enough to be a century.

From now on I want to carry you home every day.
Let the magpie fail to sing; let the flowers fly in the sky.

—C.B. and C.W.

Little Alarm Clock

It is not so difficult to hear what you are saying in your heart.
In the intervals of your breath, I can hear you singing softly a song.

The little alarm clock is running dida-dida. So much water that finds no use
Has pumped all the nights out. So many years have gone.

Life and death will meet, speaking nonsense only.
Let silence drink hard liquor and fall drunk.

My love has good eyes; she can't be bypassed in the leaves carried by ants
Or the disorderly paths covered with fallen flowers.

When the hard days come to their end, what shall my love do?
Though the woods are big enough, they can't hold a fruit plate.

The sun is dying out above the water. The stars are twinkling
On the trees. It seems that my love is still in her dreams.

She cannot recognize my face or recall my name
As if day had came before daybreak. It snows

White and fine, betraying all the claw-prints
Both inside and outside, and I find no way to hide my mind.

To learn what you are thinking, I must ask myself to listen,
Then you will run to me at my first thought.

           –C.B. *and* C.W.

清平

乡村即景

一声声，魔鬼的青蛙
在稻田里，旅游者的足迹
被贫穷地毁坏。
烤玉米的香气穿过一个中年人
出自悔恨的欣喜，
一阵风吹来，吉普车的后窗
向着广阔的陈旧敞开。
凭着对旧事物的隔膜和热爱，
年轻的导游打开了
众人的心扉，使他们成为
往昔的，错误的预言家。
乡村美景在望，饥饿的浮云
在蔚蓝的天空渐渐飘散，
方圆十里的酷热被
突然涌来的秋天消融掉。

童年的素歌

从六岁起，寒冷在记忆里扎下根。
一晃十几年，一桩不幸的婚姻和
一场不幸的革命，携手埋下温暖的种子。
如今发黄的回忆正是当年
被错误估计的新式的棉鞋。

阳光照着暗棕色的电线杆。
作为猎物和作为美景的麻雀
在蔚蓝的天空留下快乐的污点。
但是，快乐不全由遗忘带来，
更奇妙的，对于往昔的憧憬
朝向我尚未出生的年代。

Qing Ping

translations by Christopher Mattison, Gao Xiaoqin
with Jody Beenk and Zhang Er

A Rural Landscape

Frogs croaking like monsters
Through a rice paddy blurred
By travelers' steps. The smell of roasted
Corn eases middle age's remorse.
A gust of wind blows open the jeep's
Rear window to a vast and stale expanse.
Lack of communication and nostalgia allows
The young guide to open hearts to former
Times, false prophets.
A bucolic landscape, emaciated clouds
Limp through the blue of the sky.
Sweltering heat over the surrounding land
Cooled by a sudden blast of fall.

A Simple Childhood Song

From age of six, this coolness has been planted in my memory.
Decades passed, an unlucky marriage and
An unfortunate revolution warmed the seeds in unison.
Today, these memories fade for the latest style of cotton shoes
That seemed so chic.

The sun shines on a drab brown telegraph pole.
Sparrows diving as prey and as scenery
Cheerfully litter the blue of the sky.
But happiness is not brought by oblivion.
What's more intriguing is longing for an
Age before I was born.

拖拉机，草帽，金沙江的
挖泥船，这些美的魔法师
在一年之内篡改了时代。
灰色，金黄色的华丽图卷
犹如不朽的海伦引导着混乱的希腊，
向一个儿童指明了纵欲的方向。

在大地的远方，令人吃惊的
祖国的绿宝石闪着不应有的光芒，
在风暴的中心驱散了风暴。
书籍崇拜结束了，又开始。
对于图书馆的普遍失望使我踏上
凭借小聪明的人生旅途。

从十岁到二十岁，记忆的宝库
蛊惑的废金属叮当作响。
一个苦工创造着无用。
平庸的双手一再下降。
一种天大的责任突然将它们
从信仰的底部抬高了一寸。

现在，我的童年已经过去。
人生四分之一的光阴已成为
和死亡一样坚定的虚无。
回忆之风吹来，满地的落叶，
那些不属于我的黄和绿
无不写着我僭越的姓氏。

漫长的夏季

我感到漫长的夏季
在暴戾的享乐中，
不停地推卸掉去年的责任。
一样的酷热在它的
粗俗的厌烦中长出了

Tractor, straw hat, dredger. These enchantresses tramped
Down the Jinsha river and an era changed in under a year.
Grey, spectacular gold pictures
As monumental as Helen leading a chaotic
Greece, pointing a child in the direction of desire.

Far off in the country, the motherland's emerald
Shines with an unexpected brightness,
Blowing away the storm in the storm's center.
Bibliolatry ended and then re-began.
A general disappointment with the bibliostate sent me
On a life-long journey that's relied on petty scams.

From ten to twenty, the thesaurus of memory
Rings a bewitching mental state.
Drudgery gave birth to uselessness.
Mediocre hands descended again and again.
A sense of some grand duty lifted them up
An inch from the base of beliefs.

Now my childhood is gone.
A quarter of my life has become
Nothingness, as steady as death.
The wind of memory blows, leaves fall to the ground.
Yellows and greens that do not belong to me
Are written under my pseudonym.

A Long Summer

The cruel delight of a long summer
Sweeps away the previous year's obligations.
The same sweltering heat, in its vulgarity,
Composes a patch of shade that differs from the past.
I'm in a trance, like the rose momentarily
Forgetting about withering respectably in old age.
Death did not create this vast land,
Or allow it to know the horror of eternity.

不同以往的大片的浓荫。
我有些恍惚，仿佛玫瑰
顷刻间遗忘了可敬的凋谢。
死亡未曾造就这辽阔的国土，
并使它知晓永生的可畏。
一个迟睡者可能已错过
黎明的清风和鸟啼，
他的梦想却不同于梦境：
无穷的变化就是不变。
夏日的晴空不是被恐惧
而是被热爱混淆着，
星光下阴郁的灯光也一样
无法为黑夜写下新的一页，
却像灰尘覆盖图书馆一角，
照亮了这个星球上公正的错误。

清风的倾诉

早上，一大块云遮住了我。
阳光不远，但有些少。
窗外的树影一霎时着魔似的美，
毁掉了两个人心中的恶念。
一个担着使命，忘了手中的望远镜；
另一个从厨房端出早餐，
便草草结束了漫长的一天。

我未能得到我应得的乐趣，
一册《杜工部》已读不下去。
童年的恶作剧往后退，
退到了幼年，还能去哪里？
我撒了额外的谎，不是为了
把一个坏学生往伤感的路上推，
广大的死亡难道还值得去了解？

The late-sleeper might lose the clear morning wind
And birds singing at dawn, but his day dreams
Differ greatly from evenings' dream: Infinite change is no change.
The cloudless summer sky is not confused by fear but love.
Just like the gray lamp beneath the stars, which can't give
Enough light to write a new page for the night,
As if the corner of a library covered in dust
Shines on justifiable mistakes made around the globe.

A Story of Breezes

Morning, a patch of cloud covers me.
Sunlight is not far away, but faint.
The shadow of a tree against a window
Blooms magically and wears down the
Evil in the hearts of two people.
One carries on with their mission,
Forgetting the telescope in hand;
The other brings breakfast from the kitchen.
So ends the long day.

I have not received the pleasure I deserve,
The *Dugongbu*˙ cannot continue to be read.
Childhood pranks recede
Into infancy, and to where else?
I lied more than I should, not to
Push a bad student into sentimentality.
Is it possible that it's worth figuring out the vastness of death?

The turn is far from enough, Mr. Director General, in silence.
You are not a bigger screw.
As a neighbor of someone recently deceased
My past misdeeds, like drink, amuse you

˙A book about Tang poet Du Fu

转折还差得远，沉默的局长先生。
一颗较大的螺丝钉不是你。
作为一个猝死者的邻居，
我以往的劣迹美酒一样迷住了你，
却不能改变你有限的天性。
在这个街区，你以粗暴和憎恨出名，
必定熟知一个人另外的一生。

六月，清风徐来，雨季维持两个月，
带来梦想中的凶杀案。
在我窗外，一棵树长出新枝桠，
仿佛随手可折，却已能套上绞索。
我把这座城市的一切记在了心中，
为了永生，而不是告别，
顷刻间开垦出罪恶的良田。

几乎同时，却已晚了。
一大块云从反面解决了问题。
亲爱的局长先生，我的一生不是由你
也不是由我，而是由它改变了。
一架勤恳的望远镜看不见他：
当他在人群中雨水一样流动，
衰老，死去，骄傲全无。

答友人

多少炊烟升起了又降下。
多少人去了就不再回来。
一个人活到现在，三十岁，四十岁，
什么样的苦难能使他飞身向前，
把忍受的一切再忍受一遍？
岁月大得没有边沿，
生活的火箭嗖嗖向前，
掠过的都掠过，附着的都附着，
这就是我们享乐的经过？

But cannot alter your limited self.
In this neighborhood you're famous for cruelty and hate,
And you must know a person's other life.

In June the winds move in gently, then two months of rain,
Which brings on a murder case in my dreams.
New branches growing outside my window seem so fragile,
But are sturdy enough on which to hang a noose.
I keep this city in my heart,
For eternity, not saying farewell
The villainy of fertile land in the turn of a hand.

Around the same time, but later,
A wall of clouds resolves this problem.
Dear Mr. Director General, my life has been changed
Neither by you, nor me, but by it.
A diligent telescope cannot see him:
He flows through crowds like rainwater,
Grows old, dies, pride fades.

Answering a Friend

Smoke wafts up and down.
People leave, never to return.
After he's been alive for thirty,
Forty years, what could possibly
Coerce him to bravely suffer
The same all over again?
Time is boundless.
Life surges past like a missile.
Everything that can be skimmed
Has been skimmed. Everything
That can cling, clings.
Is this the passing of joy?
Is this the adopted textbook
From someone's unauthorized life story?
O fate! I don't think so. I hope you don't either.

这就是听不出来自谁的
"命运啊"的教科书？
我不这么看，也希望你不。
在这个并不寒冷的冬天，
寒冷随时会来到我们身边，
随着一场大雪的到来，
我们仿佛又回到了当年……
太危险！
回忆泼下的脏水、蜜水，
没有一滴不出自乌有的将来，
扫帚和笤帚，旧黑与新黑
犹若千年的对子等你去对。
对吗？不对！
一对，你就对掉了午餐，
再对，你就对掉了
我们短暂生命中唯一长久的
带着罪恶感的上元灯会。

时代一日

旋转，一而三，终于停下。
这正确的生活导致错误的数学。
阴天过了多半，恋爱中又死了几个
在各方面无力支付的穷汉。
这是因为，阳光露出了端倪。

十分小心地，却又似猛烈地
摧毁了死亡的想象力：
一条命包围了两个祖国。
在蓝色的天空上，黑色几乎
完全停下了梦想的脚步。

随着雨季前一场雨的到来，
小说家进入休眠期。
他们看不到一段时间内

216

In a mild winter the chill
Can drop at any moment, along
With heavy snow. We're returning
To those years . . .
It's too dangerous!
Memory pours down dirty water and honey,
Not a drop does not come from a nonexistent future,
Broom and brush, old black vs. new
As if a thousand-year-old line is waiting for you
To come up with its antithetical couplet.
Matched? Or not!
On the first attempt, you matched "lunch,"
The second time around, "The Lantern Festival"
Where we spent the most time together
In our short life, filled with guilt.

A Day in Our Life

Keep turning endlessly, then stop.
Living correctly leads to incorrect mathematics.
The clouds have mostly passed, someone in love died.
Men who can't afford to pay.
A clue appears with the sun.

Be very careful, yet violently
Destroy death's imagination:
One life surrounds two motherlands.
In such a blue sky, the darkness nearly
Puts an end to the dream.

As rain comes before the rainy season,
Novelists go into hibernation.
For a while, they're unable to see
The power of a profound fatigue.
The freshness, so far away, lacks the confusion of chance.

作为推动力的强劲的疲惫。
那么远的新，缺少混淆的机会。

原初的胆怯、眷爱，均不必提。
一天的时光过去，只有中间的陈旧
牛肉饼一样夹在汉堡中。
在儿童手上，秩序也在发生着变化，
人物也在经历着生死，但不留下后话。

偶感

翻开五十年代的日历，看见那些
挂在岁月脖子上的人，
那么多发明家啊。
世界仿佛不是他们的家园，
而是他们的一个念头。
每一天，背着叮当作响的工具箱，
揣着粽子，热狗，小米加步枪，
摇摇晃晃，闷着头，
把我们的课堂搅成一锅粥。
我想起童年到现在，无数的
争吵和烦恼，彻夜不眠的牛角尖，
如今大都已看淡。
我好像一步步走开了，
到了人少的地方，
"结庐在人境"的山坡上。
世界仍在时光中滑行，日历已
较少承担令人烦恼的提醒。
这些，难道已将我变成另一个人？
虽然远，山脚下仍有我
招魂幡一般的电脑屏幕，
那些流水账、稻粱谋，老胡同一样等着拆迁。
要将它们一锅端，却是不可能。

Do not mention the original timidness and longing.
That time of day has passed, only the stale middle
Being pressed inside a hamburger like ground beef.
Order changes in the hands of a child,
The characters experience life and death, yet leave no tales.

Musings

Flip the 1950s era calendar
To each neck hung through the ages,
So many inventors.
The world is not their home,
But merely one of their notions.
Each day with clanging tool boxes,
Holding sticky rice dumplings,
Hotdogs, nuts and bolts in their pockets.
Waving and wobbling, dropping their heads
Our class is stirred up like a pan of conjee.
I think back on countless brawls and irritations
And the self-willed sleepless nights from childhood,
Which by now have all but faded away.
I seem to fall away step by step
To a place with few people.
The hillside of "Among the busy haunts of men
I build my hut." The world continues to slide past,
The calendar bears less worrisome reminders. Have all these
Things changed me into another?
Despite being far off, at the bottom of my hill
A computer screen waves like a streamer for the dead.
Routine diaries and schemes for the day wait
To be dismantled and moved like old alleys.
You hope to change them all at once, but it's impossible.

桑克

我年幼的时候是个杰出的孩子

我年幼的时候是个杰出的孩子
我被公众孤立。我站在校舍操场边的杨树林里
目睹同龄的男孩子女孩子歌唱
我想死去的姐姐，在薄薄的被窝里搂着我
青青的头发，蓝色花朵的书包
我知道在我身体里面住着
不止一个人，他们
教我许多谁也不懂的游戏

阳光有着三色蛋糕一样的层次，我为什么看不见？
我蹲在高高的窗台下，我的旁边是吃鱼骨的猫咪
我捏着针状的罂粟花叶放入嘴里
我感到印字硬糖一样的甜

乡村摄影师

走街串巷，骑着
破旧的自行车。老式的双眼相机
挂在脖子上，招来一群
无聊的孩子。

他不单独拍摄风景，
家庭或者人物，始终占据
底片的核心。在暗房里，他满足于
把人攒在一起的能力。

他一边喝碗里的茶，一边
计算一天的收入。露水尚重
他就离开他的小镇，去他
有限的几个辖区。

Sang Ke

translations by XiaoRong Liu and Maged Zaher with Zhang Er

I Used to be an Outstanding Kid

I used to be an outstanding kid
The public isolated me. So, I stood lonely under the poplar trees
To watch my schoolmates chanting
I missed my dead sister, who used to huddle my body under the thin quilt:

Her jet black hair, and her satchel with blue flowers
I knew that there was more than one person
Living inside my body and they
Taught me games nobody could understand

Like a Neapolitan cake, the sunshine has three layers
But why I can't see them?
When crouching under the windowsill, next to the kitty licking the fish bone
I picked the needlelike poppy flowers and put them in my mouth
And it tasted sweet like a hard candy

The Country Photographer

Wandering through lanes and alleys, he rides
On a shabby bicycle with an old-fashioned camera
Over his neck. He attracts a whole bunch of
Listless kids.

He never shoots nature only
Families or humans are always
In the center of his pictures. In the darkroom, he is satisfied
That he can gather people together

He calculates his daily income
While drinking tea from a cheap bowl

当偶然得到一本没有
封皮的《红与黑》，他认为自己的
工作多少像个教士，只不过
他不传播把人搞乱的思想。

嵇康

> 讬运遇于领会兮，寄余命于寸阴。
> ——向秀《思旧赋》

> 看那炉火烧得正红，
> 趁热打铁才能成功。
> ——欧仁·鲍狄埃《国际歌》

我以事见法。我知道这是什么"事"，但是
他们的说法与此并不相同，就像天上的鸱枭，
他们说它是在寻找腐烂的食物，只有我知道
它在代替死神巡视晚年的人世。我目睹它的
黝黑的翅膀是个摆设，像一个谎言之上
纯金的天平，即使两边锡纸包裹的砝码
相等，即使它卖力地摇动着，仿佛描花折扇
吹来阵阵的春风，但它下面飞翔的的确是
只有我才能描绘出的幽冥的马车——马蹄笃笃
一直消逝在银河牛奶一样腥甜的波光中。
日影刚刚移到篮球架斑驳的篮板，这就是说
我还有时间回顾自己颓废的人生，我写得一手
锦绣文章，至于诗歌，更是我的囊中之物。
我还博得了响亮的名声，这从淑女赠送的绢帕的
数量就可以测出，我的温柔比水还重。
但这不是主要的，我交了几个臭味相投的友人
他们自我培养的优秀的怪癖让我心动。
而我也有得意的动作——
我热爱打铁，胜过了弹琴，琴声在炉火中
仿佛一棵未曾发育的山东大葱。
但是现在我却想要一把琴，即使是商场里卖的

Then - bathing under the morning dew — he leaves his small town
To visit the rest of his limited territory

When - by chance - he got a coverless copy of "Le rouge et le noir"
He realized that his work
Is like the priest's, except
That he doesn't spread confusing thoughts.

Ji-Kang

> Rely on the destiny as what one can comprehend, and
> spend every minutes of this life wisely.
> — Hsiang Hsiu: *Lamentations for Bygone Days*

> Look, the furnace burns red,
> To succeed, we must forge the iron while it is hot.
> — Eugene Pottier: *The Internationale*

I was jailed because of my violation of the law. I know exactly
Why it happened, though their thoughts might be different,
As though the flying eagle owls, they said
That they were looking for rotten food, but only I can tell
In fact they were patrolling the remaining years of the earth
On behalf of death. I witnessed their dark wings:
Decorations, like a pure-gold balance
Above a lie, even if the weights wrapped in aluminum foil
Were exactly the same, swinging hard with a spatter of spring wind
From a flower fold fan, yet flying underneath
Was a ghost carriage that I am the only one who could describe: the hoof
      beats
Disappeared into the Milky Way-like sweetish shimmering waves.
The shadow of the sun moved up to the mottled backboard,
Which means I still have time to review my decadent life:
I can write elegant essays hand over fist, let alone poems.
I also won a splendid reputation, measured by
The number of silky handkerchiefs presented to me from ladies.
My tenderness is heavier than the flowing water.

那种也行，对于品牌和质量不再挑剔，决不是
因我藏身鸟笼，而是我知道我的技艺已使
缪斯的喉咙气得红肿，凑合着打发最后的
日常生活吧，又何必那么认真？这就是
我嵇叔夜诚恳的态度。有位观众认为我
比较做作——多少有点儿，但是静静等着开场
总不如让一群少女跳跳健美操，活跃一下
紧张的神经。我的琴声算不上悠扬，但是很有些
独特的内容：炉火渐渐熄灭，一块毛铁
在水池中升起袅袅的青烟。子期兄在旁边
轻轻吟诵——看那炉火烧得正红……
铁的幻影在琴声里翻腾，火的呻吟在隐形琴弓的
抽动下让人心惊。如果有时间，我会记下
这段旷世的曲谱，只是我的兄弟们早已离开
这沙暴狂卷的豫南京城。哪里是豫南，分明是
遇难——这个问题我为什么不能直面、挺胸？
我灵魂仓库的深处早已储满命运的寒冰。
当日影移到罚球弧，我的使命就要完成。
这是早晚的事情，每个人都将看到
我看到的那辆双轮马车幽蓝的前灯，驭者轻轻
敲打着手中的棋子，仿佛那是解放的丧钟。

晨起忆登千山遇道士事

今早起床，我的心情仿若
孤月，明亮而又冷清。
这样的时刻，去年也曾有过，
不过那是在五月，我在一座山上
和一个道士闲谈，他的枕边
放着盛开的玉米花，远处的梨树林
似乎是得道的仙人。
我感觉我的愚钝，更感觉我的心中
有沙子流过，
磕磕碰碰，制造一些复杂而婉转的
纹痕。

Yet these are not important issues. I have made friends like me
Their self-cultured eccentrics sound so attractive
But I also have my own tricks —
I love forging the hot iron better than playing harps, the sound of music
In the furnace looks like an underdeveloped Shan-Dong green onion
But now I really want to have a harp, even one of the kind
They sell in the shopping mall. I am not picky anymore
About the brand and quality, but it is not because
I am hiding myself in a birdcage, instead I understand
That my skill makes the muses' throat swollen with anger. Why so serious?
How about take it easy of my real life? And this is my, Ji-Kang's
Sincere attitude. Some audience believed that I was
Affected — more or less, yet I'd rather watching
The cheerleaders performing than waiting quietly for the beginning
Of the show. The sound of my harp
Is not melodious, but quite unique: The fire is quenching, an iron
Smoking in the water, while my friend Zi-Qi is reciting
Quietly — look the red flame is burning hot . . .
The shadow of iron lingers in the sound of violin, the murmur
Of the flame under the unreal violin string is striking. If I have time,
I would write down the astonishing tunes, but my friends have just left
The sand-storming capital of Yu-Nan. It is not Yu-Nan, obviously
It is a mishap — Why can't I just face it chest up?
The deepest side in my soul stored the chilling ice of destiny
Once the shadow passes the penalty-shot curve, my mission/job will be over.
Sooner or later, everyone will see
The blue headlight of the ghost carriage that I saw before. The cavalier
Is tapping a chess piece gently, as if it is the funeral bell's ringing for
     liberation.

At Sunrise I Remembered My Meeting with a Daoist Priest When Hiking in the Qian-Mountain

At sunrise, when I got up, my soul was like
The cold moon: bright and desolate.
I experienced the same moment last year
In May, I was in the mountain

湖上

湖上应该是冷的
我看不见它，我想着
它是如何的冷

冰块在低空中
飞舞，陪伴着渡鸦。
下面是我的肠子
它的模样看上去
多么像一截废弃的
小提琴的弦。

影子在上面走，影子
的脚尖仿佛穿上了
冰刀，锐利的
刀，它是锐利的。

风也在吹，它的
老任务。树林也在摇
它不更新的汤药……

我站在湖上，头发
还有长袍披散
头仰着，但眼睛紧闭
慢慢旋转着悲伤。

雾气起了，向我围拢
用她柔软的胳膊。

墓志铭

写在这里的句子
是给风听的。

Talking to a Daoist priest: Next to his pillow
There was blooming popcorn. The pear trees afar
Looked like flying deities.
I felt my dullness, even more in my soul
The flowing sand particles
Bump against each other, to produce a complicated
And elegant trace.

On the Lake

It is chilling on the lake
I don't feel it. I imagine it.

The hailstones were flying close by
And chaperoning the ferry crows.
Below was my small intestine
That looked like a broken
Violin string.

The shadow was walking on the surface
It seemed to be wearing
Ice skates with
sharp blades, sharp.

The wind is doing its
Old job: Blowing.
The trees are swinging the
Old-fashioned medicine soup
Without changing prescriptions.

I stood by the lake, my hair
Disheveled, so did my cloak
I looked up, but my eyes were shut
Swirling slowly my sorrow.

The mist spread out, and surrounded me
With her soft arms.

你看吧，如果你把自己当作
时有时无的风。

这里是我，或者
我的灰烬。
它比风轻，也轻于
你手中的阴影。

你不了解我的生平
这上面什么都没有。
当日的泪痕
也眠于乌有。

你只有想象
或者你只看见
石头。
你想了多少，你就得到多少。

Epitaph

These words
Are for the wind to listen to.
Listen, if you can imagine yourself
The intermittent breeze.

Here I lie
In the ashes of death
That are lighter than air, or
The shadow in your hands.

You don't know my life
There is nothing on my epitaph
But traces of old time tears
That sleep in nothingness.

In climes of imagination,
You see a stone:
What you think is what you get.

树才

莲花

我盘腿打坐度过了
许多宁静无望的暗夜。
我呼吸着人的一吐一纳——
哦世界？它几乎不存在。

另一个世界存在……
另一些风，另一些牺牲的羔羊，
另一些面孔，但也未必活生生……
总之，它们属于另一个空间。

打开的双掌，是我仅有的两朵莲花。
你说它们生长，但朝哪个方向？
你说它们赶路，但想抵达哪里？

我只是在学习遗忘——
好让偌大的宇宙不被肉眼瞥见。

马甸桥

24 小时。连续 24 小时——
这是昼和夜加在一起的份量。

在桥边，一个人滋生危险的念头。
一天一天，你伤害了多少时光！

在每一个路口，危险和危险擦肩而过。

桥上所见的纷乱，
桥下所承受的震动……

Shu Cai

translations by Leonard Schwartz, Gao Xin and Zhang Er

Lotus

I have spent many tranquil and desireless nights
Sitting, my legs crossed in meditation.
I breathe a human's breath — in and out —
eh, world? It hardly exists.

Another world exists . . .
Other winds, other sacrificial lambs,
other faces, not necessarily lively . . .
In other words, they belong to another space.

I spread my hands,
the only two lotus I own.
You say they are growing — but in what direction?
You say they are traveling/on their way — but where?

I'm merely learning to forget —
that huge university not seen by eyes of flesh.

–L.S. and Z.E.

Madian Bridge

24 hours, 24 hours non stop —
This is the weight of day plus night.

By the bridge, a man incubates a dangerous idea.
Day after day, you hurt time!

At each crossing, danger rubs shoulders with danger.

生活，在路上。家庭只是
停靠站。轮胎冒烟，出汗，滚烫……

迟早的车祸粉碎了对前途的算计。

从这边看，又从那边看，
马甸桥没有内部，只是空穴。

过路的红裙，上下颤动的乳房，
松柏的生长缺乏氧气……

茶树用浑圆理解形式主义。

24 小时。连续 24 小时——
小轿车，自行车，马车，重型卡车……

危险的预感逼迫人一次次出门。
推迟那个梦，或在梦中醒着！

有什么更好的办法对付这噪音？

还得把生活挣来，
还得把肉和蔬菜拎上楼……

天终于晴了

天终于晴了
连续三天的阴雨
差点儿让心发霉
天终于晴了
彩色小三角旗
在墙头乐得直拍手
凉凉的风
在街上欢快地吹
护城河脏乎乎的脸上

Disturbance on the bridge,
Tremors under the bridge . . .

To live on the way. Family is just
a stop. Tires smoking, sweating and hot . . .

Accidents (which will occur) sooner or later smash the plan for the future.

To look from this side, and then from the other side:
MaDian Bridge doesn't have an interior, but an empty hole.

Red skirts pass by, dangling breasts,
pines and cypresses grow in lack of oxygen . . .

Tea plants understand formalism
Judging by their roundness.

24 hours, 24 hours non-stop —
cars, bikes, horse carriages, heavy trucks . . .

The anticipation of danger forces people out of doors.
Delay that dream, or awake in the dream!

Are there any better ways to deal with this noise?

We still have to earn a living,
still have to bring meat and vegetables up the stairs . . .

                    –L.S. and Z.E.

It Finally Cleared Up

After three day's rain
it finally cleared up
nearly leaving the heart moldy.
It finally cleared up,
colorful little pennants

也有了笑容
天终于晴了
你登高可以望到远处
洗去尘土的大城
方形的塔楼结实
矮小的平房朴素
街道在涌动
人们在忙碌
刺疼天空的电视塔
高得没什么道理
天终于晴了
最好出去走走
让凉凉的风
吹一吹身上的潮气
顺便去看看护城河边的
那排柳树，芽儿
是不是壮实了，长高了
从这边望过去
密密匝匝的柳枝
已被凉凉的风
梳得整整齐齐
一颗颗随风拂动的柳树
一团团淡青色的好心情

喊

三只知了喊了一上午
院子里的人听得心乱
知了扯直了嗓子喊——
喊神经被秋风碰了一下

空气在一阵阵痉挛中弯曲

如果十年前，我一定会
冲出家门去捉这几只知了

clapped with joy,
a cold wind
blew happily
across the street.
(The city moat's
filthy face even managed a smile.)
It finally cleared up
and you can climb a long way up
to watch the city in the distance
get cleared of dust.
Square towers are solid,
one-storey houses modest:
streets surge
with busy people
and a TV tower stabs the sky,
high up for no reason.
It finally cleared up,
so you'd better take a walk
let the cool wind evaporate
moisture from your body.
You can go and see that row of willows
lining the city moat, are their buds
strong enough, are they taller than before
look, you'll see
the bunched branches of the willows
are combed neatly
by cool wind,
lines of willows waving
one by one
oh so greenly.

−L.S. and G.X.

Shouts

Three cicadae shout the whole morning.
Folks in the courtyard get upset listening to them.

在晃动的叶片间，我认准
一个黑点，然后高举网罩

把那无知的知了一下扑住

如今我深陷在岁月的沼泽
心急起火时像那三只知了
嚷嚷累了，才肯歇一会儿
心力如沙，身体怎能坦然

像知了预感到秋天的逼近

三只知了下午还会喊
它们有力气它们就喊吧
爪子到死还紧抓着树干
终于，"啪嗒"摔在地上

儿时我捡这些蝉壳卖钱

像鸟一样

假如你真是一只鸟，
你想怎么办？

你肯定想飞，
那是你多年的梦想，

也许正相反，坐在家门口，
你反而拿不准方向。

如果找不到北，你
会飞的翅膀往哪儿飞？

雪莱学习云雀，边飞边叫……
马拉美则飞上了万米高空，

Cicadea shouting at the top of their lungs!
Everyone is unnerved and

The air is a wave of convulsions.

Ten years ago, I would certainly
Have rushed out to catch these cicadae.
Amongst swaying leaves I would have aimed
For a black point and raised a net

To swat those ignoramus cicadae.

Now I'm mired deep in time's mud,
Burning with anxiety just like those cicadae
Willing to rest only when hoarse.
When the mind is like sand how can anybody be at ease

Cicadae's premonitions of the approaching autumn

Three cicadae that will go on shouting all afternoon.
Let them shout if they have the strength.
Their claws clutch hard at the trunk
when at last they die they will crunch on the ground.

In childhood I collected cicadae shells and sold them

–L.S. and G.X.

Like a Bird

If you are a bird,
What do you want to do?

You want to fly of course.
That is your dream of many years

越来越微妙，越来越费劲……
维庸闪进胡同口，躲警察，

那是另一个方向：向下
……爪子也挖到了麦粒。

飞到谁也看不见你的地方，
或飞到市场上的小推车旁。

有了翅膀，还找不到
天空的门，那你就惨了！

海子跳上驶向太阳站的火箭，
戈麦向天鹅湖的虚空处沉去……

由于缺乏带点儿腥味的口头语，
你失去了一个完整的人的乐趣。

越来越玄，望见古代的人，
越来越狂，找不到尺子的人，

而那些退回冥冥天国的人，
需要你从你的生活出发

想象他们的人情味儿，
再次得到简化和充实。

假如你真的想飞，
此刻你就能做到。

看

我这是怎么了——
在街上瞎转悠？

Or maybe, quite the contrary, sitting at home,
You are not sure of the direction.

If you can't find north, where will those flying
Wings of yours fly you?

Learning from larks, Shelley shouted when he flew . . .
Mallarmé flew to unprecedented heights

Ever more delicate, ever more hard . . .
Villon flew down the lane, to avoid policemen,

And there's another direction: downward
. . . paws excavating the wheat.

Fly to the place where nobody can find you,
Or fly to the market to sit beside a small cart.

If with wings you still can't find the gate of heaven
then you really are a miserable thing!

Hai Zi lept on the rocket flying towards Sun Station,[*]
Ge Mai throwing himself into the empty deeps of Swan Lake . . .[†]

For lack of a colloquial phrase with a fishy smell
You have lost the pleasure of being a complete man.

More and more abstruse, those who observe the ancient.
More and more arrogant, those who can't find a measure.

---

[*]Hai Zi (1964-1989), original name Zha Haisheng, poet, commited suicide by lying on a train track on March 26, 1989.

[†]Ge Mai (1967-1991), original name Chu Fujun, poet, commited suicide by jumping into a lake on September 24, 1991.

我的目光，一路打量，
而众人忙着赶路……

有人结伴而行为了说话，
有人在站牌下探头张望，

我看一古怪老头，光裸上身，
一动不动，在胡同口，坐着，

他的枯瘦让我想起我外公，
去年盛夏，他肚皮凹陷，

一边等我，一边老死……
而非洲离我的村子太远！

我看另一对老人活得更艰难，
老妪坐着，老叟费劲地推车，

他们终于挪到了一个小摊旁，
老头儿想挑一只称心的乌鸡。

鸡贩！你坑谁也别坑这老俩口。

我看一滚圆壮汉正从公厕
出口的窄墙挺肚而出，随即

啐一口痰，差点击中一块碎砖，
他面有愠色，甩手甩脚地离去。

我这是怎么了——
走了一路，看了一路？

每一个路口都让我感到
一种危险正从斜刺里杀出。

And those who retreated to a dark heaven
Need you, from your point of view,

To imagine their human touch
Once again simple and rich.

If you really want to fly,
You can do it right now.

–L.S. and G.X.

Look

What's the matter with me
Wandering so in the street?

My eyes watch things to their limit,
But people are busy hurrying on . . .

Someone is walking with a companion just to talk,
Someone is standing at a bus stop just to look around

I saw a strange old man, half naked,
Sitting motionlessly at the entrance to a lane,

His skinny figure reminded me of my grandpa,
Last summer, his belly sunken,

My dying grandpa, waiting for me far away in Africa . . .
too far from my own village!

I saw an old couple living an even harder life:
the old lady sitting in a cart, the old man pushing it

They inch forward to a stall,
the man shuffling to buy a black-boned chicken:

黄昏中这条街簌簌作响，
被两排老槐树夹在中间。

我看红色夏利车来回空跑，
司机的脸色比暮色更灰暗。

天空真的就暗下来了！

我于是拐进一家小酒馆，
三张条桌，九把方凳……

我要了一盘煮毛豆，一碟
田螺，一盘炒苦瓜，外加

一碗刀削面……我挨窗
坐下，眼睛还往街上瞧……

我这是怎么了——
黑乎乎的外面能看见啥？

小酒馆渐渐满了人，
啤酒味熏得人脸红。

我看一浙江老乡喝斥
他三岁的胖墩墩的小儿子，

大儿子一声不响，闷头扒饭，
小儿子吓得从方凳跌坐在地。

我看瘦瘦的女服务员忙得欢喜，
不时向小窗口里尖声禀报菜名，

她的灰格子衬衫泛出平民的朴素。
这时，我听见又挨着父亲坐下的

Chicken-peddler! You can cheat anyone but this old couple.

I saw a burly man, his big belly
Sticking out of a public john, spitting,

The spit nearly hitting a broken brick, a bit
Angry, swinging his arms as he returns to the street.

What's the matter with me,
Walking all the way and watching always?

Every crossing makes me feel
some danger rushing forward.

At dusk this street rustles,
between two lines of old Chinese scholar trees.

I saw a dilapidated taxi without any passengers,
The face of the driver darker than dusk.

It really is getting dark!

So I enter a small restaurant,
Three tables, nine square stools . . .

I order a plate of boiled soya bean, a dish
Of river snails, a plate of bitter gourds

A bowl of knife-cut noodles . . .I sit beside
a window, my eyes resting again on the street . . .

What's the matter with me?
What can I see when it's so dark outside?

The restaurant gets more and more crowded,
Customers flushing to the smell of beer.

I see a native of Zhejiang scolding
His fat three-year old son,

小儿子在喊："爸爸，爸爸……"
一边把嘴吐得圆圆的，伸过去，

我看那父亲把一匙豆腐吹凉了，
小心翼翼地，送进儿子的嘴里……

过去过去过去

"过去过去过去……
过不去过不去过不去……"

有个人念念有词——
这个苦恼的人正走在幸福大街上。

过去它肯定能过去，
但这个人的脑门太窄了。

他还在跟自己过不去，
而他的过去早过去了。

过不去？那你再试一试。
生活就是让一天天过去，

就像麻雀在低空飞，
就像泥鳅从泥里钻，

就像大人答不出孩子的问题，
就像死者不愿讲死亡的秘密。

有人急了，有人眼红了，
全因为不明白这个道理。

过去，过去，过去……
是啊，一切都会过去的。

The elder son eating silently
While the little boy falls to the ground in fear.

I see a skinny waitress joyfully serving,
Shrieking the names of dishes through a small window

Her shirt reflecting the common touch.
Then I heard the little son shouting

At his father: papa, papa . . .
Stretching his round mouth forward

And I saw the father blow on a spoonful of bean curd,
Carefully put it into the mouth of the boy . . .

–L.S. and G.X.

It's Over, Over, Over

"It's over, over, over . . .
It's not over, not over, not over . . ."

Someone is reading aloud:
The Worried Man walking the Street of Happiness.

It is surely all over:
you note the man's forehead is too narrow.

He is hard on himself,
His past has already left without him.

It's not over? Lets try again.
Life consists of letting days pass

Like sparrows flying at low-altitude,
like eels writhing in mud

但一个小男孩被两根铁栅卡住了。
他在喊。他在挣扎。他的未来。

弱小的

一只蚂蚁向一根草的顶端爬去……
摔了下来，但没有受伤。
一些松针从枝丫间跌落，
有几根直直地插进泥地。
一个孩子用玩具车拉着
另一辆更小的玩具车，
嘴巴模仿喇叭：嘟嘟嘟……

各种各样的弱小的生物，
此刻在阳光里各忙各的，
享受着自己的最普通的瞬间，
没有抱怨，也不去冥想明天。
今天的风刮出今天的凉意，
今天的阳光也不是宣传画，
今天总是值得珍惜。
你的皮肤有一点儿凉，
他的心头有一丝欢喜。

这些弱小的从不声张的生物，
我们常常因忙碌而忽略它们。
而当我无事可干的时候，
病中或病后虚弱的时候，
当我被虚无拽紧衣领的时候，
或被烦恼拖住脚后跟的时候，
我会目光向下，看见它们，
我会蹲下身子，在泥地或
水泥地上，静心地看一会儿，
我会在屁股底下垫一块碎砖，
单独坐一坐，听一听风
和风从远处带来的响声，

Like adults who can't answer children's questions,
like cadavers who don't want to reveal the secret of death.

One person is angry, another is jealous,
and all because they don't understand.

It's over, over, over . . .
Yes, everything will pass.

But there is a little boy wedged between two iron bars.
He is crying. He is struggling. His future.

–L.S. and G.X.

Small and Weak

An ant is crawling towards the top of a grass blade . . .
It falls but doesn't get hurt.
Pine needles fall from branches,
sticking straight into the mud.
A little boy is pulling an even smaller toy car
with another toy car,
shouting du du du and imitating a car horn

All kinds of small and weak living things
Are busy doing things in the sunshine,
enjoying these ordinary moments
without complaint and thought of tomorrow.
Today's wind blows in today's coolness,
today's sunshine is not a poster.
Your skin is a little cold,
your heart a tiny joy.

These small, weak and silent living things,
I often neglect on busy days.
However, when I have nothing to do
When I'm ill or weak,
When nihility grabs me by the collar,

我会像一条活生生的溪流，
一路溅起幻象，又一路放弃，
然后我会起身，接着走我的路……
我发觉思想并不能记录，
因为能思想的只是我的灵魂。

窗子响，不是想招呼谁。
太阳落，不是想抛弃谁。
这些因弱小而格外善良的生物，
我应该更多地和你们在一起，
哪怕仅仅是坐一坐，坐在
我自己有头有脸的影子里，
让衣角在风中像风一样起伏。

弱小的……总是弱小的善！

安宁

我想写出此刻的安宁
我心中枯草一样驯服的安宁
被风吹送着一直升向天庭的安宁
我想写出这住宅小区的安宁
汽车开走了停车场空荡荡的安宁
儿童们奔跑奶奶们闲聊的安宁
我想写出这风中的清亮的安宁
草茎颤动着咝咝响的安宁
老人裤管里瘦骨的安宁
我想写出这泥地上湿乎乎的安宁
阳光铺出的淡黄色的安宁
断枝裂隙间干巴巴的安宁
我想写出这树影笼罩着的安宁
以及树影之外的安宁
以及天地间青蓝色的安宁
我这么想着没功夫再想别的
我这么想着一路都这么想着

When sorrow pulls at my feet,
I look down and see them,
I squat down on the ground,
On the cement, to watch them quietly.
I sit on a broken brick
Listening to wind and sounds
Brought by wind from a distance.
I want to be like a living stream
Splashing phantoms as I rushed,
Then I would get up and go on my way . . .
I find that thoughts can't record things,
Because it's only my soul that thinks.

The window makes sounds, not trying to call anybody.
The sun is setting, not wanting to abandon anybody.
You living things especially kind just because of
Your smallness and weakness
I should spend more time with you,
Even sitting for a little while, sitting in
The shadow of my own head and face,
Letting my clothing wave in the wind as wind itself.

Small and weak . . .always the kindness of small and weak!

–L.S. and G.X.

Tranquility

I want to write this moment's tranquility.
My inner tranquility like a humble grass blade, dried.
This tranquility flies to the heavens in the wind.
I want to write this neighborhood's tranquility.
The empty tranquility in the parking lot after all the cars have gone
The tranquility of grandmas chatting while the kids are running
I want to write a clean and bright tranquility in this wind.
The rustling tranquility of shivering grass
The skinny tranquility, the trousers of an old man.
I want to write the wet tranquility of the earth,

占据我全身心的，就是这
——安宁

The yellowish tranquility spread by sunshine
The dry tranquility among the broken twigs.
I want to write the tranquility under the shadow of a tree
And the tranquility beyond the shadow
And the blue and greenish tranquility between sky and earth
So thinking, I have no time to think of other things.
So thinking, I think this to the end.
It is this tranquility which
Keeps my mind so completely busy.

–L.S. and G.X.

唐丹鸿

突然吊桥升起……

突然吊桥升起行人止步并看见
河水正在流逝，仿佛随着合奏
高抬的左腿正在抵达彩虹
突然光从后面照来阴影朝前倾覆
她躬身亲吻，她的乳房被衬衣遮掩

在黑暗里，在芬芳中，乐队的狂潮
并不比情欲猛烈，乌鸦们欢呼着
扑向我的胸膛，除了花腔还有姐姐
在我耳中，她嘹亮的裸体正四蹄狂奔

突然吊桥降下行人朝彼岸走去
高抬的左腿像我的头一样耷拉下来
突然青春的激动的追光经不住流水摧残
那伟大子宫的大门在我回来前已经关闭
我抚摸你萎缩打皱的苹果脸，我热爱

看不见的玫瑰的袖子拭拂着玻璃窗

由漆黑和温存组成的大块头之夜
刚刚翻身

红窗帘扭腰站定到角落
白窗帘哗地一声敞开胸襟
扁平透明的玻璃乳房
朝老板和秘书响亮地坦露

玻璃乳房啊，玻璃，你不会相信

Tang Danhong

translations by Eleni Sikelianos and Jennifer Feeley

Suddenly the Drawbridge Raises

Suddenly the drawbridge raises a pedestrian stops catches sight
of river water slipping by as if after a musical ensemble
left leg lifts high, brushes a rainbow
suddenly in the back light lights up, shadows topple to the front
her arched body kisses, breasts encrypted in a shirt

In the perfumed dark, the orchestra's swelling tide
is nowhere near as fevered as desire, crows applaud
thrashing my chest, besides coloratura in my ear there's an older sister
her deafening naked body four hoofs rushing like mad

Suddenly the drawbridge descends the pedestrian is off for the farther shore
left leg that was lifted high wilts so does my head
suddenly youth's impatient spotlight can't stand rushing water's destruction
The front door of that great uterus shut before I returned
I stroke your wasted apple face, I furiously love

The Invisible Rose's Sleeve Dabs the Windowpane

The night large in stature made of pitch-black compassion
just turned over

The red curtain twists its waist halts at the corner
The white curtain rips open the garment's bodice - rip
A flat terrain, translucent glass breast
laid bare to boss, secretary with a tearing crack

Glass breast oh, glass, you won't believe it

阳光已渡过泪水亲吻眼睛的眯缝
葡萄酒把光辉的脚迈进了心坎

复印机秋波回睇，她激动的纸舌
抵进写字台秘密的口腔，她翻卷

金指环的牙齿，高压电的牙齿
吻着，又薄又白的吻，对吧？

既然墨在往下滴
浸染了公函洁白的花边内裤
那么从 8 点到 11 点为何不高高隆起

玻璃乳房啊，玻璃，你在哆嗦
看不见的玫瑰陪你过夜
你风流面又磨蹭

看不见的玫瑰挂断了电话
看不见的玫瑰在我心中哭泣

看不见的玫瑰有她的急事
看不见的玫瑰的袖子拭拂着玻璃窗

玻璃乳房啊，玻璃，我说过
"闪光的胴体才有锋利的乳汁"

难道说我错了？
难道说玫瑰不该别在你的左边？

从梨子到蝴蝶

裙裾从春季的腰身滑到脚踝
我看见难堪中出汗的夏天的丰臀
我看见闪光灯闪了又闪，啊，浑圆的，微酸的

254

Sunlight has waded through tears, kisses the eyes' squint
With bright feet, wine steps to the bottom of the heart

The copy machine glances backward beguilingly, her agitated paper tongue
unfurls in the writing desk's private cavity, she spins

Gold ringed tooth, high voltage tooth
kissing, a kiss that is both light and white, right?

Since ink is dripping down
fouling the official virginal white lace underwear missive
why doesn't 8 o'clock to 11 bulge high noon?

Glass breast oh, glass, you're trembling
The invisible rose escorts you through the night
You are wanton, and dawdle too

The invisible rose has hung up the phone
The invisible rose sobs in my heart

The invisible rose has her emergencies
The invisible rose's sleeve dabs the windowpane

Glass breast oh, glass, I said
"Only the flickering body holds rough milk"

How could I be wrong?
Shouldn't the rose be pinned on your left breast?

From Pears to Butterflies

A gown's lapel slips from springtime's waistline to the ankles
I see summer's full rumps, embarrassed and sweating
I see the photoflash flash and flash, perfectly round, slightly sour
autumn pears copiously occupy the free market, long poles
slap their butts, some violently shaken in both hands

秋日的梨子坐满了自由市场，她们的屁股
有的被长杆打击，有的被双手摇撼

大腿负担着肉体梨子形的部分
大腿间夹着失控的凤凰自行车
我看见车轴转身了又转身，润滑油温柔地催促
啊，胀鼓鼓的、像胶味的轮子高弹
她们的屁股，跟随飞掠的凤凰飞掠

除了梨子的幽灵还有一把闪乐的提琴
她扪着胸温存地索要指挥的手势
我看见弦紧了又紧，长杆和双手要求泛音荡起
我看见擦时她拉开翅膀，露出了光着的蝴蝶形
啊，一粒、又一粒，产卵的蝴蝶，涉及她们的痛楚

斜线皇后

是谁曾一左一右倾谈？
并非波浪或父母亲
因为父亲要捏烂桃子
漩涡淹死了他的中指
是谁一高一矮宣布：
刀俘虏了敌人
绷带裹往了食物
因为母亲迈步而来
她哺育天使成疾，一个趔趄
她糜烂的上身：斜坡向阳的一侧

她拉直了甜蜜的波浪线
让果实由二滚到了一
她说：让花作螺旋的借口吧
让父亲摇着残废的桃树
她给了颂词一记耳光
让左边的括号空对右边的省略
她说：不许伏在我胸上哭泣

What holds up the pear-shaped part of the body?
An undisciplined Phoenix bike gripped between thighs
I see the axles spin round and round, lubricating oil lovingly pushed
oh, inflated, like rubber-flavored wheels catapulting
their rumps brushing the Phoenixes as they brush past

Aside from the specter of pears here's a sparkling violin
She puts her hands on her breast tenderly asks for the conductor's signal
I see strings tighten and tighten, long bow and both hands demand a
    trembling overtone
I see in rubbing she draws out wings, exposing the naked shape of the
    butterfly
oh, one grain, then another, egg-laying butterfly, touches upon their suffering

Queen of Oblique Lines

Who are those two facing each other
(one on the left, one on the right)
Who has ever had a good heart-to-heart?
It's by no means breaking waves or parents
Because father pinches rotten peaches
the eddy drowning his middle finger
Who (one taller, one shorter) declares:
a knife captures the enemy
a bandage wraps the food
Because mother takes a step, draws closer
she falls ill from nursing angels, her rotten torso
stumbling: a slope leaning toward the sun

She straightens the sweet wave-lines
makes fruit from two roll into one
she says: let flowers justify the spiral
let father shake the crippled tree
she gives tribute, a box on the ears
so the brackets' left side faces the vacancy, the right side's omission
she says: don't bury yourself in my chest sobbing
tears might soak my back

因为眼泪会浸湿我的背
她倦怠了对称，一个呵欠
她糜烂的身上：斜坡向阳的一侧

正如探戈舞那严肃的停顿
疾风会搂住暴雨折腰
正如焰火沿夜空而下
鲜血在狂喜中挺身而出
而你，你是天使饥饿的骷髅
难道你不感谢她的食物——

正如光芒危险地蹑着髋
她的上身：从海拔六千到漩涡的中心
尽可能地——糜烂
尽可能地——倾斜

次曲美人

如果我口里含着一枚琥珀
决不说出"棕色的手肘"
意味着次曲：一位美丽的人
包藏在松涛中的反扭的腕骨

还不如说挽起袖子
暴露了雕花匕首——
额头情愿燃烧抚慰它

如果我口里含着一片云母
决不说出"羚羊的眼睛"
渗出闪光的液体淋湿了次曲——
可是，美丽的人是谁？
还不如说：

"次"就是
松开衣襟，撩起长袍

She has exhausted symmetry, her rotten torso
a yawn: a slope leaning toward the sun

Like the tango, that somber pause,
a strong wind hugs pounding rain, sinking
as fireworks arcing into the night sky descend
blood in wolfish joy strikes out
Yet you, you are an angel's ravening skeleton
how can you not be grateful for her food

Like rays of light dangerously jutting out from the hips
her torso: from 20,000 above sea level to the center of the eddy
all-rotten
all-slanting

Ci Qu Beauty

If the inside of my mouth were to hold a medallion of amber
I'd never say brown forearm
signifies Ci Qu: a beauty's
twisted wristbone hidden in the sloughing of pines

It's better to say roll up your sleeves
exposing a carved dagger —
a forehead is willing to soothe it by burning

If the inside of my mouth were to hold a sheet of mica
I'd never say antelope's eyes
seep dazzling liquid drenching Ci Qu —
but who is the beauty?
Better to say:

"Ci" equals
loosening lapels, the lifting of a long gown
"Qu" equals
sweeping off piles of snow so the snow lotus may recklessly grow,
pulling out thick clouds to reveal absolute blue

"曲"就是
拂去积雪任雪莲疯长
拨开浓云露出纯粹的蓝色

如果我口里含着一颗流星
决不说出"被吹灭的油灯"
曾经把裸体映红、放大——
整个草原都目睹了帐篷上摇晃的次曲
还不如说：

"她举起手肘"表达
舒展翅膀掠过了岩石
"她转过脸来"化作
猛然跌入夜晚的细胞的雪崩
"她起伏"，就是从黎明挪出银河的后腿
"她凝结"，当快感飞逝
停滞于琥珀的窒息，云母的光芒

可是，我嘴里都含过一些什么呢？
我很想执一把雕花匕首
推搡着纸张的后背追问——

如果，在成都，"次"
是指我厌倦了自己的理智
在拉萨，"曲"承认梦改变了我的太阳穴
还不如告诉她，一位美丽的人

向白云伸出的是我的舌头
写在纸上的是我的尸骨。

我的坏在哀求我的好

坏孩子的冤魂在揪我
是为了控诉他
坏孩子的附身物就是我

If the inside of my mouth were to hold a falling star
I'd never say a snuffed-out oil lamp
once made the naked body shine red, magnified —
the entire prairie saw Ci Qu swaying on the tent
Better to say:

"She raises her forearm" communicates
unfolded wings sweeping past rock
"she turns back her face" transforms
into an avalanche of cells suddenly dropping into night
"she rises and falls" is precisely
drawing the Milky Way's hind legs out from dawn

"she congeals" equals: at the quick lapse of orgasm she stagnates
in amber's suffocation, mica's radiance

But what has the inside of my mouth held?
How I'd like to clutch a carved dagger
heaving and thrusting the paper's verso, probing in detail

If, in Chengdu, "Ci"
refers to my being tired of my own intellect
in Lhasa, "Qu" recognizes that dreams have transformed my brow
Better to tell her: beauty,

what's stretching out toward white clouds is my tongue
what's written on paper is my bones

My Bad Begs My Good

The wronged ghost of the bad child snatches
at my sleeve, says to denounce him
Who haunts me is the bad child
beaten to death at age ten, playing an elegy
When I come to the prairie to photograph the spring scenery
I sit on the chaste nun's vagina

十岁被打死，玩弄着哀歌
当我来到草原上拍摄春色
却坐在守戒尼姑的阴道上

花啊，你叫什么名字？
你是说叫你野花？
你是说该叫鲜花？
叫你什么纯属枉然——
压扁了你
不爱你
对你没感觉
我在草原上做什么？

我躺在草原上揪住花朵
我被好孩子糟蹋了！

好孩子的附身物就是我
十岁被复制，涂改了舌头
当我揪住自己说原谅他吧
我的嘴
就像那守戒尼姑的阴道

草原啊，你是说到了春天？
你是说你在爆炸？
你是说什么也不说？
你说什么纯属枉然——
当我来到草原上拍摄春色
那守戒尼姑的阴道
像我的坏在哀求我的好

Oh flower, what's your name?
Did you say to call you wild flower?
Did you say to call you fresh flower?
To call you anything is a waste —
I've crushed you
don't love you
have no feelings toward you
What am I doing on the prairie?

Lounging here plucking
I'm devastated by the good child!

Who the good child haunts is me
cloned at age ten, altered tongue
plucking at my own sleeve, tell myself to forgive him
my mouth
like the chaste nun's vagina

Oh prairie, are you speaking of spring?
Did you say you're exploding?
Did you say you didn't say anything?
Whatever you say is a waste —
When I come to the prairie to photograph the spring scenery
the chaste nun's vagina
is like my bad begging my good

杨键

懂得

一座坟静卧着，
一块碑竖立着，
就像我自己在静卧，在竖立着，
风轻轻地吹过荒草，
一层一层地吹过去，
就像我自己在吹过去，
无动于衷地吹过去。
狗不断地在远处叫着，
又被寂静的虚空包容，
就像我自己在叫着，在包容着，
没有什么彼此，
也没有什么先后，
呵，只有迷茫的人才会去伤害，
只有糊涂的人才会去憎恨。

小木船

你为什么要把生活弄得这样僵硬？
你连一条小木船的轻松自如都没有，
连一棵树都不如啊，
比如说柳树，榆树，香樟树，
一年四季都在自然地变化着，
一年四季
都很美好。
你为什么连这些树，
连一条小木船都不如啊！

Yang Jian

translations by John High, Kokho with Zhang Er

Understanding

A grave in stillness,
The headstone upright,
as if it is I in stillness and upright,
A breeze flickering across wild grasses
fluttering wave upon wave,
as if it is this self flickering,
Unattached and outside feeling flickering
and the dog's bark incessant, somewhere distant
as if it is this self barking, embracing
this no you no me,
no earlier no later,
Only the lost ones, yes, choose to damage
only the confused choose to hate.

A Wooden Boat

Why make your life so stiff?
You even lack the ease of a wooden boat,
You're not even worthy of the tree,
a willow, an elm, a camphor, for instance —
change with the four seasons naturally,
the year's four seasons
all very beautiful.
Say, you're not even worthy of these trees,
or for all that, a wooden boat!

在浮世

野鸭子在半空
沙哑，单调地叫着
"啊，啊"
多么像我们，
虽然面部安详地走着和坐着，
但心里总有一种
隐约的凶兆，
朦胧的担忧……

生死恋

一个人死后的生活
是活人对他的回忆……
当他死去很久以后，
他用过的镜子开口说话了，
他坐过的椅子喃喃低语了，
连小路也在回想着他的脚步。

在窗外，
缓缓的落日，
是他惯用的语调。
一个活人的生活，
是对死人的回忆……

在过了很久以后，
活人的语调，动作，
跟死去的人一样了。

柳树

温良的乳母一样的柳丝，
在沉静的水边，

In the Floating World

A duck quacking mid-air
course monotonous
"ach, ach!"
Strutting then squatting calm face,
so much like us,
but inside ill
an omen faint
some vague stress . . .

Life-Death-Love

After death a man's
his memory among the living.
For a long long time a mirror
starts to open a mouth to speak,
the chair where he once sat begins utterance
even a road recalls his tracks.

The window's other side,
the slow of sunset,
this is the man's usual tone.
The life of a living one
is a memory of the dead.

For a long long time
the tone and gesture of those alive
Becomes the same as the dead.

Willow Tree

Leaning arms of a willow,
gentle as the mother breast feeding,
rocking back and forth by a calm water line,
a look of no discontent.

轻拂着，
看上去，那么容易。

它安慰每一个怒火中烧者，
并为悲痛的失恋者讲述：
"一切不过是过眼云烟，
一切，也会反过来，温暖可亲。"

迷路

在森林里
一个迷路的人，
开始恐惧起来，
他的心不由自主地
变出了老虎和狮子。
小时候听到的，
阴曹地府的鬼魂，
也从记忆里，
活灵活现地跑出来了。
他先是慢慢地走着，
装做若无其事的样子
走着，走着，
身后簌簌响起的声音，
就像有一个人在追赶。
他快速地走了起来，
连头也不敢问一下。
森林里渐渐暗下来，
他心里的老虎、狮子和鬼魂，
越来越生动。
这样，
他就跑起来了，
一会儿向东，
一会儿向西。
随后，
他再也不知道路在哪里了。

Consoling all ravage all raging inside,
as if murmuring "O broken and jilted lover —
it's all passing clouds and fog over the eyes,
reversely, it may all grow tender."

Lost Way

A being
wandering the wood
enters fear
and the mind can't help
lions and tigers coming forth
and those hungry ghosts
of childhood's hell mirrored
as if alive now, parading out of the past.
At first he walks slow
Pretense of the benign and no worry in
One step and another and then the stalking
rushing rustle from behind,
as if pursued, so dare not
turn the face back to see it.
The wood darkening,
tigers, lions, and these ghosts of the heart
more vivacious, movie-like.
Alas, fleeing
one foot eastward
one westward,
and then suddenly where is
the road after all.
The real tiger may have ravaged him,
or was it his own fear.
The wood remains as its usual self
radiating in a gold-rimmed dusk.
The way clear enough
a vivid light —
only few recognize
and walk out on it.

他会被真的老虎吃掉，
也会被自己的恐惧吓死。
而森林还跟往常一样，
笼罩着金黄的夕光。
一条小路干净地卧在那里，
亮晃晃的，
只有很少的人，
看到了，
并且走了出去。

相依

1
你手上抓着一根柳枝，
在那条小径上走着。

那条小径，通向一座寺院
寺院里，塔身庄严、肃穆。

你就像那片风景中一粒灰色小斑点，
一粒没有爹没有娘的灰色小斑点，

一粒没有头没有尾的脆弱小斑点，
使我的眼睛模糊，喉咙哽咽。

你又来到水边轻拂着柳枝
而我在一个小亭子里看着。

眼睛由模糊变为明亮，
由不安变为平静。

2
多少次，
我们又背道而驰。

Leaning on the Other

1.

Holding a branch, a willow,
that set of tracks you trailing

the set of tracks, to a monastery
that place a silent pagoda stands solemn.

You a fleck of grey in a scene
a fleck, a grey speck, no father nor mother,

Fragile, a clueless speck
vanquishing sight choking my breath.

Again you appear at water's edge, branch willow sway,
while here I study you from a small pavilion.

My eyes translucent from haze
tranquilized from unease.

2.

How often we
walk in contradictions of motion.

How often we
fall into grieving
not so fine not finished together.

Longing for a girl like wispy dusk, I'm reminded.

Then one day
the heart
suddenly blown over —
you're my dead father,
actually, my own mother, alive
how could I forget?

多少次，
我们为不能好好在一起，
伤心难过。

这让我希冀着一个像薄暮一样的女孩。

有一天，
我的心，
猛地震动起来，
你就是我死去的父亲，
你就是我活着的母亲，
我怎么都忘掉了？

在你的泪水濡湿的枕巾上，
是我的手臂。
而使我们拥抱得如此紧密的，
不再是爱情了。

我们可以共存，
与窗外的景色同在。

   3
在经过了很久以后
我们有一点知道
生活有着比我们早年所幻想的
肉体的爱更为重要的东西。

我们一度以为冻僵就是我们的真相，
不知道我们还可以变化，
坚硬的可以变成柔软的，
蛮横的可以变成慈悲的。

在古老运河的小径上，
根本就不存在受难者和施虐者。
我们丧失了颜色
混进了四周。

On the pillow-cover, my arm
your wet tears.
What makes us cling so tight is
our gone love.

Maybe we coexist and merge
with all of that outside the window.

3.

After awhile a reckoning
occurs we come to
life more fertile than the body,
the fantasy of a juvenile love.

Back then — our truth was rigid, fossilized
Blind to change
to the hard that softens,
arrogance and rudeness becoming compassion.

On those tracks of an ancient canal,
There never were victim and victimizer,
blanched and without intention
we become the landscape.

Steps unheard and bodies
leaning into the other,
the spirit stilled
without suffering.

Hands joined we slipped
through the ruin of the city wall —
effortless, speechless,
our face the same as withered grass.

No sound no breath a night descends
and leaves come home,
as if this is the great secret of salvation
we've forgotten.

脚步轻柔
相偎的身体
不再损害
灵魂的寂静。

我们手挽着手，
在所剩无几的城墙下经过
无须用力，也无须说话
我们的神情就同地上的枯草一样。

夜晚无声无息地来了，
树叶无声无息地落了。
好像这就是得救的奥秘，
我们还不知道呢。

一个孤独者的山和湖

1
一段时间以后，
我又要到山上去坐一坐，
去调我破琴一样的心。
我会选择一块抬眼就能看到落日的地方，
我想坐下去，一直到石化。
可是我的老母亲怎么办，
如果我就此石化了？
留恋就像一阵寒风，吹着我回家，
在窗前，月亮在我的脸上洒下苦涩的泪滴。
我不会忘记怎样让母亲幸福
仍然是我们所追求的最伟大的艺术。

2
多美啊，
逆来顺受的柳树，
那是在河岸上。
那条河

The Mountain and Lake of a Loner

1.

After some time
I'll rest on the mountain cliff
clearing a heart — this broken music box . . .
pick a stone where the sun peaks,
just sitting 'til this body itself is stone.
But what about my mom,
if I've turned to stone, then what?
The longing a cold wind carrying homeward
and there by the window pane the moon rains down hard tears.
Not forgetting to make mother happy
is the greatest art we pursue.

2.

How stunning, yes —
these always accepting willows
shoring up the riverbank.
The river itself
abandons no traces no distinction —
we become the abysmal
yet may be shining,
drinking this red dust of air.
Happiness will sprout a lung's leaf.
Though I've gathered no wood for the frames
I'm planning for a window.

Brushing

In a bed we hold each other in kisses,
a few decades afterward, you touch my corpse,
in the bed of our love-making,
will wisdom then pour out of your eyes —
seeing the breeze brush the curtain is our life.

不会留下任何擦痕——
我们变成了最不好的，
但完全可以是最好的，
痛饮这空气里阴沉沉的泥泞，
我的欢乐就要长出一只肺叶了。
虽然我还没有木头，
但我已经想好了一扇窗户。

吹拂

在一张床上，我们抱着亲吻，
几十年后，你抱着我的尸体
在我们曾经相爱的床上，
那时，智慧是否会从你的泪眼中涌现
认清吹拂窗帘的微风就是我们的生命。

1967 年

他们说：
"这把二胡的弦要扯断，
琴身要砸碎。"
我们就没有了琴声。

他们说：
"这棵大树要锯断，
主要是古树，全部要锯掉。"
我们就没有了荫凉。

他们说：
"这个石匠要除掉，
那个木匠也要除掉，要立即执行。"
我们就没有了好看的石桥，
我们就没有了好看的房子。

Year of 1967

They said —
Ravage the strings of the Chinese violin,
Smash it,
and now we don't have music.

They said —
Raze the miracle trees,
All the ancient ones,
and now there's no shade or coolness.

They said —
Ditch the stonemason
and the carpenter too, pronto —
and now the good-looking stone bridges are all gone,
the good-looking houses too.

They said —
Trash the books of the sages and those of virtue,
Bring down these Confucius temples,
Send the home-leavers home again
and now we have no prudence,
no remaining conscience.

Born during the collapsing year of 1967,
Fated to see the world through one-sided eyes,
I was damaged shortly after birth,
Fated to see the world through damaged eyes.

To witness all of you die,
Fated not to die,
Fated to speak among these ruins,
Fated to open the dust-sealed iron gate.

他们说：
"这些圣贤书要烧掉，
这些文庙要毁掉，
这些出家人要赶回家。"
我们就没有了道德，
我们就没有了良知。

我生于崩溃的 1967 年，
我注定了要以毁灭的眼光来看待一切，
我生下来不久就生病了，
我注定了要以生病的眼光来看待一切。

看着你们都在死去，
我注定了不能死去，
我注定了要在废墟上开口说话，
我注定了要推开尘封的铁门。

运河

这不是一座城市，
这是灰蒙蒙的水泥厂。
老房子拆掉了，
狗也死了，
倒在运河边，
像家里的一个老人，
眼睛睁得比平常大一点，
运河上一条船也没有，
我们的桥，半月形的，
在远处，
令人想起生命是柔和的，绵延无尽的，
（如果生命不是永恒的，活着干什么呢？）
只是我们的烦躁，
越来越小的耐心，
使我们再也造不出那么精细的护栏，
而柳树的枝条还是轻松地悬挂着，

Canal

This is not a city,
just an ashen cement factory
the old houses demolished,
the dog dead too,
stretched out by the canal,
like an old master come home.
No boats in the canal,
our crescent bridge out
there reminds us —
life's tender shoots, and endless spreading,
if it's all impermanent, why bother to breathe?
Our anxiety and shrinking patience
separate us
from carving again such delicate railings,
while the willow branches linger, at ease
thanks to the unyielding earth.
Looking out at today's river
my life fades —
nightfall taking in the late dusk,
so that the eye
moves beyond and sees
all the people after work
heaving like the train out
there rushing over the crescent bridge.

那都是不屈的泥土的功劳。
我凝望着今天的河水，
我的生命暗淡了，
它好像正处在薄暮向夜晚转换的时刻。
随后，
我的视野展开了，
看见每一个下班的人，
都像一列气喘吁吁的火车，
在那半月形的桥梁上通过。

杨小滨

裸露

她走进旧照片洗澡，把水搅混
象表层的泛黄。我
用雾气擦亮镜框，但看不清
是谁，藏在浴廉背后。

"一个少女，"她解释说，
"但不是我。"她扔出
更多的鳞片、污垢、内衣
婚礼上的歌谱。"是美人鱼吗？"
我问得她大笑，水珠
溅在我脸上。"让我念一段
诗经，"她声音宛转而空洞

我听不懂。我捂住耳朵
我飞逃，撞在她身上
才从梦里醒来："原来
你在这儿。"她漂在玻璃上
默许："因为
你在梦中跑得太快。"

她擦干，一边哼歌
一边打喷嚏。远远地
她下颌的倒影
悬挂在春天的颈项。
"那是一件礼品，"她喃喃而语，
"我遗忘已久。"

她脱去无数冬天的积雪。
我给她点烟。照片在火苗里
弯曲。"对不起，"我说，
而她消逝无踪。

Yang Xiaobin

translations by Karla Kelsey and John Gery with the author

Nude

She entered an old photograph to bathe,
stirring the water, a murky yellow glaze. I
rubbed the foggy glass but couldn't make out
the figure concealed behind the curtain.

"A young woman," she offered,
"but not me." She tossed out
bloodstained scales, specks of dirt, lingerie,
the songbook for a wedding. "Are you a mermaid?"
She laughed at my question, splashing water
onto my face. "Let me recite for you,"
she purred, but in her disembodied voice her words

faded into nothing. I covered my ears
and fled, until I crashed into her body,
jolting me awake: "Ah ha,
so there you are." Floating on the glass,
she smiled compliantly. "You were
running too fast in your dream."

Humming, she dried herself off,
then sneezed. In the distance
the reflection of her chin
glimmered around the neck of spring.
"Here is my gift for you," she murmured,
"something I long ago overlooked,"

as she stripped thick layers of snow from her body.
I lit her a cigarette. The photograph,
catching fire, began to warp. "Forgive me," I sighed,
as she vanished in a wisp of smoke.

景色与情节

她湿漉漉地跑过来，身后的影子
像慧星，雪白，她说
"我们去看电影。"我
听见更多的呼吸声。在夜里
"我们去吃冰激凌。"她说

但我没有时间。我转身
她又站在我身边，从胸前
掏出半只苹果，手上血红
好像苹果是头颅。但
我要赶去梦里。我急急
穿好睡衣，坐到藤椅上。
她拨动纽扣："我要回到晴天。"

那真是一个鲜艳的周末。我们赶路
没有看见碾在路旁的松鼠
只看见湖，易碎的湖面
我不忍心跳进。她的手颤抖着
好像频死的鱼。她的眼睛
充溢着泪水，最后滴在丁当的船舷。
"太甜了，"她舔着阳光
舌尖一闪一闪，像灯塔
从黑洞洞的嘴里。

但我没有时间。我回头
是另一个她，"我们去挖牡蛎。"
我听见雷声。她说
"快，快，"一边脱下外衣
风刮着两颊，枝叶间的笑声
越来越冷，她挎着篮子
手和双乳陷在泥沙里。
"午睡，然后才是晚餐。"
我的目光朝着水而移动。
但她并未察觉："就一会儿。"

The Setting and the Plot

Drenched, she rushed up to me, the shadow behind her
white as a comet, and proclaimed,
"Let's go to the movies!" I,
because it was night, could only hear her panting.
"Let's go out for ice cream!" she begged me

but I had no time. I turned away
and there she was, beside me again, plucking an apple
from her chest, her hands bloody
as though she'd pulled out a baby's head. Still,
I was sucked deeper into the dream. Quickly
I slipped into my pajamas and settled into the wicker chair.
Tugging at my buttons, she cried, "I want to go back into tomorrow."

It turned out to be a colorful weekend. We pushed on with our journey
not even detecting a single squirrel along the road beside us
but only the lake, with its shimmering surface
I didn't have the heart to leap into. Her hands twitched
like two fish dying. Her opaque eyes,
welling over with tears, suddenly caused our boat to rock.
Licking the sunlight, she exclaimed, "It tastes too sweet,"
as her tongue glistened, beaming like a beacon
from the dark hole of her mouth.

But I had no time. I turned my back
only to find another her: "Let's go digging for oysters!"
I heard a thunderclap. She shouted,
"Hurry! Hurry!" as she tore off her coat.
Wind battered her cheeks, and a cackle in the bushes
grew colder and colder. She grabbed a bucket
and burrowed with her hands, her breasts brushing the sand.
"First, a nap, then dinner."
My eyes looked toward the water.
But she didn't notice: "Just for a little while."

我脸上爬满了蚂蚁，像交响乐里
一支柔板的咬啮。
我是否把脸遗忘在原地？
但谁也没有找到。在梦里
我只听见她又说
"把窗帘打开。"但我害怕
阳光般的鸟。我披上窗帘
躺在过去的船上，等待梦中之梦。

她说，"最后一次吧。"
好像几年前的声音。我抬头
她从门后一闪而过。我再次
闭上眼睛，阳光涌进整个房间。
"是咖啡还是焦味？"她尖叫。

离题的情歌

　1
我睁开你的眼睛。我无法凝视的
眼睛，让我失明。
让我瞥见的花朵
在你的春意中阑珊，你一回眸
我的美人就苍老无比。
你一转眼，风景把我席卷而去。
我看见的，就是你
眼底的海，是你的目光
淹没了我。是我清晨醒来的时分
一只瞳人般的鸟飞去
带走了你，和你镜中的睡姿。

　2
我张开你的嘴唇。我无法亲吻的
嘴唇，你饮的酒
灌醉了我。我歌唱
你的声音刺痛我。我忍受

Soon ants began to crawl across my cheeks
in a symphonic adagio.
Did I abandon my face there?
But no one has found it. In the dream
I could hear her voice once again:
"Raise the curtain." But I feared
the birdlike sunlight. I held the curtain draped over my shoulders
reclining in what had once been the boat, waiting for the dream inside my
    dream.

She whispered, "How about one more time?"
in a voice familiar from years before. I lifted my head
only to see her flash by the door. Finally,
I closed my eyes. Sunlight gushed into the room.
"Do you smell coffee or is something burning?" she cried.

Love Song Gone Awry

1

I am blinking your eyes, the eyes
I cannot gaze at that blind me.
Whatever flowers I glimpse
wither in spring. When you look behind,
my beautiful woman there grows wrinkled.
When you look to the side, the landscape sweeps me away.
If I peer into the ocean at the bottom of your eyes,
your vision
drowns me. When I awake at dawn
a bird flies from your eyes, taking in its beak
the image in the mirror of you sleeping.

2

I am pouting with your lips, the lips
I cannot kiss. The wine you drink
befuddles me. When I start singing,

你的饥渴，我吞食
你嘴里的花园纷纷飘落
我吐出你的早餐
你的絮语，你的尖叫。
静下来，让我用你的舌头
说话，那一句
你的梦呓，我遗忘已久。

　3
我伸出你的手。我无法握住的手
穿过黑夜，拥抱我的阴影。
我捏成你的拳头
你用手背上的月色
掀倒了我。是我握住的指甲
刻出你的掌纹，是我
用窗外的风抚摸你的伤口
我疼痛。我的手指战栗
插入你的呼救，用你
在我胸前的双手
剪断我的祷词，扼住我的呼吸。

信件·面包·书签

　信件

午餐之前，你听见信封里的叫喊。
你把它打开：一封
寄自本埠的情书，落款是
小夜曲。

你坚持把它封死。就像
埋掉一只夜莺。你怕

your voice pierces me. I suffer
your thirst. I swallow
the gardens inside your mouth drifting
downward from the sky
and exhale your breakfast, your whisper, your scream.
Quiet now: Let me speak with your tongue
the words you whisper in your sleep, the words I
have never heard.

     3

I extend your hand, the hand
I fail to touch, seizing my shadow, piercing the night.
When my hand closes into your fist, you
push me away
into moonlight. These are my fingernails
that carve your palm print, fondling
your bruises in the night breeze,

causing me pain. My fingers tremble,
breaking through your cry, as your
hands reach inside my chest,
cut short my pleading, and begin to strangle me.

Three Short Poems

1. The Letter

Before lunch, you heard a cry come from inside the envelope.
You opened it: a
love letter from across town, signed
Serenade.

You carefully resealed it, as though
burying a nightingale. Such pure music

那首歌。你把它扔回邮筒
直到第二天
它又在你的信箱里呻吟

面包

你用梳子切开面包。那里
有死者的发丝，娇嗔
烤热的爱。

面包越来越黑，碎屑
越来越理不清：

梳洗之前，你的脸已烧焦。
难以下咽的五官
带着美的饥饿。

书签

你打开一来尘封已久的书：
一只手
夹在书签的位置。

它不愿意离开，它死死地
抓住这个字
一个句号。
枯萎的手，书页上的化石
等待另一只手的掌声

风暴
（《毒蛇世纪》三首之一）

一片屋顶掀掉另一片屋顶
一座城市毁掉另一座城市
一个人死在另一个人身上

terrifies you. You dropped it off at the post office
but the next day again
you heard it in your mailbox, weeping.

    2. Bread

You sliced the loaf of bread with a comb,
finding inside it hairs of the dead, a squeamish voice,
and dry, warmed-over love.

The bread darkened and darkened, its crumbs
more and more seared and shriveled:

Before you could wash and dress, your face, too, was burnt:
its features, not easy to swallow,
burgeon with a hunger for beauty.

    3. The Bookmark

You opened a long neglected book:
A hand
was inserted in place of a bookmark.

Unwilling to let go, it held on tightly,
grasping at characters,
clinging to a period.

That little hand, a relic on the page,
still waiting for another hand to clap with

Storm

A roof tears off another roof
A city destroys another city
A person dies in another person

风暴将替身轻轻删去
将世界甩出手掌，不让它模仿
风暴是家乡的敌人

因为在世的不再记得
去世的更加沉默

只有风暴在说。它扔出我们的肺
拒绝其它声音

于是我们只剩下一口气来表演革命
表演缝隙中长大的蝎子
卷在心里，长在红旗下
唯一的痉挛来自末日
从雷电向遗骸横扫

这是风暴在说。这是一声惨叫
狂喜的鸟压迫一次
瘟疫就洒遍了整个原野

博物馆
（《文化》五首之一）

把亚洲放在坛子里
腌干。亚洲就会成为古董

或者把非洲的骨头剔开
非洲古色古香，瘦得令人心酸

它的肝脏流着黑色的血
泼在地图册上显得异常枯萎

如果有钱，就能买下整个世界
以及它每一年的战争和尸骸

The storm lightly deletes its stuntman
And tosses out the world, refusing imitation
It is the enemy of the village, the enemy of home

Because the living no longer remember
While the dead remain silent
Only the storm speaks. It throws out our lungs
And rejects other voices

Thus we have the only remaining breath to perform revolution
And play scorpion, creeping out of crevices
Etched in the heart and growing under the red flag
The only spasm comes out of doomsday
Sweeping from thunder to dead bodies

This is the storm speaking. This is an agonized cry
Whenever the ecstatic bird crushes
The epidemic will spread entire wildernesses

Museum

Put Asia in a jar
And pickle it. Asia will become a curio.

Or pick the bones out of Africa.
Africa is so archaic, so skinny that it hurts the heart

As its liver oozes black blood
That withers when spilled on album.

If you are rich you can buy the whole world
Along with its annual wars and corpses

And the tribal chiefs' prayer when drumbeats, stopped in the dry season,
Get recorded, elegantly interwoven with chamber music.

以及酋长们的祷文，鼓点在旱季中止
移到室内乐里优雅地敲打

那些随手写来的敕令，也比牲口贵重
因为它并不耕田，只是一味地肝脑涂地

记录在最隐秘的部分，好象伤口
为了公开而不得愈合

并且这些伤口已经分类，
所有的类别都看不见血迹。

只有疼痛从不提起，被刀镞锈住
疼痛悬挂在很久以前，早已一代代地臣服

在我们祖先的祭典里
强盗佩戴了女人，成为皇帝

但是活的群众从来不被收藏
因为他们太不整齐，毫无经典性

那时的青春，那时的劳动！
饥饿在观赏中变得美丽

过去的一切都禁止抚摸，一旦触及
我们就会立刻老去。

四季歌

　春

为了春天，我们不惜迎著东风的媚眼和杨柳的鞭子
为了春天，我们把泪滴解冻在抒情的伤口里
春天啊，我们因为比牡丹丑陋而自杀未遂

Even the randomly written edicts are dearer than livestock
Since they do not plow, but only pour out brains

Recorded in the most secret parts like wounds
Which are not allowed to heal in order to be public.

The wounds have been categorized
And none of the categories show bloodstains.

Only pain is never mentioned. Stuck in the rust of knives,
Pain was hung a long time ago, subjugated generation after generation

In the sacrificial rites of our ancestors,
The robbers wore women and became emperors

Yet living masses are never collected
Because they are too irregular, beneath the classical level.

Youth at the time! Labor at the time!
Hunger gets prettier in enjoyment:

Everything in the past is forbidden
As soon as it's touched, we'd grow old.

Seasons

Spring

For the spring we face the charming eyes of the east wind and the whips of
    willows
For the spring we melt tears into lyrical wounds
Oh spring, we failed in our suicide because we are uglier than the peony

For the spring we are infected with pistils before taking off our coats
Disguised as butterflies and honeybees, brewing boundless acnes
For the spring we divulge the secrets of love
Scaring out snakes before chasing off cows

为了春天，我们脱掉上衣之前就感染了花蕊
装扮成蝴蝶和蜜蜂，酿出无边的粉刺
为了春天，我们走漏了爱情的风声
刚要虚张声势就已经打草惊蛇

就是为了春天，我们才把嗓子吊到树梢上
唱出的麻雀也不管东方的青红皂白
为了春天的幸福我们拍卖所有其他的幸福
降价处理，概不退货

为了春天，我们把夏天斩尽杀绝，禁止它出场
为了春天，我们也开除不合格的春天
让它们和冬天呆在一起，永世不得翻身

都是为了春天啊，这个
耸人听闻的、花枝招展的春天！

哦，春天，我们还没等到你就已经苍老

　　夏

看见夏天，才知道春天的虚伪
赤裸裸的夏天迎面走来
没有教养的腿，一步就跨在我们肩上

夏天，颠来倒去还是夏天
而我们累得汗津津，一夜间熟透

尝到夏天就是尝到自己，依旧贪得无厌
夏天刚出炉，就端在我们面前
喝下一锅热乎乎的夏天，尿出金子
服用过量，还至死不渝

血却白白流掉，无非是冲著一个无耻的夏天
这样，我们就比夏天更烫

Just for the spring we hang our voices in the tops of trees
The sparrows we sing are careless of dark or bright horizons
For the happiness of spring we auction all other happiness
Discounted, with no return

For the spring we eradicate summer and forbid its entrance
For the spring we dismiss disqualified springs
Let them stay with winter and never stand out

All for the spring —
This astounding, glamorous spring

Spring, we get old before you arrive

Summer

Seeing summer we realize the hypocrisy of spring
Naked summer comes before us
Uneducated, with a step it straddles our shoulders

Summer is still summer even upside down
But we get sweaty out of fatigue, grow ripe overnight

To taste summer is to taste of oneself and remain greedy
Newly cooked, summer is served before us
Drinking a pot of hot summer and urinating gold
Overdosed but unyielding

Bloodshed for nothing, just for a shameless summer
Thus we are more scorched than summer
Contracting SARS and mad cow
Having a fever until death, leaving only a corpse

And peddling our remaining souls in another summer
Touching summer, licking summer, and tolerating summer

从疟疾一直患到梅毒
高烧至死，仅仅留下一具焦尸

在另一个夏天里叫卖用剩的灵魂
摸著夏天，舔著夏天，忍受著夏天

夏天，年龄不详，籍贯不详
在五月的某一日强暴了春天
将立即押往秋天执行枪决

　　秋

接著，秋天收割了我们的头颅
以丰年的速度掠过

秋高气爽的日子，我们的爱情都凉了半截
和出走的器官一起萧条起来

只有内心的老气愈加横秋
用枯萎的伤口装点枫叶

一片叶子还没落下，秋天就认出了我们
来自夏天的逃犯，衣裳还来不及打扮

即使伪装成蟋蟀，也要露出知了的马脚
爱出风头，受不了黑夜的孤独

而一旦被秋天吟诵，我们又清高起来
在菊花下把腰肢扯得一瘦再瘦

想到落木正等著萧萧的时刻即将来临
我们走在山水画里也忍不住瑟瑟发抖

这是最寂静的时刻，我们被夕阳窒息
而一顿深秋的夕阳却填不饱被夏天喂过的肚子

298

Summer, age unknown and national origin indistinct,
Raped the spring on a certain day in May
And will be escorted toward autumn for execution

Autumn

Then, the autumn harvests over our heads
Flying with the swift speed of a bountiful year

A fresh autumn day, our loves all get cooled down,
becoming scarce along with eloping organs

Not a single leaf has fallen but autumn already recognizes us,
Runaways from summer, without much time to get dressed

Even disguised as crickets we still show traces of cicadas
We love to show off and can't stand lonely nights

Once recited by autumn we become haughty
Pulling our waists under chrysanthemum until they're thinner and thinner

Aware of the upcoming moment of falling twigs
We can't help shivering in the landscape painting

At this most quiet moment, we are stifled by the setting sun
But the late autumn sun cannot stuff stomachs fed on summer

Oh my setting sun, your immortal ghost haunts us
With autumnal retaliation while sending autumnal seduction

Winter

We freeze after taking away the fallen leaves and fly
Over the philosophical wasteland as we put on down jackets
Looking at the horizon we don't see the spring river in the near future
Where warm ducks might stay within the rhymes of Song Dynasty poetry

夕阳啊，你万寿无疆的阴魂追随著我们
一边秋后算帐，一边暗送秋波

冬

我们脱掉落叶就冻成雪人，穿上羽绒
就飞在思想的荒原之上
眺望地平线，却不见未来的春水
暖洋洋的鸭子从来游不出宋诗的韵脚

在冬天的童话里，明天的天鹅将被无限地延迟
丑小鸭翻过这一页湖泊就进入了梦乡

梦见蜂拥而来的圣诞老人都比去年老了一岁
减去我们还不够春天那么年轻
加上，又过了死亡线
那儿有虚拟的天鹅吹著英国管

而一个真实的冬天会咳嗽不止
于是我们把它裹在被子里，挂在壁炉上
用松枝勒住冬天的脖子，不让它北风吹

这样的冬天就可以安心地滋补我们
用冰柱痛击我们的冬眠
直到僵硬的言辞诉诸熊胆
听另一个冬天在窗外无产阶级地咆哮

听另一个冬天流浪在灵魂的月色中
在卖掉最后一根火柴之前
先卖掉一首无家可归的诗歌

In the fairytale of winter, tomorrow's swan is delayed forever
Turning over this page of lake, the ugly duck enters a sweet dream

In which all Santa Clauses are one year older than they were last year
Not as young as spring, even if we were subtracted from it,
Or beyond the death line if we were added
To hear a virtual swan blowing an English horn

But a real winter will cough over and over again
Thus we wrap it in a quilt, hang it above the fireplace,
And strangle it with pine branches, refusing its north wind

Such a winter can give us seasonal nutrition
And strike our hibernation with icicles
Until rigid words resort to bear bile
Listening to another winter roaring in a proletarian way outside the window

Listening to another winter wandering in the moonlight of the soul which,
Before selling the last match,
Sells a homeless poem first

Flood

Under water we see nothing. Water
suffocates. Along with us.

All summer long water grows crowded with corpses.
People spread turning into fin-de-siecle roes,
Some swim toward the next century to nibble steel on the shore
While others sit in banked pools.

There is no water on a sunny day, a day of air.
You wait until air turns to the end, page by page
Water arrives. Water —
The world cries out only once and gets lost on its way

But we continue to be drunk by water. Water
Is death in every second following air,
Yet gloomy and severe it is hotter than a teenage girl.

大水

在水下，我们看不见什么。水是
窒息的。和我们一起。

整个夏季，水和尸骸显得拥挤。
人蔓延开来，成为世纪末的鱼种
有的游往下一个世纪，啃岸上的钢
更多的坐往水的花瓣上。

晴天没有水。晴天是空气的日子。
等到空气一页页地翻完
水降临了。水！
世界只喊了一声，就不知所终

而我们继续被水喝光。水
是每一秒钟内的死亡
紧跟在空气之后，但它阴沉，严重
它比少女更淫荡。
水用冷峻的笔将人口轻轻删去。
一个有风的夜里，水比我们还要渴
因而它极端仇恨。它锋芒毕露！

水是尖叫的神。在水里散步，我们的灵魂
属于你，我们的肉体
献给你，热爱水的人民，赶快死去！
不要等到来人及死的时候后悔莫及

看见水，就是看见母亲，一生的水
从泥里出来，添加在水上
仍然没有水丰盛，贫脊如土
而无边的诱惑，顺着腰肢在茎叶间生长
年复一年，双腿透明，我们的母亲
和水相互吞噬着，拥抱着

Water deletes a population with its cold pen.
On a windy night, water is thirstier than we are
And it hates us, it shows us its blade.

Water is a shrieking god. Walking in water our souls
Belong to it and our flesh
Is sacrificed. Those who love water die quickly,
Don't wait until you cannot die or feel regret.

Seeing water is seeing our mother. The water of life
Comes out of soil added to water,
Not as ample as water but barren as land

Yet year after year boundless temptation grows in stems
and leaves along the waist with transparent legs. Our mother
Engulfing water is engulfed, hugging —

All summer long sons are older than mothers.
All summer long water damages more than the sun.

Struggling and drowning until we get fished into coral
We hum a requiem tune:
"Floating and floating
In our vast tear!"

整个夏季，儿子比母亲更老。
整个夏季，水比太阳更刺痛！

一边扑腾，一边淹没，
直到被鱼群打捞成珊瑚
我们哼着安魂的曲调：
"漂流啊，漂流！
在我们盛大的眼泪中！"

叶辉

在乡村

在乡村，我们开始谈论命运
我们在一张屠桌上
铺上白桌布，它就变成一张会议桌
那样我们可以安心地
把两只手放上去

在其它情形里，有人说：床已经铺好了
但我不知道说话的是谁
是怎样的一只手
还有油灯边那张年轻姑娘的脸
悲哀，还是羞怯
以及户外是哪个时代的迷雾

漫延开来，在我站着的窗前
象在一面镜子前
白雪落到了镜中

老式电话

进入老年我父亲的身体开始好转
越加灵活。他爬到围墙上修剪树枝，紧张地
站在风中，他在沉默中独自干着，如果
谁和他搭话，他就会咆哮。因为他知道那将是危险的
也不管电话铃声，他总说没有什么要紧的事
有一天傍晚我从外面回家
听到铃声在响，一部老式电话，发了疯似的
我跑上楼，拿起来却是一个打错的电话
灯光从户外照到地板上，一个倒放的楔形
我想起另一些日子，多么相象，但又不知道是那些日子
记得和另一个男孩，站在刚刚雨睛的蓝色背景中

Ye Hui

translations by Joshua Beckman, Zhang Er and Zhao Xia

In the Country

In the country, we talk about fate
We spread a white table-cloth
on a killing table which turns into a meeting table
so we can be at ease
and put both hands on it

In other situations, someone says: the bed has been made
But I don't know who the speaker is
what kind of hand
and that young girl's face beside the oil lamp
whether it is sad, or shy
and outside, from what time the dense fog creeps

in front of the window where I stand
as in front of a mirror
White snow falling into the mirror

–J.B. and Z.X.

The Old Telephone

Entering old age, my father's body feels better
more flexible. He climbs on top of the surrounding wall
to trim the branches, nervously
he stands in wind, silently he works alone, if
anyone talks to him, he growls, because he gets the danger
Never mind the ringing, he always says there's nothing urgent
One evening I come in from outside
I hear the crazed ringing of an old-fashioned phone
I run upstairs, pick it up, but it's the wrong number

在一根暗黑的杂树做的电话线杆下
一个男人正向我们走来，瘦长、急促像是我父亲

小镇的考古学家

小镇的考古学家终身未娶，他年轻时
爱上一个女人，那时她刚刚出土
用楠木棺材存放。在一个阴雨天气里
当地农民将她暴露于众
她一丝不挂连皮肉也没有
她的丝质衬衣早已变成泥土，金子发夹
已放入一位主任的口袋。他看看她的牙齿
年仅十六。他看看她的盆骨嘭然心动
她的耻骨光洁饱满像从未有过
压痕，她的胸前似有乳峰的影子
微微颤动。她头枕玉枕
表明她的身份高贵而不可侵犯
因此也不可死亡。那是七十年代
他将她小心藏于阁楼
从此无人提及。八十年代他替她戴上
发套。九十年代他让她
挤进一件粉红色比基尼，整天躺在他床上
但骨架有了损伤，有几处被压断
用石膏小修，下半身绑上坚固的钢筋
只有她的头骨还完好如初
双颚开合自如像这样：嗒 、嗒 、嗒

在糖果店

有一回我在糖果店的柜台上
写下一行诗，但是
我不是在写糖果店
也不是写那个称秤的妇人
我想着其他的事情：一匹马或一个人

308

Lamp light from outside falls on the wood floor, an inverted wedge
I remember some days, how similar, yet don't know which days
I remember I was with another boy, standing in the blue background just
after the rain had cleared up
under a telephone post made of a dark tree of no particular use
a man walked towards us, lean and elongated, stepping quickly as if
he were my father

–J.B. and Z.E.

The Archeologist in the Little Town

The archeologist in the little town never married. When he was young
he fell in love with a woman. At the time she had just been excavated
and was stored in a strong coffin. One gloomy rainy day
local farmers exposed her to the public
she didn't have a stitch on, not even flesh
her silk blouse had turned to earth, her gold hair pin
had been put into the chief's pocket. He examined her teeth —
she was only sixteen. He examined her pelvis, his heart pumping hard
Her pubic bone shining smooth and full, as if there had never been a
trace of being pressed, on her chest as if there were shadows of breasts
trembling. Her head laid on a jade pillow
demonstrating a noble origin, thus inviolable
therefore immortal. That was in the 70s
He carefully hid her in the attic
since then no one mentioned her. In the 80s, he made her wear
a hair piece. In the 90s, he made her
squeeze into a pink bikini, spending the whole day lying in his bed
but her skeleton was broken, a few places crushed
He used plaster to mend it, bound the bottom of the body with solid steel
Only her skull is as perfect as before
Her jaw opens and closes smoothly like this: Da, Da, Da

–J.B. and Z.E.

在陌生的地方，展开
全部生活的戏剧，告别 、相聚
一个泪水和信件的国度
我躺在想像的暖流中
不想成为我看到的每个人
如同一座小山上长着
本该长在荒凉庭院里的杂草

量身高

在我幼时的每个除夕之夜
我把身高刻在门口一棵梧桐树上
在以后的日子里
我发现自己在缩小，并怀着退回到
根部的恐惧

在以后的一个晚上，我看到灯光明亮的房间里
两个恋人像是玩着同样的
量身高的游戏：他与她
是并肩的，他只长到她胸前，然后
滑至她腰部。一个肚脐眼
一个奇妙的树洞

我知道每棵树上都有
附近某人的生活，一棵树被砍掉了
但生活仍在延续
它变成木板，打造成一张新婚的床铺
在那里生儿育女，如此
循环不已

一个年轻木匠的故事

年轻的木匠不爱说笑，行事利索
他从墨斗里扯出一根线来，如同一只

In a Candy Store

Once I wrote a line of poetry on the counter
in a candy store, but
I was not writing about the candy store
or that woman weighing the candy
I was thinking of other things: a horse or a man
In strange places,
the drama of an entire life unfolds
the farewell and the coming together
A country of tears and letters
I lay in the warm current of imagination
and I don't want to become any of these people around me
Like on a little hill
Growing a weed, which should only grow in an abandoned court yard

–J.B. and Z.X.

Measuring the Height

On every new year's eve when I was small
I carved my height on to the Chinese parasol tree by the gate
Years later
I found myself shrinking, and was terrified by
my retreat to the root

On one evening, I saw in a brightly lit room
two lovers seeming to play the same game
measuring their height: he and she
shoulder to shoulder, now he is to her breasts, then
down to her waist. A belly button
a wonder tree hole

I understand with every tree there is
a life of someone living, a tree cut down
but its life still extends
it turns into board, is made into a wedding bed

黑色的大蜘蛛，吐出一根丝在木板上
但错了。我说去找块橡皮
他没有睬我，只用刨子轻轻一抹
没了。我怎么就没想到
木板锯开来，还是不对，尺寸比我想要的小
他拉起锯子，变成两条腿
但矮了，又剖成四根档。现在行了吧。他说
然后俯向另一块木板。而我忍不住问他
要是又错了呢。那可以削成十六只楔子
他不假思索地答道。接着他师傅来了
我说给他听，问他，这些经验是谁传给他的
师傅笑着说：是斧子

遗传

我上班的地方
有一张五十年代的
办公桌。平时
我把脚架上去
当有人来时，我就移开
让他们看
桌沿上的压痕：一道很深的
腿的压痕
人们往往会惊讶道
如此逼真
而我告诉他们
这不是我一个人的缘故
还有其他人
它以前的主人，是
集体创造
就像楼上那个女同事
她有一双漂亮的眼睛
那也同样不是她的
独创，那可能是她母亲的
也可能是她祖母的

on which people bear sons and raise daughters, so on
and so forth, circling without end

The Story of a Young Carpenter

The young carpenter doesn't like to joke around
He draws out a line from his ink marker
like a big black spider, spinning a string of silk on the wood board
but it is wrong. I say I am going to find an eraser
He doesn't answer me, only pushes the plane lightly
It is gone. How come I never think of it
The wood plank sawed open, but still not right, smaller than what I have
    imaged
He picks up the saw, makes two legs
but they are too short, then they are cut into four crosspieces. Okay? He says
and then bends over another wood plank. I can't resist asking him
if it'd still be wrong. Then trim them into sixteen wedges
he answered without having to think. Later his master came back
I told him the story, asking, who passed this all on to him
The master laughs: it is the ax.

Inheritance

Where I work
there is a desk
from the fifties. Often
I put my feet on it
When people come to visit me
I move my feet away
let them see the indent
on the edge of the desk:
a deep groove indented

甚至有可能
是我爷爷的一个伯父的，它们
一代接着
一代

信徒

在郊外一座小寺庙里
并排放着刚运来的佛像
装着它们的木框
看上去犹如古代的囚笼

天下着雨，前来的信徒
一个个跪下，燃起焚香
一些在地上垫一块手帕
还有些跪在脱下的外套上

对此，一旁站着的主持认为
这些人是真正的信徒
因为他们懂得
怜惜自己的膝盖

在寺院另一面，有块被隔离在外的池塘
杂草从生，深蓝色的池水在寂静中反映着天空
雪青色的蚊蝇飞舞、
一个墨绿色的青蛙和乌黑的蝌蚪
共处的天堂

People are always surprised
It's so real
Then I tell them
it is not just me
there were others
there were other owners
it's a collective creation
like the female colleague upstairs
she has a pair of pretty eyes
that are also not her own
unique invention, it might be her mother's
might be her grandmother's
even possibly
my grandfather's uncle's
It gets passed on
one generation after
another generation

–J.B. and Z.E.

Believers

In a small temple on the outskirts of the city
the Buddhas, just shipped, lie in formation
still with wood frames
like ancient prison-cages

It rains, the believers come
to kneel down one by one, lighting incense
Some put handkerchiefs on the ground
Some kneel on their jackets

As for this, the monk, standing aside
holds them to be real believers
since they know
to take pity on their knees

On the other side of the temple, there's a pond, isolated beyond
Weeds overgrown, dark-blue water reflects the sky with quietness
A heaven where lilac colored mosquitoes and flies dance around
the coexisting ink-green frog and black tadpoles

–J.B. and Z.X.

臧棣

夏天的车站

天气也许有助于判断
某些迹象，但不适合
推进内部的审判：
这些已开始让嗓子冒烟的
热气仍显得不够准确，
它们仍没有交成蒸汽，
虽然温度看起来已经达标。
我们沿胡同向外走，
油腻腻的细汗像是在
重新界定排泄的概念似地
将我的文化衫打湿。
而真正陷入麻烦的是幽灵——
它以为用分层法就能
把火辣辣的东西留在表面；
以使用象征的恒温笼屉
长期存放暄而软的纪念物。
你穿的短裙上印有八月
硕大的花朵，取材自
寂静的池塘中的荷花。
但现在是六月，似乎只有
下沉的渴念才能产生涟漪。
我知道没有任何理由
可以把嗅不到花香归咎于
这些过分美丽的图案。
至少它们曾用夺目的细节
阻止人生滑向无度的乏味。
我并不需要比让事情变成
插曲的时间更多的时间。
我的变形记始于胡同的拐角：
我从裤兜里掏出自行车钥匙，
问你想不想留下它——

Zang Di

translations by Martin Corless-Smith and John Balcom with Zhang Er

Summer Station

Perhaps the weather
can help in judging
some of these signs
but its not suited
for an inner trial:
The heat inside that makes
The throat so hot
seems imprecise
Is not quite steam,
although the temperature seems right.
The alley leads us out
where oily pearls of sweat
soak through my cultured shirt
seeming to redefine
what it means to perspire.
But it's the spirit that's in dire trouble
thinking it might keep this burning
to the surface stratum — in an attempt
to store some dumpling souvenir
in a metaphoric food steamer.
That huge August bloom
printed on your short skirt
was inspired by the lotus
in a still pond.
But its June — it seems
only sinking desires
can raise a ripple
There's no reason for me
to blame these overblown designs
for a flowery fragrance
I cannot smell

让它成为临时的小礼物。
它看上去不比一只小虾更大，
而坠链上挂着的仿佛是只
刚刚跳过龙门的鲤鱼。
它们全都是由黄铜做的，
也闪着只有阳光下的黄铜
才能溢出的那种光——
不是很强烈，但却显得镇定。
你困惑于我的举动：
草帽的阴影下。你的眼珠
不停地眨动，就像两只热带鱼
正在游出假山的岩缝。
你的时间很紧，还要赶赴
城东的一处涉外机构，领取
证明自己身份的上面盖有
各种红印章的文件。
你如此年轻，就在忙于
帮助别人搞清自己的身份。
这的确让我感叹。而我
更是惊讶于我们的步调一致：
缓中有快，那节奏
就像是在和影子跳舞。
我们走到站牌下时，106 路电车
刚巧进站。由于是午休时间，
车厢里几乎没人站着，
显得空荡荡的；你从后门上车，
车门关拢时出的响声
就像是有人用扇子拍苍蝇。
我目送着电车驶离，盼望
能从后车窗上看到你的身影，
但是没有。又一辆电车靠站，
下车的人刚才还被称为乘客，
现在立刻变成行人，
并把我也卷入移动的行列。

— at least they prevent life
sliding into drabness
with their dazzling particulars.
I don't necessarily need
more time than required
for things to become
an interlude.
My metamorphosis begins at a bend in the alley
I take my bicycle key
from my pocket and ask you
if you'd care to keep it
as a small parting gift.
It looks no bigger than a tiny shrimp
and hanging on my chain
is what looks like a lucky fish
all made of brass
refulgent in the light
of the sun — as only brass can be
Not hot but cool.
You find my movement
perplexing: In the shade of your straw hat
Your eyes ceaselessly blinking
Like two tropical fish
Swimming out of a rockery . . .
You must hurry to the office
for foreign affairs
on the east side of town
to pick up your papers
covered with red seals
so busy and so young
helping others clarify
their own identity.
It makes me sigh. But I am
more amazed we walk at the same pace
a slow haste — the rhythm of which
could give the impression that we dance
with our shadows.
As we reach the sign

戴维斯的夏天

这里的阳光像是在冲刺。
热，用寂静对折着
传奇故事中的荒凉。
我到达时，这工作
仍然没有停止的迹象。
这工作仍然显得非常自然。

一条河也显得极其自然。
虽然从外观上看，它一半像引水渠，
一半像小湖。怎样的激情对折
产生了它？一条鱼从水中
啪地跃出，样子就像一只炒勺
在出锅前的最后一刻翻弄一道菜。

阳光下的石头看上去像只小旅行箱。
我拍打着它。在我之前，
一阵风干过同样的事情。
这之后，石头给石头带去了什么呢？
是否一些旅行也是这样？
无须动手动脚，但是有一个过程。

一棵橡树也许记得更多的事情，
但是，它能纪念的只是
一道时间中的褶痕。说一棵橡树
产生于一次对折，并不意味着
我想肯定什么或者我能否定什么。
而我也不是碰巧正站在树底下。

他们说生命是一种现象，
他们也说过生命是一条线。
而树阴里，蝴蝶正忙着
把这两种说法串联在自己身上。
蝴蝶美丽于我每一次看见的
为什么都是它这样一个简单的事实。

the 106 electric trolley
pulls into the station —
being nap time its empty
you board from the rear
the door slams shut
like swatting a fly. I watch
as it leaves — longing
for a glimpse of you
But, no luck. Another pulls in
and passengers become pedestrians
sweeping me off into their ranks.

Summer in Davis

The sunshine here seems to gush.
The heat folds the desolation
of legendary tales with quietness.
When I arrived the job
showed no signs of stopping.
The job still seems all too natural

though outwardly it half-resembles a channel
half a small lake. What half-hidden passion
produced it? A fish jumps out of the water
like food tossed in the wok
before serving. Under the sun

the stone looks like a suitcase.
I pat it. A gust of wind did the same
just before me. Afterwards
what does a stone take to a stone?
Are some journeys the same?
No need to take a step, though there is a route.

The oak might remember more.
But commemorates only
a crimp in a span of time.

它用舞蹈留下一条虚线——
为下一次对折充当着向导。
这美丽自然于惊人，并且需要一段时间
才能变成"惊人的美丽"。
而我，好奇于成年，希望
这段时间能被延迟得更长久些。

石器

爱上一个女人后
我喜次收集石头。
用手触摸时：一个太轻，
一个稍重，至少
表面上是如此；就像有一次
一个严格的收藏石头的人
带着评估的口吻对我说：
"它们还称不上石头，
充其量是一些石块。"
我赞同他的敏锐。因是我想
至少在表面上他说的有道理。
石头和石块应该有一些
像他这样的人能看出的区别。
还有一些更浅显的道理
流溢在石头的纹路中，
很像一种我们的邻居中
有人渴望模仿的语言；
部分是线索，部分是痕迹，
它们重申着我们在最高的虚构中
遭遇的事情：就像时间
有一张公认的嘴巴，
我们看不见它的形状，
但我们能认出它的歌词。
这也是为什么吐露
要比流露更成功，溢出了
更多的湿润；虽然

To say this oak
was produced by a dismissive folding
does not mean I approve or deny something
and I'm certainly not under this tree by chance.

They say life is a phenomenon
also life is a thread.
In the shade of the tree
a butterfly is busy
joining these views in its wings.
Each butterfly I see is more lovely than "why"
it is always such a simple fact.

Dancing, it leaves a dotted line —
a guide for the next folding
such beauty amazes — needing
a greater span of time to become
an "amazing beauty."
And curious about such aging
I wish this span of time could last much longer.

Stone Artifacts

When I fall in love with a woman
I like to collect stones.
Take them in my hands:
one is too light, one a little heavy,
that's the way appearances are.
A serious collector once told me
with a connoisseur's tone
"They cannot be called stones yet,
at most they are just rocks."
I welcomed his acuity,
believed he was right — at least
stones and rocks
ought to be distinct.
Shallow reasons are effused

我并不想辨称至少在本质上
灵魂更像是一片湿润。
这也是为什么我喜欢
一些理由来自湿润，哪怕是
间接的，哪怕表面上看去
仅仅是在搜集大大小小的石头。
一个秋天的下午，像是很偶然地
我想到在我的生活中，
从未有什么东西曾被称为石器。
我似乎收集了足够多的石头，
每一块都因为美丽而显得可疑，
但它们仍不能被叫做石器：
就好像我们不会把磨刀石
叫做石器一样，至少在看上去
正常的生活中，我们如此行事。
偶尔，我会用我搜集的石头
压住一些轻飘的东西：
比如一件起皱的衬衣，比如
一张浸泡过的邮票，或是
上厕所前正翻看的书页。
但即使这样，这些石头
还是不能被称为石器：就仿佛
我所做的，不过是挪动了一下
它们的位置，至于它们的本性，
则丝毫没有改变。

——给唐晓渡　2000.11

飘泊

一些水在炉子上
嘶嘶冒着热气，活跃着
早上的气氛。一些水
在杯子里使哲学变浅。
一些水你刚刚喝下，

in the pattern of stone
like a neighbor's mimicking language
part clue, part trace,
restating our encounters
in our highest fictions — like time
thought to have a mouth
we cannot discern
but we understand its song.
Just as telling something is better
than letting it slip — effusing it with more moisture
and while I don't want to argue about it —
the soul is more like a damp spot.
That is also why I like some reasons
that arise from moisture
even if superficially they appear
like large and small collected stones.
Perhaps by chance one autumn afternoon
it occurred to me that my life has been without
stone artifacts. I had many stones
each beautiful and therefore suspicious
but no stone artifacts.
Just as we never call a grindstone
an artifact in its daily life.
Occasionally I would use stones
as weights — to hold down a wrinkled shirt
a soaked stamp, or the pages of a book
I was reading before going to the toilet.
Even so, these stones are still not artifacts
for all I did was change their location
without seeming to change their natures
in the slightest.

— for Tang Xiaodu

但不是用同一个杯子。
一些水中有糖，
却不能代替汁液——
那里，黏度的宪法构成了
我们精神中的什么浅滩呢？
一些水泡着今年的新茶。
而另一些水泡着今晚的新闻
一些水汹涌着，
使我们进入专注角色。
一些水散发着浊气，
而一座铁桥和它交叉成十字。
一些水上有蜻蜓的留言，
而波纹的早操为它们分行。
一些水的一半用于
过滤我们的成年，
另一半用于挽救
我们的缺席。
一些水偏僻，而蝴蝶
把它们变成泉源。
一些水逃不出镜子的帝国，
就这样，一些罪
纯洁于我们的困惑。
一些水被子抽上堤岸
在锈迹斑驳的管子里旅行着。
一些水滴着，让你萦怀于
三个词：小、慢、亮。
一些水忙上忙下，
但这情形并不指一些人
正脱掉工装或面具，
在厕所里洗凉水澡。
一些水中有鱼，
一些水上有野鸭或鸳鸯，
它们渐渐汇合于风景的政治。
一些水无法搅动，
因为良知，或是因为

Drifting

Some water sizzles on the stovetop,
sending up steam, enlivening
the morning. Some water
in a cup makes for shallow philosophy.
Some water you just drank,
not from the same cup.
Some water contains sugar,
but it's no substitute for juice —
where in our soul
is this viscous shoal Composed?
Some water is used to brew this year's new tea.
Some other water is used to brew the evening news,
Some water surges
us into absorbing characters.
Some water is turbid,
where an iron bridge crosses it, a cross is formed. On
some water dragonflies leave messages,
the morning exercises of the ripples break them into lines.
Half of some water is used
to filter our adulthood,
the other half is used
to rescue our absences.
Some waters are remote, and butterflies
change them into fountainheads.
Some water is unable to escape from the mirror's empire.
In this way some sins are
washed by our confusion.
Some water is pumped over an embankment
traveling through rusty pipes.
Some water drips, let your mind linger on
three words: small, slow, bright.
Some water is busy with this and that.
But this doesn't necessarily indicate that
some people are taking off their work clothes and masks,
and taking cold showers in their homes.
Some water contains fish, on

第三个人告诉第二个人
第一个人的心死了。
一些水使他们脱水。
但是另一些水仍然从里到外。
一些水提前流着，
而你还是习惯扯起衣角
擦幸福的眼泪。
一些水响着，我知道
你想对我说："它真好听。"

未名湖

一个传奇就是一次问候。
当然，也不是所有的人都赞同
这样的想法。中秋过后，
小湖安静得就像刚从橱柜里
拿出的一张小毛毯。

花纹如同皱纹——
带你一块玩时，他们才能看到
荡漾的波纹。小秘密
就是不解心头恨。如同掠过湖面的蝙蝠，
万古愁飞得确实有点低。

这里，风情多于风景。
散步就是兜圈子，
一会儿甜得要命，一会儿咸得要死。
几个人懂得欣赏渺茫
的确不能把大伙怎么样？以后仍会如此。

偶尔，美好的天赋拗不过
天赋多么美好。前者是
一个人躺在草地上时，

some water there are wild ducks or mandarin ducks
they slowly float together
In a politics of landscape.
Some water is unable to stir,
because of its good conscience, or because
the third person tells the second person
that the heart of the first person is dead.
Some water dehydrates them. But
some other water goes from inside to outside
some water flows in advance, and
you are still accustomed to lifting a corner of your dress
to wipe the tears of happiness away.
Some water makes sounds, I know
you want to tell me: "It sounds so sweet."

Weiming Lake

A legend is a greeting.
Of course not all people think so.
After the mid-Autumn festival,
the small lake is still and calm like a woolen blanket
taken out of a chest.

Patterns like wrinkles. Only when playing with you
they see ripples. The small secret
that it can't quench our regrets.
Like bats skimming the lake,
old sadness flies a little low.

Here, amorous feelings outnumber landscapes.
Taking a walk is no more than moving in circles,
one moment too sweet, the next too salty.
Do the few who appreciate this uncertainty
really not influence others? On it goes.

Occasionally a wonderful gift can't be dissuaded of
the wonderfulness of its gift.

周围站着的全是
低沉的有魅力的陌生男人。

后者呢？似乎从未有过
准确的形迹。旁证到是有一些，
比如，一点点自然就可以松开几只喜鹊。
或是，落叶晃动如纸条
为自我和自我之间的缝隙免费催眠。

也不妨说，孤独即自由。
矛盾于爱意味着你还有很多次机会，
就像这秋湖，它差不多能融和
所有的事情。例外在别处——
有时，这样真的很了不起。

看不见的门

有一天，你告圻他们
你的生活中有一扇
看不见的门。你想知道
他们的情形是否也和你一样？
你想知道是否有一个底线
说的是一个人是另一个人的
一扇门？在那种境况里
看不见的又是哪一部分呢？
一次，你闭上眼睛，
深入，迂回，穿插，这一切之后
你想象它是蓝色的。
这并非没有先例。譬如，
在比利时人马格利特的一些绘画中，
梦，既是背景，又是角色，
所以，很自然地，门
被画成了蓝色——
不深不浅，但，蓝得真实。
站在旁边，他们看久了，

Such as when a person
lies on the grass surrounded by
unfamiliar men who are charming and degraded.

What of the latter? Its exact bearing seems unknown.
But there is circumstantial evidence,
like how a piece of nature might loosen
some magpies. Or how falling leaves
flutter like paper strips

Lulling the chink between oneself and oneself
to sleep for free. It might well be said that solitude is freedom.
Contradiction in love means you still have many chances,
just like the lake in autumn.
which nearly fuses with all things. The exception is elsewhere —
sometimes, it is really wonderful.

Invisible Doors

One day you told them
there was an invisible door
in your life. Did you want to know
if it was the same for them?
was one person the door
for another person? In such a situation
what part is invisible?
One time you closed your eyes,
entered, turned, passed through
after which you imagined it was blue.
This is not unprecedented. In Magritte
Dreams are both backdrop and subject.
It was natural for the door
to be painted blue —
neither deep blue nor light blue but actual blue.
After long study they became accustomed to it.
Another time,
carrying a teapot out of the kitchen

自然也会习惯的。
另一次，
从厨房里提着茶壶出来，
抱怨杯子时，你忽然又觉得
你的生活中其实不仅仅
只有一扇看不见的门。
你的玩笑开得新颖而又大胆——
你确信，你不再为无法触摸到它们
感到烦恼。这些看不见的门！
当你停止呼吸，你会一个不留，
把它们从这里全部带走。

宇宙是扁的

从收音机里听到这个新闻时，
我正在厨房里
切黄瓜片。两根黄瓜，
我刮去表皮，
将它们切得又圆又扁，
这只是一种结局。
将切好的黄瓜浸泡在
香油、盐、米醋的小世界里，
则牵扯到另一种结局。
多少人来吃晚饭？
有没有不速之客？
多少真正的营养互相矛盾！
或者，同样涉及到结局，
为什么我喜欢听到
有人在黄金时间里播报说
宇宙是扁的。
妙，还是真的有点妙？
我的预感说不上准确，
但强烈如光的潮汐。
正如短时间内，
我在厨房里看到的和想到的——

complaining about the teacups
you suddenly felt
that your life possessed more than
one invisible door.
A joke that was novel and audacious.
You were certain, and being unable to touch them
no longer concerned you.
Those invisible doors!
When you stop breathing — you won't leave even one —
you'll take them all with you.

The Universe is as Flat as a Pancake

I hear the news on the radio
while slicing cucumbers
in the kitchen. Two cucumbers
peeled, and sliced
round and flat
as an end result of sorts.
I soak the slices
in a small world of sesame oil,
salt and rice vinegar.
Another end of sorts.
How many are coming to dinner?
Will there be any unexpected guests?
How much real nutrition is there in contradiction?
Or, why, by the same token
touching upon the same end result
I am so happy to hear
someone on primetime news say
the Universe is as flat as a pancake.
Wonderful, isn't it just a little wonderful?
My premonition wasn't accurate —
but as strong as the ebb and flow of light,
perfectly coinciding with
the brief moment in the kitchen
when I saw the cutting board is flat,

案板是扁的，刀是扁的，
不论大小，所有的盖子
都是扁的；图纹并貌，
只有盘子不仅仅是扁的。
面具是扁的，真真假假，
药片也是扁的；甚至
最美的女人躺下时，
神也是扁的。

我们如何写一首诗

秋天的早晨，天空飘着小雨。
我靠着窗户坐下，开始写一首诗。
很快，诗中出现了一扇门，
它就像昨天才粉刷过似的，
白得镇静、一些鲜红的痕迹
已被抹去。什么东西
是你特别想知道的。真相
还是迷？在我看来
谜就是不宿命。和诗有关的迷
尤其如此。我打开那扇门，
顺势走下台阶。那里
生活果然开阔多了。
一条在东西向的街道
已按计划躺在了小说中。
这部小说，我已读过多遍。
其实，你也一样。
你甚至读得比我还多。
只是你不愿承认，就仿佛坦率是
一个是非太多的空间。
另有许多人等待着
进入适合他们的场所。
你更贴近他们，
不像是我创造出的一个人物。
转身看我时，你的脸

the knife is flat, no matter how
big or small, àll the lids are flat
only the plates — with their marvelous patterns
are more than flat.
The masks are flat, true and false,
the pills are flat; even
when the most beautiful woman lies down
the gods too are flat.

How We Write a Poem

A drizzling autumn morning,
I sit down by the window to write a poem.
Soon, a door appears
as if it were painted only yesterday,
white and composed. All traces of red
have been erased — what is it that you
really want to know? The truth
or riddles? In my opinion
riddles do not equal fatalism.
Especially those related to poetry.
I open the door, taking
the opportunity to descend a flight of stairs
to where life really is more expansive.
A street runs east and west
stretching out in a novel,
according to plan.
A novel I have read many times.
Actually, so have you.
You have read it even more times than I have.
You just don't want to admit it,
as though frankness opens a space
planted with discord.
Besides, crowds are eager
to enter that place.
You press close to them,
no longer one of my characters

才显露出几分变化不大，
如同一扇早晨的窗户。
而在写作过程中，我确实
曾打开过身边的窗户，
并几次起身去调整
窗缝的大小，以便
风透进来时，纸不会冷得发抖。

turning to look at me
your face only then
showing a few small changes
like the window this morning.
I actually opened the window
and got up several times
to adjust the crack
so that when the wind came through
the paper wouldn't tremble with cold.

张耳

古事问

光的背后
是坚硬如石的卵
是瞳如深水的眼

光的背后
有风
有白日的异想，没有夜的确定

季候性的水族密集成阵
沉稳地循游
步步逼近脉冲边缘

混沌不定，无动无静
庞然
中心，一只尚未受精的巨卵

剥去坚壳，向内部窥视
穿过浆液，插入弹动的原核
自射之箭指向记忆积层

向外部飞去
向洪玄张开
下一世纪的星蜂拥倒转，**雾瀑迷离**

企图固化时间的眼执迷于
那行诗句的温柔，那只草莓的红粉，那次云雨的欢愉
一尊窄小的墓碑

青草蔽天
最早的泥土结不出粉红的诗句
只见萤火虫发光的尾部，和不安宁的地衣

Zhang Er

translations by Bob Holman, Susan M. Schultz
and Leonard Schwartz with the author

Story

Behind the light
there is an egg as hard as stone,
an eye, its pupil the depth of water.

Behind the light
there is the wind,
the reverie of day, not the certainties of night.

Seasonal sea-life in compact formation
calmly cruises by,
steadily approaches the periphery of the pulse.

Void, static yet in flux,
the colossal
center, a giant ovum unfertilized.

Peel off the hard shell, peep into the interior;
penetrate protoplasm, thrusting into the throbbing nucleus:
the arrow of vision reversed in the direction of memory.

To be flung towards an exterior,
to open up to an impenetrable torrent
swarm and swirl of the next centuries stars,
       misty waterfall.

Attempting to freeze time, eyes transfixed
by the sensuality in one line of a poem,
pinkness of strawberry, comfort after love-making:
       narrow tomb.

在脚下滑移
两块玉石撞击
沉淀在骨骼里的经文，耳廓燥热

反复抚摸光滑如卵的石
仓惶若瞽者震颤的手指
黑暗吞食黑暗

如果天是地，阴是阳，东是西，水是火
则我亦非我，知亦非知
这一边亦那一边吗？

玄武岩上透明的枯叶沉睡如思
随意解析太极之圆
五彩四溅

有梦
将玄学的嫩枝任意组合着
河龟背上十三条甲纹，凶吉非常卜

河神失落
原雨蒸腾
唯一的独木舟早已演为缤纷的水族

大泽浮世，瞳孔迅速下潜
余下的问讯窿张天穹，鱼坠如雨
微光从背后环抱

猛回身
空无一物，闷雷
起自单立之蛋，巍挺若坚岩，有风

Green grass blots out the sky
older soils know nothing of this pinkish poetic
only the fluorescent sparks
       of the fireflies, the ancient lichen.

Slidings under the feet.
Two pieces of jade tinkle
a chant is tripped from the bone,
       the ear unrides.

Caress the stone tablet as smooth as an ovum:
letterless hands shaking like those of the blind.
Darkness swallows darkness.

If heaven is earth, yin is yang, east is west, and water, fire,
the self become the nonself, the known, unknown,
and this, that, for sure?

Leaves asleep in mineral thought
casually spun on the wheel of events,
the splashes of color.

A dream
composes at random the tender branches of Thought
into the thirteen cracks on a turtle shell,
       pattern of divination.

God of rivers that sinks into oblivion,
original rain vapor:
an ark becomes the sea.

Land emerges, the pupils submerging.
A sky created by questioning, fish falling like rain.
A dim light embracing it all from behind.

女书

贯穿一致
你袭一身黑衣，偏不甘寂寞
从深沉的河底醒来
很久很久以来

我们一直年轻，也一直惦记着你
沿着雪花飞扬的街巷叫卖热包子
和冻硬的稀粥
很久很久以来

我们只专心地生一个孩子
而且面对没有路障的广场大动肝火
这里应该长树，应该生风
很久很久以来

我们蹲在园子里吸烟
坐在屋子里谈话
议论着你的身世
看着你再一次浸没
你那墨色的纤指

渔人与作家

　　一

这条路我总走错：出地铁往西
就误入东方的中国城，黑咖啡
酸辣汤，餐桌花瓶里也埋着镇鱼的冰。
混淆的汤水，鲜花与鱼腥。

只有我一个茶客，明亮的地板，手绘彩漆
方桌。书没人翻动，每人都可以是一部。

Turning suddenly
there is this nothingness, muffled thunder
arising from the egg towering like a cliff

And there is the wind.

–L.S.

Nushu (Female script)

all in black
halo to sole
but don't leave
me lone wake
me up oh
from river bed for
a long long time

forever young, us
forever worried we
or remember you
running snowflakes streets
hawking hot Bao/dumplings
Jook/soup get it
while it's frozen for
a long long time

obsessed one child birth
bawling at square of no one
not even a roadblock
there should be trees
should have wind for
a long long time

smoking in the garden
talking in no particular
room yak it up about

今天钓上来的鱼，昨天早已制过标本
装了镜框，钉上墙。

河依然从窗外流过，桅杆竖立在巨型家俱店
后面，与我相隔源源不断的街。龙骨悬空
空为某种头上的情致。没见过渔人，或者作家
也许他们病了，也许他们已经出城。

诗流于这混杂的日常，清洁如旧的
布置。走进来的都是过路人，不着急地
吐纳——安然已经美丽，即便没有漆花
香花。诗是城。

只是这条路总错，不断犹疑的坐标
像沙漠季河，渔人每十年走出来一次
用鱼干换佐料，粮米和书，这碟急需的青菜
证明，他们回来了，拎一小串诗。

　　二

还是先确定自我的身份，生产者－消费者
兼顾？出海时你看见什么？看不见鱼
上钩的是鱼死的过程。非常难过，却出神
张着嘴，因为你不可能控制两极化冰。

船板咯吱咯吱在脚下挣扎，时刻准备
离你而去。除了站着，小心垂下
这偶然一线，你只能高举双手，希望
更象祈祷，愿你为我殷勤的姿态殉情。

这难道不如一次婚约——
茫茫复盲盲，丢个眼波给过路的鱼
你和他一口把月亮咬住，咬紧不放
海浪翻身，连太阳一起抓落。

ancestors watch you from river bed
dip your finger
black ink
slender

–B.H.

Anglers and Writers, Hudson Street

1.
Always get the way wrong: exiting the subway to the west
end up in Chinatown to the east: to black coffee,
hot and sour soup, iced fish, ice-filled flower vase
on the table. Blurry liquid, fresh flowers, fish.

I'm the only one for tea. Lacquer table, shiny
wood floor. No one ever riffles the pages here, everyone can be
a book. Today's catch — yesterday's cast — hangs
framed, on the wall.

The Hudson flows beyond the window, masts erect
behind the furniture depot, past the street's incessant traffic. A boat's hull
suspended in air, empty, as a mood. I've never seen an angler or a writer here;
perhaps they're sick, or they left the city.

Poetry blurs unto the blurred routine, old, yet clean.
Passers-by walk in, breathe easily; at ease is already
beautiful, even without the painted flowers,
fragrant flowers. Poetry is a city.

But this is the wrong way, maps like moving dunes
a desert river which emerges every ten years, with anglers
exchange dried fish for spices, grains and books; this dish of urgent greens
proves they've returned with their string of small poems.

退潮时，你们对坐桌旁，不经意地剖开
彼此，把每根神经从头嚼到尾，还有心肝
和不再看见的眼珠。听得见肠胃
叽咕，直到彼此全部吃掉，首尾嵌合。

每次下网，都找不到水，因为月历的关系。
每一条鱼，布满刺，非出血才香。鱼汤
溶入所有想象，月光，血光，尝一口
尝一口，你就数得出月亮下所有的浪。

三

在我们的推断里，生活曾经淳朴——
渔人与作家，这个海滨城市真正需要的
职业。可眼下打鱼不如卖鱼，不如端上桌面的
小小卖弄。一眼便认出这个季节流行。

他曾经让人们在水边满足，从而跟他进入
天堂。现在，地上的我一边没水一边没顶——
闪光发亮、无穷尽计算、声嘶力竭之后，把心
抛向何方？真地钓上什么就是什么？鱼、我。

坐在酒吧前的俏女人过来问我是不是演电影的
女侠，在北京砖墙大院铁灰屋顶上飞奔？是啊，
梦的布景路过这河岸飞雪的小饭馆
是谁？曾经是谁？他、鱼。盘子里。

不管是谁，捕捉住，才是你的。写下
才活过。只是玻璃的海里，盛不下你，颂扬他
不如描述这把刀，先问问彼此的身份？炒作之后
依旧蒙着哪处的风沙？色味真地永不减褪？

那些辨不清的航线水情，转眼间使你和他
仇敌，兄弟，母女，悬在高处墙上眼神离散。
桌子上，最后的雪下个不停，串串黑脚丫
向东，向西，将通向那里的路一再掩埋。

2.

First fix your identity, whether producer, consumer
or both? What do you see out on the sea? You don't see fish.
Who dies on the hook, mouth hinged wide in a desperate
process: you can't control the arctic melting.

Boat's wooden deck squeaks, struggles, threatens to leave you
behind. You stand, carefully let fall
this accidental thread, pressing palms together — more in prayer
than in hope — please do sacrifice yourself for my ardent pose.

It's not unlike a marriage contract,
this sense of being out to sea, blind, throwing
glances to passing fish; you and he both bite down on the moon
refuse to let go, as waves turn to drag down the sun.

At low tide you sit across the table, heartlessly
dissecting each other, chewing every nerve from end to end
heart, liver, and eyes that no longer see. The gut's rumble
heard, until all is eaten, inlaid from head to tail.

Not every net finds water in this lunar calendar.
Every fish has bones, delicious when it bleeds. Fish soup dissolves
the imagination, its moonlight, bloodlight, the one taste that enables
you to count each and every wave beneath the moon.

3.

The implication is life was once honest —
anglers and writers, professions this city needs. Yet now
the catching of fish is no match for selling them, or the little show-off
served on the table. One look captures this season's fashion.

He once satisfied those on the water's edge, who followed Him
to heaven. Now I'm caught between drought and flood, between light
and its reflection, calculations, shouting myself hoarse, yet not knowing
        where to cast
the heart. Are we really whatever is caught, caught up? Fish, I.

饮茶

偶然被挤在一起做最基本的事，他
竟是从另一个生活里走来的故人：
雨林边缘的小镇，雨溪和满含雨水
想象的远山——那里怕就是中国？

上海时间。午间饮茶配百年经典，
殷实的面碗和许多讲不清名堂，比如
旱季里罂粟的收成，军管和 CIA，现实
过时转身变成时髦的历史，摄影的摄影

制片的制片，小街遍地烂泥，小街
酒吧里躲避空袭、与吧女调笑、观赏
来前线视察的将军，种种多功能的无聊。
记起来了？编成娱乐吧，让大家忘了

眼下这张圆桌的深度，已经活过的梦和
正在一起做的事情。这不可能，能在一起
喝茶而没浇在身上？有这份上海人的
冷静和可以让人放心插手的口实？

巴西鸡尾酒、凉水和青柠檬。你坐对面。
面对冰和酸的老套，看报纸争执纽约郊外
公共湖泊能否对公众开放，全面游泳。思考
葛州坝超常低水位对坝体和发电的影响。

我只想叫一杯茶，一杯热茶让寒毛孔全面
开放。再野性的梦不过设下另外的局限
这我懂。毕竟此刻霓虹灯下海滨棕榈
被暴雨洗得流光，发丝依顺，像不像

以前雨林里的梦？这里是迈阿密抑或
新加坡？也许我们该去吃冰激凌？那样
糖和凉就溶为一体，让我们回到年轻时
一切都可以重做的心情。在水之湄，闲逛。

The pretty woman at the bar comes to ask if I'm the GongFu heroine
in the movie, galloping over Beijing's gray roofs
and walled yards. Sure, this small restaurant beside the river under the
    drifting
snow passes for a dream stage. Who is it? Was it? Him, the fish in the dish.

No matter what it is, when it's caught, it's yours. Writing is living.
But the glass sea doesn't make you content. Praising Him proves no better
than describing this knife. First ask the identity of each. After flaying, the fish
    is still
covered with sand, and from where? The flavor doesn't fade?

These hidden sea routes make him your enemy, your brother, mother,
    daughters,
hanging on the wall, expressions blank. On the table, the last of the snow
    falls
constantly, where black footprints again bury
both ways: east and west, the way leads there.

                    –S.M.S

Dim Sum

Accidentally tossed together, doing the natural thing,
unexpectedly he becomes an old acquaintance from another life:
the little town at the edge of the rain forest, rivulet rain,
mountain of the imagination soaked in rain — is that China over there?

Shanghai time. Dim Sum at noon, a century of culinary evolution
results in one substantial bowl of noodles filled with indescribable
flavors: poppy seeds harvested in the dry season, yum, military control
and CIA, delicious, aged reality turned into popular history, incredible!

Now the photographer photographs, the producer produces.
Here's a muddy little lane lined with bars you run into
to escape from air strikes, flirt with prostitutes and catch the general
visiting the front lines. A multi-functional joint named Boredom. Now do you
remember it? Transform it into entertainment and forget

软席候车室叙事

二叔二婶陷在皮沙发里
宽大地微笑。不愧是老铁道
在涌来涌去的混乱中，　一针把大车站的
牛皮戳破，舒服地坐下去
等我们定下神再继续两年前的谈话：
"那里已经没草了，沙化，他们说"。
才写了几首诗，生了个孩子，就没草了？

暴雨打在蒙古包上，暴雨的羊
穿碧绿长裙金马甲的红脸小姑娘？

二叔没变，又胖了，"只吃菜
不吃饭也胖"，全球减肥的难题。
"什么都可以吃，什么都不要多吃"
我听见自己说。希望真理就这么简单——
而我现在就想吃禁忌的冰激凌
难以分离的手感在屁股上变成累赘
我身体罪恶又最不明朗的一部分。

怎么办？恐怖分子，感情陷井，经济危机
晚生的孩子，抑郁症，失眠，失眠……

二叔消瘦的时候反右，犯错误，离婚
支边放羊，（像我现在一样），本来铁定的
结果，却像那只童话里的聚宝盆：
"拉出一个老头，又一个老头……"
抓住一根贪婪的尾巴，举起道德的鞭
二叔讲故事的时候却总是笑呵呵的
讲一次笑一次——

平时背得重，出门越提越少，二叔。
我现在也有这种趋向。

how deep this is, let our dreams dream that they have already
been lived and the things we are doing right now
we are doing right now. Is it possible to be together drinking tea and not
pour it over each other's body? We have the calmness
of the Shanghainese and the excuses that allow them to relax.

Try a Brazilian cocktail, cold water and lime? You sit across from me.
Face the stale routine of ice and acid, read in the Times about the ongoing
environmental debate about the lakes in the suburbs, whether they
should be open to the public, whether they should be fully swum. Think
    about
how the unusual low water level at Gezhou Dam affects the dam
itself and the undulating flow as it generates electricity.

I only want a cup of tea, a hot cup to expand my sweat glands
to the ultimate. The wildest dream only sets up other limitations —
I understand that. Yet at the moment, under the neon lights on the sea
    shore,
the palm trees are washed shiny by the storm, hair suddenly becomes
    obedient.

Doesn't it resemble the dream we had that night in the rain?
Was it Miami or Singapore? Maybe we should go and have some ice cream.
That way, sugar and cold will melt into each other, enabling us to go
back to the mood of our youth when everything could restart.
Say, let's take a little walk along the water's edge and go nowhere.

                –B.H.

In the Soft Sleeper Waiting Lounge

Second Uncle Second Aunt sink
into leather sofa which generously sighs.
First Class Waiting Lounge. Hooray! Working
on the railroad, all the live long day long. Easy
enough to puncture hauptbanhof. Thick dermis.
Comfortably arrayed around this secret

四哥

肯定是那顶鸭舌帽
在暗中使劲，他有把握地走近：
"你们也回？南坡李家？"
怎么会看不出来，一家人
笑得都像。其他深层的表情和着
慢车摇曳的拍子，模糊出
满座席温柔的背景，阳光

从早晨到正午，聊家里的事——
黄土坡，窑洞，道边的树一闪一闪

像没有注册的偏方，贴得满街晃眼
谜底却藏在你手里，自己研制
又一说是祖传，就好比根深叶茂的
道理和一针就好的性病，支持
我们深信的模糊逻辑。打烧饼的
医师助理和正在进行时的葬礼
信与不信，日子一样过得端正正。

只有一个表面，四哥的侧脸肖像
右边过道该是我拍照，也面目晴朗？

决定

放下去的
天，碧蓝如我们相识的
下午，等待
意外让我们走到一起
再各自走开。可以给出
一切，却决定什么都
不给。微笑着走开
去拥抱街上婚车喇叭
决定地一路欢乐。

the chaos of outside tides in tides out.
— pause — waits for us to calm all the way down. Now
continue conversation
started two years ago: "There is no grassland any more,
       desertization they say."
             Wrote a few poems,
              had a child,
                    now there's no grass left?

Rain beats down on yurt, a sheep of rain—
where's ruby-faced girl in long apple
green skirt, gold-trimmed vest?

Second Uncle hasn't changed, only fatter, "Eat only vegetable dishes,
no more rice, still get fat!" The easier said than done problem of global diet,
solved: "Eat everything, overeat nothing," I hear myself saying —
wish a simple truth — now time for forbidden maple ice-cream!
Hand inseparable from butt grows into a burden,
a part of my body shameful, ambivalent.

What to do? Terrorists, emotional trap, recession,
late born child, depression, insomnia, insomnia . . .

When Second Uncle was thin, anti-rightist movement, committed mistakes,
    divorced,
transported to border region to herd sheep, the iron-
clad conclusion — ah! it's the fable's ever-full treasure chest!
She pushes her annoying old man in, accidentally
during their fight over what is the worthiest thing to put in
and what does she pull out? Why, the old man after the old man!
Catch the tail of greed, the whip of ethics.
Second Uncle always laughs
when he tells the Husband Parade story,
laughs over and over when he tells —

Every day he shoulders the heavy heavy,
so when he travels he

不过是风
不能决定自己
树叶在室外小幅度摆动
不小心擦过这扇蒙尘的窗
划破多年哀怨。
感谢失控
是一个决定：
右转弯。这样
剪接技术就能救我们——
记录过去和将来
这就是全部。翻过
现在，以及
枝条在阳光里不知情的
舞蹈。决定——
吃东西
写这些句子。四两轻。

carries less and less, Second Uncle;
I myself have the same tendency now.

                    –B.H.

On the Train: Fourth Brother

                    The cap's beak must have exerted a
quiet pressure — Fourth Brother confidently approaches:
"You on your way home too? You're Li family, NanPo, south slope, yes?"
Of course he can tell, family
even smile the same way. Under smile,
other expressions of molecular genetics syncopate
shrugs to the slow train's
swaying rhythm. Sound blurs visuals,
the background of the soft sleeper softens. Sun.

Morning till noon, chatter gossip —
yellow soil, caves' people build houses into hills,
a geologic fact, trees track along the flicker . . .
Local folk medicine advertised all over town, dazzling.
The real cure is in your hands, did the research yourself!
Or — legend has it that your ancestors passed the secret down to you.
Folks, the prowess of this remedy is so strong, these here leaves so fecund
that one punctuation of acupuncture and your STD's will be banished
        forever!
Take a deep breath of the profoundly ambiguous logic we believe in.

            Like flipping a wheat cake, the doctor's assistant
and the funeral coexist in present tense — believe it!
                    or don't, life g-g-g-going on, eminently

stable.

                            There's only one surface
and that's Fourth Brother's silhouette.

I was the one who took the picture, on the other
side of the passageway. The same sunny expression
                                    in my face, in my eyes?

       –B.H.

Resolution

Put it down
to the sky
turquoise and transparent
like the afternoon
we met, wait
this time let us
walk towards each other
and keep walking.
Could give everything,
but nothing. Walk
on by, smile, ok, whirl
to the horns
of the wedding procession
damn cheerful all the way.
It is only the wind
that can't control itself. Leaves
make tiny lapping waves outside,
unintentionally brush dust
from the window, and then
Cut to sepia: accumulated sadness.
Resentment even. Crap
indignation. OK, be grateful
for this loss of control
go on go ahead make a right
turn. This way
the montage technique will save us —
graft the past on the future,
that's all. Turn over
the present, blaze dance

of unknowing branches
in the sun. Resolved:
eat something. Resolved:
write these sentences.
Light as feather.
Four ounces.

–B.H.

张枣

悠悠

顶楼，语音室。
　　　　　　　　秋天哐地一声来临，
清辉给四壁换上宇宙的新玻璃，
大伙儿戴好耳机，表情团结如玉。

怀孕的女老师也在听。迷离声音的
　　　　　　　　　　吉光片羽：
"晚报，晚报"，磁带绕地球呼啸快进。
紧张的单词，不肯逝去，如街景和
喷泉，如几个天外客站在某边缘，
拨弄着夕照，他们猛地泻下一匹锦绣：
虚空少于一朵花！

她看了看四周的
新格局，每个人嘴里都有一台织布机，
正喃喃讲述同一个
好的故事。
每个人都沉浸在倾听中，
每个人都裸着器官，工作着，

全不察觉。

海底被囚的魔王

一百年后我又等待一千年；几千年
过去了，海面仍漂泛我无力的诺言

帆船更换了姿态驶向惆帐的海岸
飞鸟一代代衰老了，返回不死的太阳

Zhang Zao

translations by Lihua Ying and Sam Hamill

Remote

On the top floor, the language lab.
With a bang, autumn arrives,
its translucent rays casting a new layer of glass on the walls,
everyone putting on earphones, expression as uniform as jade.

Listening too is the pregnant teacher.
Fragments of ancient words belong to the elusive voice:
"Evening Post, Evening Post," the tape turning around the globe
at a deafening speed.
Intense vocabulary refuses to disappear, like a street scene,
a bursting spring, like a couple of aliens standing transfixed
at a certain edge.
Playing with sunset, all of a sudden they unfold a bolt
of colorful brocade:
the great void is smaller than a flower!

She looks around
at the new set-up: in everyone's mouth is a loom,
spinning in quiet murmurs the same good tale.
Everyone is engrossed in listening;
everyone is at work, organs exposed.

Completely unaware.

The Fiend Imprisoned at the Bottom of the Ocean

after a hundred years, I waited for another thousand; several millennia gone
    missing
my feeble promise remains on the surface of the ocean, floating

人的尸首如邪恶的珠宝盘旋下沉
乌贼鱼优哉悠哉，梦着陆地上的明灯

这海底好比一只古代的鼻子
天天嗅着那囚得我变形了的瓶子

看看我的世界吧，这些剪纸，这些贴花
懒洋洋的假东西；哦，让我死吧！

有一天大海晴朗地上下打开，我读到
那个像我的渔夫，我便朝我倾身走来

楚王梦雨

我要衔接过去一个人的梦，
纷纷雨滴同享的一朵闲云；
我的心儿要跳得同样迷乱，
宫殿春叶般生，酒沫鱼样跃，
让那个对饮的，也举落我的手。
我的手扪脉，空亭吐纳云雾，
我的梦正梦见另一个梦呢。

枯木上的灵芝，水腰系上绢帛，
西边的飞蛾探听夕照的虚实。
它们刚辞别幽居，必定见过
那个一直轻呼我名字的人，
那个可能鸣翔，也可能开落，
给人佩玉，又叫人狐疑的空址。
她的践约可能是渐渐潮湿的。

真奇怪，雨滴还未发落的前夕，
我已感到了周身潮湿呢：
青翠的竹子可以拧出水，
山谷来的风吹入它们的内心，
而我的耳朵似乎飞到了半空，

sailboats, with new positions, travel toward melancholy shores
flying birds, aged after generations; returning, the sun that never dies
human corpses, like wicked jewels, swirl, sinking to the bottom
Inkfish, free and relaxed, dream of bright lights on land

the ocean floor is like an ancient nose
sniffing at the bottle that imprisons and deforms me
look at my world: these paper cut-outs, these glued-on flowers
such languid counterfeits; oh, just let me perish!

one day when the ocean parts from top to bottom, clear and sunny; when I
    meet
the fisherman in a book, my likeness, I will lean aside to walk toward myself
    indeed.

King Chu Dreaming of Rain

I want to enter the dream of a person in the past had,
An idle cloud shared by the incessantly dripping rain.
My heart wishes to jump in the same disarray.
Palaces emerge like spring leaves; wine froth leaps like fish.
Let the one drinking across from me also lift and drop my hand.
My hand takes pulse, the vacant pavilion breathing mist and clouds, in and
    out.
My dream is dreaming of another dream.

A glossy ganoderma on a decayed tree, a silk scarf
Tied around a willowy waist,
A flying moth in the west inquiring about sunset.
Since they have just bid farewell to secluded abodes, they must have met
The person who has been whispering my name;
That unoccupied address, capable of soaring and falling,
Bestows jade pendants, but also arouses suspicions.
Her failure to turn up for the appointment may be dripping wet.

How strange: before raindrops fall,
I am already feeling soaked, yeah, soaked.
From the lush green bamboo leaves, water could be wrung out;

或者是凝伫了而燃烧吧，燃烧那个
一直戏睡在它里面，那湫隘的人。

还燃烧她的耳朵，烧成灰烟，
决不叫她偷听我心的饥饿。
你看，这醉我的世界含满了酒
竹子也含了晨曦和岁月。
它们萧萧的声音多痛，多痛，
愈痛我愈要剥它，剥成七孔
那么我的痛也是世界的痛。

请你不要再聆听我了，莫名的人。
我知道你在某处，隔风嬉戏。
空白的梦中之梦，假的荷叶，
令我彻底难眠的住址。
如果雨滴有你，火焰岂不是我？
人神道殊，而殊途同归，
我要，我要，爱上你神的热泪。

预感

像酒有时预感到黑夜和
它的迷醉者，未来也预感到
我们。她突然扬声问：你敢吗？
虽然轻细的对话已经开始。

我们不能预感永恒，
现实也不能说：现在。
于是，在一间未点灯的房间，
夜便孤立起来，
我们也被十点钟胀满。

但这到底是时日的哪个部件
当我们说：请来临吧！？
有谁便踮足过来。

From the valley, wind blows into their hearts.
But my ears seem to have flown up into midair.
Or perhaps they stand still to burn, burning the person
Who pretends to be sleeping inside, that tiny wet person.

Burning her ears as well, into ashes,
So that she will never have a chance to hear the hunger in my heart.
Look! The world that intoxicates me is filled with wine.
Even the bamboos are imbued with rays of the morning sun and the passing
    years.
How painful are their shushing sounds, how painful.
The more painful they are, the more I want to peel them, into seven holes.
So my pain is also the pain of the world.

You, the person without a name, please stop listening to me.
I know you are somewhere, playing behind the wind.
An empty dream within a dream, a fake lotus leaf,
An address that gives me sleepless nights.
If raindrops contain you, am I not a flame?
Gods and humans take different paths, yet they lead to the same destination.
I want, I want to fall in love with your sacred tears.

Premonition

Like wine that portends dark nights
And its addicts, future also foresees
Us. She suddenly raises her voice with a challenge: Do you dare?
Though a soft dialog has already begun.

We cannot forecast permanence;
Even the present cannot say: at present.
Hence, in a room without a lit lamp,
Night has been isolated.
We are also bloated with 10 O'clock.

But which part of the time is it,
When we say: please arrive?

把浓茶和咖啡
通过轻柔的指尖
放在我们醉态的旁边。

真是你吗？虽然我们预感到了。
但还是忍不住问了一声。

星辉灿烂，在天上。

南京

醒来，雷电正袭在五月的窗上，
昨夜的星辰坠满松林间。
我坐起，在等着什么。一些碎片
闪耀，像在五年前的南京车站：
你迎上来，你已经是一个

英语教员。暗红的灯芯绒上装
结着细白的芝麻点。你领我
换几次车，丢开全城的陌生人。
这是郊外，"这是我们的住房——
今夜它像水变成酒一样

没有谁会看出异样。"灯，用门
抵住夜的尾巴，窗帘掐紧夜的髦毛，
于是在夜宽柔的怀抱，时间
便像欢醉的蟋蟀放肆起来。
隔壁，四邻的长梦陡然现出恶兆。

茶杯提心吊胆地注视这十天。
像神害怕两片同样的树叶，
门，害怕外面来的同一片钥匙。
但它没有来。我想，如果我
现在归去，一定会把你惊呆。

Someone tiptoes over,
Placing strong tea and coffee,
With gentle finger tips,
Next to our drunken state.

Is it really you? Though we have a hunch,
we cannot help but inquire.

Brilliant stars, in the sky.

Nanjing

I wake up when lightening attacks the May windows,
Last night's stars hanging among pine trees.
I sit up, waiting for something to happen. Several broken pieces
Glisten, like the Nanjing Train Station five years ago:
You came over, already

An English teacher. On your crimson corduroy jacket
Tiny white sesame seeds congregated. You led me
To make a few transfers, leaving behind all the strangers in the city.
This was the suburb, "This is our house;
Tonight it is like water turning into wine?

No one can detect any difference." The light, using the door
Blocked the tail of the night, the curtains clutching its hair.
Hence, in the expansive gentle embrace of night, time was
Set loose like an ecstatic drunken cricket.
Next door, in the long dreams of the neighbors, suddenly appeared ominous
   signs.

The teacups carefully observed those ten days.
Like gods fearing two identical leaves,
The door feared the same key coming from the outside.
But it did not come. I think, if I returned
Now, you would be stunned.

我坐在这儿。同样的钥匙却通向
别的里面。嘴在道歉。我的头
偎着光明像偎着你的乳房。
陌生的灯泡像儿子,吊在我们
中间——我们中间的山水

结满正午的果实。航着子夜的航帆。
我坐着,嗅着雷电后的焦糊味。
我冥想远方。别哭,我的忒勒玛科斯
这封密信得瞒过母亲,直到
我们的钢矛刺尽她周身的黑暗。

死囚与道路

从京都到荒莽
海阔天空,而我的头
被锁在长枷里,我的声音
五花大绑,阡陌风铃花,
吐露出死
给修远的行走者加冕的
某种含义;

我走着,
难免一死,这可
不是政治。渴了,我就
勾勒出一个小小林仙:
蹦跳的双乳. 鲜嫩的陌生,
跑过未名的水流,
而刀片般的小鹿,
正克制清荫脆影;

如果我失眠.
我就唯美地假想
我正睡着睡,
沉甸甸地;

I'm seated here. But the same key passes through
Another interior. The mouth is apologizing, my head
Leaning against light as if against your breasts,
The unfamiliar bulb, like a son, hanging between
Us — the landscape between us

Filled with noon fruits, sails the midnight boat.
I'm seated, sniffing the burned smell after the lightening.
I'm pondering a faraway place. Don't cry, my Taylor Marcus.
This secret letter has to be hidden from mother, till
Our steel spears pierce through the darkness all over her body.

On Death Roll and the Road

From the capital city to the wilderness,
The ocean is wide and the sky spacious, but my head is
Locked in the long cangue, my voice
tightly roped. The wind-bell flowers on the crossing paths
Reveal the meaning of death
crowning the distant traveler.

I'm on the road.
Death is unavoidable; however, it is not
Politics. When thirsty, I picture
A small forest angel, whose leaping breasts are tenderly foreign,
running over nameless streams,
But the doe, sharp as a blade,
Is restraining the cool shade and dancing shadows.

If I fail to sleep,
I would pretend in aesthetical terms that
I was sleeping,
deeply sleeping.

If I fear, if I fear,
I would presume that
I'm already dead, that I've sent death to death, while

如果我怕，如果我怕
我就想当然地以为
我已经死了，我
死掉了死。并且还

带走了那正被我看见的一切：
褪色风景的普罗情调，
酒楼，轮渡，翡翠鸟，
几个外省的鱼米乡，
几个邋遢地搓着麻将的妓女.
几只像烂袜子被人撇弃在
人之外的猛虎
和远处的一只塔影，

更远一点，是那小小林仙，
玲珑的，悠扬的，可呼其乳名的
小妈妈，她的世界飘香

像大家一样，
一个赴死者的梦，
一个人外人的梦，
是不纯的，像纯诗一样。

祖母

   1

她的清晨，我在西边正憋着午夜。
她起床。叠好放子，去堤岸练仙鹤拳。
迷雾的翅膀激荡，河像一根傲骨
于冰封中收敛起一切不可见的仪典。
"空"，她冲天一喨，"而不止是
肉身，贯满了这些姿式"；她蓦地收功，
原型般凝定在一点，一个被发明的中心。

Taking away everything that I'm witnessing:
Popular sentiments of faded sceneries,

Restaurants, commuter boats, halcyons,
Several fish-rice villages in another province,
Several unkempt mahjong-playing prostitutes,
A few fierce tigers abandoned like worn socks

Outside the human realm,
And the shadow of a pagoda in the distance.

Farther ahead is that small forest angel,
The delicate and melodious little mother,
Whose pet name you can call. Her world is fragrant

Like everybody else;

A dream of the person on the journey to death,
A dream of the person excluded from others,
Is, like pure poetry, not pure.

Grandmother

1

Her early morning, I'm in the west stifled at midnight.
She gets up, makes her bed, and goes to the river bank
To practice Crane Boxing.
The wings of the mist are surging; the river,
Like an unyielding bone,
Holds off in the frozenness all invisible ceremonies.

"Emptiness," she cries out toward the sky, "not just
Flesh and blood, fills up these poses,"
She abruptly gathers in her energy,
Rooted to the spot like a prototype, an invented center.

    2
　给那一切不可见的，注射一针共鸣剂，
以便地球上的窗户一齐敞开。

以便我端坐不倦，眼睛凑近
显微镜，逼视一个细胞里的众说纷纭
和它的螺旋体，那里面，谁正头戴矿灯，
一层层挖向莫名的尽头。星星，
太空的胎儿，汇聚在耳鸣中，以便

物，膨胀，排它，又被眼睛切分成
原子，夸克和无穷尽？
　　　　　　　　以便这一幕本身
也演变成一个细胞，一个地球似的细胞，
搏动在那冥冥浩邈者的显微镜下：一个
母性的，湿腻的，被分泌的"0"；以便

室内满是星期三。
眼睛，脱离幻境，掠过桌面的金鱼缸
和灯影下暴君模样的套层玩偶，嵌入
夜之阑珊。

    3
　夜里的中午，春风猝起。我祖母
走在回居民点的路上，篮子满是青菜和蛋。
四周，吊车鹤立。忍着嘻笑的小偷翻窗而入，
去偷她的挑木匣子；他闯祸，以便与我们
对称成三个点，协调在某个突破之中。
圆。

2

Into all that is invisible, inject a dose of resonance,
So that all windows on earth will open wide at once.

So that I can sit upright, invigorated, eyes coming close
To the microscope, focusing on the various debates within a cell
And its helix, inside which is a man, a miner's cap on the head, digging layer
After layer towards the mysterious end. Stars,
Fetuses of the outer space, assemble in tinnitus, so that

Matter, swelling and excluding, is segmented into
Atoms, quarks, and infinity?
So that this scene itself
Evolves into a cell, an earth-like cell,
Pulsing under the microscope of the person who roams the immense
        universe:
A maternal, wet and creamy "O," so that

The room is filled with Wednesdays.
Eyes, having left the illusory world, glance over
The gold fish tank on the table
And the nesting doll that looks like a tyrant under the light, implant
        themselves
In the waning darkness of the night.

3

Noon at midnight, spring wind suddenly rises. My grandmother
Is walking on the road back to her neighborhood, basket brimmed
With green vegetables and eggs.
All around her, construction cranes perch high. A thief, suppressing a
Giggle, enters her house from the window,
To steal her cherry wood box. He gets himself into trouble,
In order to form with us
A triangle, harmonized in a certain breakthrough.
A circle.

张真

愿望之三

离开盛大的宴会
跟跟跄跄穿过链节般的街巷
低垂的街灯追随着我的声息
像猎犬的牙齿咬我的影子
目的地不明，又是无月之夜
黏糯的蓝雾使我迷路
我歌唱着，每一个弱音消逝时
有一绺头发飞扬上
邻近的屋顶
于是我哭，哭成大雨淋漓
天亮的时候
被掩埋的城市显现出未
它背负茫茫的草原
每一株白色的草尖上
都闪耀着
一粒黑色的音符

愿望十一

简陋的闷罐式火车
蠕行在热带红沼泽里
我们不约而同地上了车

车厢带着天文台的圆顶
惟一的窗户被裹上重重石膏
父亲带着男人们进进出出
他们手持计算尺和铁锤
铸造一只大蜘蛛
在漆黑一片中没有人出声
通向其他车厢的门敞着

Zhang Zhen

translations by Bob Holman and Xiangyang Chen with the author

Music

Stumbling out of the grand reception
I tripped across the low white chains to the raw street
My breath boomeranged off the low-hung street lamps
Like the fangs of a terrier biting my shadow
Destinationless, moonless
Lost in the glutinous blue fog
I chanted, and when each note decrescendoed
And disappeared back between my lips
Strands of hair, C#
Rise to the eaves
So I cried, until it poured
When light dawned
The buried city began to emerge
Encumbered with a vast grassland
And glistening on the tip of each grass blade,
A single black note.

Train

ramshackle, watertight, snaking
through the tropical red marsh
You got no ticket.
You get on board.

Carriage domed like an observatory,
The only window covered with layers of plaster.
Father comes in, goes out. A long line
Of men, dressed like him, files through. They
carry measuring tapes and hammers and
start back in on the big Spider they are building.

涌进热浪和腥味
却无法看见无从想象
那里在进行的事业

现在好了
竣工的大蜘蛛如同枝形灯
优美地撑满穹顶
我们姐妹们爬上梯子
默默地给蛛脚插满蜡烛
我们的裙子被一阵意外的阴风鼓满
也一道燃烧起来
那美丽的形象噼噼啪啪着化为灰烬
我瞥见被打开的窗户焕然一新
浓烈而刺鼻的白光涌入车厢
一条干涸的红河里
缓缓走来硕大的河马
它扇动鼻翼
以不可思议的速度
强调奇迹的降临

漂亮的河马贴近窗棂便消失了
而身后留下的一行尸体
像人在睡眠中蜷伏
它们是难以名状的使者
是恐龙的后代或是中国的红虾
它们透明的肉体和尖利的长须
在赤道烈日的舔食下
发出咒语般的光芒

我想欢呼
想召唤身后的人们
却哑然失声
我感到身体在失去水分
在变轻
却无能为力
气急败坏的父亲冲进来

No noise. Pitch black. The door to the next
car is ajar — heat and spunk gushes in
but there is no way to see what's going on.

Ok, it's finished. The Spider
hangs over us, an elegant chandelier
canopying the dome. My sisters
and I climb up the ladders in silence
and begin to light the candles
in the Spider's legs. A sudden gust
balloons our dresses, they catch on fire!
a beautiful image which soon sizzles to ash.
The window is open — through it I see the
brand new future. A sharp strong white shaft
penetrates the carriage from the red dry river bed,
lopes along towards us, a gargantuan hippo,
its nostrils flaring, riffling, transmutating,
underscoring the descent of wonders.

Our beautiful hippo vanishes. Sigh.
Our attention is drawn to the window where
we now see a line of dead bodies, like men
left behind huddled in sleep. These are
the unnamable messengers, descendents
of dinosaurs, or perhaps Chinese red shrimps.
The tropical sun laps their translucent bodies,
their razor sharp beards, like a curse. I want to shout

with joy, hailing all, living and dead!
But my voice has evaporated. I feel
my whole body dehydrating, becoming light . . .
Helpless . . . Father rushes in in exasperation.
I block the window with my body.
The light pours round my silhouette.
My eyes occupy the bodies. A secret
flashes by and moves on, never
to return to the window on the train which
continues snaking through the red marsh,

我堵着窗口
强光从我轮廓线后溢出
我深深地望着他们
一个秘密就是这样闪现过
又在永恒地离开
离开这惟一的窗口
离开我们的轨道所在的红色沼泽

正午的会面

一个红头发的汉子走过去了
他低斜的左肩上坐着一只金丝猴
它看见我，叹了一口气

一个瞎子走过去了
他双眼圆睁，闪闪发出磷光
胸口挂着巨大的"红挑"扑克

一个系俄罗斯头巾的老妪走过去了
她的菜篮里满是青蛙
它们渲泄欲望的歌声久久地回响

一个穿开裆裤的女孩走过去了
她在沿途的每一根电线杆上刻上一刀
它们流出乳汁，像茁壮的产妇
广场风磨似的旋转起来
太阳带着所有的人翻了个身
我等的人却始终没有来

梦中楼阁

它展开庄重平整的肩膊
那纯色的白铅像少年的皮肤
我没有联想到重量与体积

ramshackle, watertight. I have no ticket.
I get on board.

Meeting at the Square at Noon on the Dot

One-armed red-head man walks past
Monkey clinging to his stump sighs
At the sight of me me me

Wide-eyed blind man walks past
Orbs teeming with iridescent light
Big red spade dangling from the chest

Old lady in babushka walks past
Hauling a frog basket
Their croak desire drowns the landscape

Girl in slit trousers walks past
Gashes each electrical pole she passes
Milk gushes like a woman after delivery

The square begins to whirl — it's a windmill
The sun has vanished taking everything with her
Hey. I'm here. You're not. On the dot.

Dream Mansion

like an architectural drawing unfolds
square, somber and white as lead
skin of a teenager. No clue

of size, scale. Just walk up the steps
how you do it without touching earth
I do not know I can't even

在我踏而上的时候
感觉不到鞋底与地球的接触

没有试着扔一个苹果，或者石块
也没有向上或者向下瞩目
阶梯普通得以致看不清轮廓
脚步声必然流入了一个秘密的通道
不知身外哪一层，没有任何门洞

它的整体消失在我的攀援里
记忆再也不能临摹出
我深深凝视过的它的面貌
一只白鸟掠过密集的静寂
"外边是什么样的？"我问

它怜悯地望我一眼飞了出去
或者说不见了，这就是回答
我留在自己的脚印里无法自拔
好吧，现在让我占有你
你的虚无的四壁，你的存在

革命

来呀，天神
这些人又在闹了
且趁我飞离之机
我不知道为何泪水流淌
为何撕破了报纸为何
躲进衣柜寻求黑暗的庇护

我低低地却用尽全力呐喊
我觉得喉咙在流血而词语无力
天花板上面有老鼠在乱蹿
电灯摇晃着像钟摆一下一下无情
我恍然大悟：

throw an apple or a stone
up is down now hello stairs drip
a secret passage where the hell

am I? without a door the whole place
gone my memory hole I throw
myself into and ask the white bird

"What's the weather like outside?"
It's already gone. Flew away. Or
Vanished, who knows, was never . . . Aha!

I am forever stuck to my footsteps.
But you are with me, I won't let go.
Your four walls. Your existence. Dream stuck.

Revolution (1989)

Come, O heavenly God!
These people are making such a scene
I'll never be able to make my flight
Real tears, real tears I'm crying,
Confetti, I am tearing the newspaper to confetti
Why why why I'm running into a broom closet now

How can I scream when my throat is bleeding.
Nuts-o! Roof rats are rollerskating helter-skelter
Lightbulbs swing, passion on a pendulum
Suddenly the whole damn thing dawns on me:
I'm getting what I deserve!
I'm not fit enough to have an enemy
Nobody bothers to look at me
I am a zit-covered teenager in love
You are big? You must be my mother!
Laugh laugh shake pain and pass out

我那被卸掉的耻辱正是我
那应有的责任
我已不配有这敌人
没有人召唤我
我只是一个自作多情的小鸡仔
将随便遇到的庞然大物当生母
这一切真好笑
我笑痛了肚子笑昏了过去

革命已与我无缘
热血无处抛洒就倒进制冰盒吧
用来调酒美味极了

但这又错了，天神说
他的手放在我的心口
说他的脸贴在我的发梢：
小女子，你本身就是革命
是呵，我每天目击救火车掠过
只要我愿意火势就无法收拾

驮上自由这轻如羽毛的行李
我游遍各处扇风点火
惟当盛夏来临
在我诞生的节日里
天神与我相会，和我跳舞
在白夜下流连

时差

这几天
我注意到一种似有若无的清香
拐角上私人庭园里的梅树
突然探出矮墙
令人顿足翘望

Revolution and I have parted company
Pour my sangfroid into the refrigerator

God places His hand on my heart,
His face upon the tip of my hair
Says, You made a mistake
Little girl, for you yourself are the Revolution.
Fire trucks speed by every day
First one way, then all the others, woo woo
A circling wagon train of fire trucks, woo woo
I watch them as the flames race out of control

Pack animal carries featherweight luggage of freedom
Striking sparks and dousing the fire with gasoline.
It's a crazy hot July day. I suddenly remember
This is my birthday, and dear heavenly God has
Kept his appointment.
He dances with me.
We linger in the pale night.

Jet Lag Satori

These days
the slightest fragrance
invites my attention.

The plum tree in the corner
of my neighbor's garden
stretches its head out of the yard.

I stop. I can see time.
There's a tangerine in the parking lot.
I am tiptoeing past the past, lest

the fruits fall, a blizzard of stars.
I am pregnable, I'm the plum tree,
thick, suffocating, coagulating.

而停车场中的那棵橘树上
依然悬着去秋的果实
我得踮着脚经过
怕那灿烂的东西在眼前损落

我和梅一起怀春
浓艳得使心窒息使血凝结
经验使我痛苦使我预知花埋春泥
秋橘在夜间飘落落在另一个庭园里

那个地方似曾相识
四季的花开在一处奇香无比
我见到自己午睡正酣
而静脉被割破血轻轻流入池塘

这几天
时间之河在倒流
一些名称与另一些混杂
花哨的或破烂的形象从雨雾中越出

我故意表现得令人失望
我会枯坐长久感受微弱的地震
也许消极的意愿倒能产生奇迹
天空在最黑之时会轰然打开

这闰月又短又湿
穿着一身丧服便匆匆出走
我独享这一树梅这一树橘
喜不自禁而忧心忡忡

洗衣

这些被拧成面团的布片
会比用它的身体长久

Flowers are blossoming in my sight, losing
petals, tangerines are dropping one by one
into a strange garden, and only at night.

This Twilight Zone is so familiar.
Flowers of all seasons, a raucous symphony of odor.
I see myself napping. My blood trickles into the pond.

The river of time is flooding.
Names confound, conflating with other names.
Flashy trashy brashy bursting through foggy rain . . .

I'm going to be a bad girl.
I'm - a sit here and earthquake orgasm.
Heave ho! Split the sky!

This leap month is short and wet
and hurrying to the funeral .
It's me! Me and the plum!

Now everything is!
Eat a plum, eat me, eat a treeful of tangerines
Fill joy, overflow sorrow. Home.

Laundry

Laundry wrung, laundry crumpled
Lasts longer than the bodies that wear it
My daughter should join a carnival
To dig out the faded fabric of my history

Raw colors and abstract forms of the century
Palette of emotions and silhouettes of thoughts
I toss them all into the machine, plop
Scrub them clean of tears and memory

我的女儿在未来的狂欢节
会挖出我的褪色的历史

这个时代有这些色彩这些造型
情感的颜料思想的剪影
我将它们塞进机器
机器将眼泪和记忆甩净

在某些口袋里放入字条
这将是我延长生命的努力
一个缺少的扣子或一个裂口
让承承者去猜测

我多么愿意和她们交谈
在衣柜被打开的时候现出微笑
而她们会如临大敌
她们不认识我

我的首饰被送进当铺
我的情书作为壁炉的燃料
月亮夜复一夜地升起
却不再有我的凝视

传说

哪个旧情人对我说过：
生活可以在磨杵里捣烂
阳光剪着透明窗花
永远织不完的毛衣——(给谁的?)
发出樟脑丸的气味

梦见神农架的老树里
飞出凤凰——我啜着咖啡
讲着老掉牙的民间传说

Secret notes dropped in anonymous pockets
This is the way to prolong life
A missing button or a tear
Is speculation for the heir

I want to talk with them!
Flash a smile when the dryer door is flung open
Why do they confront me like enemies?
Act like we haven't met?

The jewelry my lover gave me, send to the pawnshop
My love letters fuel the fireplace
A missing button or a tear
Is speculation for the heir

Legend

An old lover once said to me:
Go ahead. Pulverize life in a mortar.
Watch the sun cut through windows
Slicing the paper flower cut-outs.

Darn a sweater. Don't know who it's for.
Doesn't matter anymore. You
Can never finish it.
Smells like camphor anyway.

I dreamed in Shennongjia:
From out of an old tree a phoenix flew.
We are sipping coffee. I start to narrate
An old folk story, clichéd, boring. I want

To see your reaction. The red leather sofa steams,
Your pants get wet and wetter,
The hybrid boy of our dreams
Demands an ice cream cone.

.

红皮沙发冒出热气　尿了裤的
混血男孩要吃冰激凌

对，走到哪儿都带上墨镜
腋下夹一本厚字典——（什么语言都行）
电饭煲开始吐气的刹那
土星被撞出一个大洞　眯眼
你可以看见满天异彩

Sure, wear dark glasses wherever you go,
Carry a thick dictionary under your arm,
Doesn't matter which language. The rice cooker
Begins to steam. Saturn has smashed a big hole

In the universe. You are so over. Screw up your eyes.
It's not me you see. It's a sky of blood and rainbows.
It's all you. And it's all for you.
Let me tell you a story.

赵霞

书生

一本仍是处子的书，页和页紧咬得多厉害，
我还未从风雪中来，它们却已备好
茶水和饺、静电扎成的欢迎词。

蜡光纸在胡乱闪耀，深居简出的仿宋体
袖着手向外张望：好象体面的乡绅
约好了县城的郎中，女人们耸着新拢的髻，
把炊烟高高地甩上天空。

蒙昧中的七朵百合

　1
不斟满
我们手中的杯
也不雀跃

屯溪的农妇把草场收拾得整洁
咥咥的朗诵家开始了默读

　2
我何时竟成了身外
携书进食，读和游出

医师的厅堂大开着一蓬花
运动着的和拘谨的
拉锯的两个讷言的木匠

　3
墙的尖棱角
使额头多么不幸

Zhao Xia

translations by Rachel Levitsky, Zhang Er and the author

Scholar

An uncracked virgin of a book, holds tight to its pages like a locked embrace
I've yet to come in from a storm though they've already prepared
Tea, dumplings, welcoming words, static and bound.

The wax paper wildly shines, as Fang Song font
Secluded type, looks around with
Hands in sleeves — an honorable squire meeting the town doctor
Women tower in their newly combed coils
Cook-smoke thrown high in the sky.

–R.L. and Z.X.

Seven Lilies in Barbarism

1.
Not to fill
the glasses in our hands
not to jump for joy

A woman farming in Tunxi arranges her grasslands
A *bang-bang* reader of out-loud text reads with no sound

2.
From when I became an external body
eating with book, reading and swimming

The doctor's lobby was filled with blossom
one was in motion, the other reserved:
taciturn carpenters working a two-handed saw

393

棱和弧
怎么在学堂外再次相遇

羊们吮吃冬天的水果
再没有舞来一条挑衅的龙

   4

哦，她端着她的赘腰
在收银台砌出一座小分币山
女士们用旧了的皱纹
于是，嵌得下水嫩的中国豆芽

   5
你的美
搭筑了铅的山墙
门楣还有牌楼

你之外的
都极尽萧飒

我更快地走
村道逼仄，夜黑得
好象人类没有来过

   6
她的背面繁复，逆着光
却明亮如菊
行走委蛇，绳结的一个姻亲

规矩地等绿灯放行
两排过路人，互相提醒着
颧骨和人中，追溯艳情史

3.
A wall's sharp edge brings a
grand misfortune to your forehead
Edges and arc
How will they meet after school?

Sheep sucking winter fruits
Gone dance of provoking dragon

4.
Oh. Bearing bulky waist she builds
a little hill of coins on the cashier's desk

The women's overworked wrinkles could
by now be populated with
tender Chinese bean sprouts

5.
Your beauty
lifts the lead gable
then lintel, archway

The rest is beyond
bleak, desolate

I walk faster. The village path narrows,
the night's so dark as if human life
was never here

6.
Her elaborate back against the light
but bright, as chrysanthemum
Her tortured walk, bound to marriage

Two rows of pedestrians remind each other —
Behave well through the wait for a green light
Cheekbones and philtrums track mark old stories of love.

7
你把自己当作破线团了
钓得起水藻和蜉蝣

那颠沛的移民说说说了
同样的渣屑
你就抽出凹角里相应的低贱

伯阳

邻居是一组魁梧的汉子和
个别的几个女人，晚间的院子
就是共产化的澡堂，小崽子们
光腚颠颠地跑
几张稔熟的大脸，假模假式
像行人一样，在半敞的门户外

滑过。窗帘的蓝色布匹竟有些
冷胀热缩？而烈雨，是毫不腼腆地
来了，亲吻斜纹的衬衣，和一切
香脂粉黛的细小物什，白纱裙裾的
一小声娇柔的尖叫，引我在
润湿的木门——驻足片刻

近旁的两家 24 小时超市售卖
澄黄的桔汁，和永恒欢乐的护身符
我手揣一封薄纸的书信，为小片
五角的邮票奔忙，稍后未果而
折回，上个月猛响的链条撑脚
遗憾地已被彻底修理（哦，摆平！）

游水时吴勇说我偌大一只好肺，以及
头在上必沉头在下必浮的
若干鬼话，我重塌塌登陆上岸
尾巴甩水，自觉风情万种

7.
You see yourself as a ragged reel of fish line
good for algae, mayfly
That vagrant immigrant, again and again and again
mouthing the same shit, until you produce
some correspondent lowliness, from the hollow

–R.L. and Z.X.

Bo Yang

I share the communal yard with a group of
enormous men, a few women. As night falls
their bare-assed children run around
our common bath house
its few familiar faces pretending
as passers-by glide outside

the half opened door. Does the blue curtain
material expand in cold and contract in heat? The downpour
isn't shy, it comes and intimately kisses the twill
shirt and every little frilly cosmetic detail and
the white gauze skirt that screams a tiny little scream
calling me to stop in front of the wet wood door

Two 24 hour supermarkets nearby sell orange yellow
tangerine juice and the talisman of eternal joy. I hold
the thin sheet of a letter, rushing around for a 50 cent stamp,
give up and turn back to the bottom bracket,
the chain set that sounded loud for a month and now
must be completely rebuilt (Ha! Handled!)

When swimming, Wu Yong says that I have big
strong lungs "Head up, sink. Head down, float."
Such nonsense! I climb heavily to shore, tail flicking
water, charming (so I think) in a thousand ways

再其后冷面店爆发过一场
艺术政治家的空前狂笑

邻居们在露天餐桌上吐露心声
和鱼刺，壮年男子在街上
劝说猴子务必翻一只漂亮的筋斗
溶解咖啡的室温中摆放着
几个季度前暗香的水瓶
皮肤可以触到时间——
在黏滞地流走

新出版的刊物上，一篇世纪末的
玩笑情怀，另有于姓作家
对其一日的，玩笑性描写。
就我所知而言，玩笑莫过
伯阳不回信笺，哪怕
这一行假设的汉字，都令我
不胜寒噤

锐角的铁丝中央，腾空的雌性蜘蛛
难得的狂欢的放纵
以绝妙的构图，将美感铺陈
阳光下我抖落布衣的一片尘埃
身着它，我去赴那海鲜的盛宴

做粗活的工人在早晨
攀爬上屋顶，我像婴儿般安睡
如此哀伤，光线清朗得无邪
墙布是迷乱的方格，关于他的相片
倒伏在我七月的慌张之上
影片、铃声，房门在午后
被随意地敲响

我的身体，是一堆朴素
而迷惘的废墟
酒吧间

Later a cold noodle shop explodes in the wild
unprecedented laughter of politician artists

Neighbors at the outdoor table their guts spill
spit fish bones as a grown man in the street
persuades the monkey to perform
a pretty somersault. The room temperature
is high enough to dissolve the coffee, a few
bottles that were perfume a few seasons ago
skin can sense time as it slinks away

In a recent journal is an article by Yu
teasing himself erotically making jokes
through feelings of the day
one day at the end of the century and
for me the best joke is that Bo Yang
doesn't write me back, that single line
presumably in Chinese character
would make me tremble with cold

At the point of the acute angle
on an iron wire, a female spider suspended
in air brings an orgy of joy hard to come by
this ultimate composition, spreads beauty
under the sun I shake dust off my simple cotton
clothing and wearing it, go to a fresh seafood buffet?

The workmen in the morning climb up to the roof
as I peacefully sleep like an infant
so sad, the light is clear without twist though
on the wall cloth are confusing squared patterns
as his photo falls on top of my July rush
the flurry of films, the door bell, careless
pleasures of the door knock in the afternoons

My body, is a pile of plain
yet confused ruin
bars twisting dance hall

扭动的舞场
他人之间的亲密恰像
废墟四周，孪生的座座高楼

我所能看见的，全都柔软地后退
从微微反光的店铺的门扇走出
我骑车越过了，炎热季节的
枣核般微小的孤独
转角是上了绿漆的栅栏
蜿蜒的小径，继而穿过南大
希腊竞技场的校园，于是我就度过了
我九十岁前的
全部爱情。

宝蓝色的陀螺

发生了什么事，发生了
什么事？什么人生活在
一个怎样的
单向的世界？

　树叶只有一面，镜子也照不全
　第二张相反的脸。

发生了什么事，发生了
什么事？哪一轮时间的圆圈
往复出了
重叠的墨点？

　正在做的已完成，曾忧伤的
　仍经历着欢欣。

发生了什么事，发生了
什么事？何处的河流有两个

intimacy between others
the identical high-rises around

All I see retreats softly walking
out from doors of stores in soft light
riding on the bicycle, passing the hot season's
solitude, tiny as the pit of a jujube date
The corner of the fence painted green
winding alleys that cut through Nanjing University
campus, the Greek arena, thus I'll spend
all love before I turn 90.

−R.L. and Z.E.

Sapphire Blue Top

What's happened? What has
happened? Who lives
in which kind
of the unidirectional world?

>   One sided leaves. Reflection incomplete, mirror
>   won't reflect their other side.

What's happened? What has
happened? Which circle of time
returns the ink spot
in duplicate?

>   The things being done are done, the once worried
>   continues toward exultation.

What's happened? What has
happened? Where is the mortise-
tenon river, of Yin and Yang
opposite names?

卯榫阴阳的
矛盾的名字？

　背影代表凝视，说着密切的话
　却愈发沉默。

暖风南倾

清晨呲呲刷牙，下午兢兢读书，
舔一口喜剧的白糖，嗅一丝男女的醋香。

再剪指甲，掉下十弯月亮。去院落，
摘下衣架上晾干的豆荚。

兰花迅长，好似我们未来的喧天娃，
太阳时退时显，哪里学来的狡黠？

你将胡须在水斗逐个敲碎，又去跑步
把球鞋的泥底左右翻出，

暖风南倾，拽歪你绚烂的菟丝发，
你咧嘴浅笑，春天就象纸鸢般跟随。

托马斯的音乐生活

邻居托马斯每天听晦涩的歌，
嘴里叼着车库钥匙，走进走出。

他不厌倦世上的一切，包括
换汤不换药的爱，和万变不离其宗的乱。

女孩全都栽在他的琴弦下，
栽了以后，他把她们
轧成香馥的乐谱。

View of a back means earnest gaze, intimate words
of a greater reserve.

                    –R.L. and Z.X.

Warm Wind Leaning South

Swooshing of the morning tooth brushing, ci-ci
Afternoon book reading vigilance, jing-jing

Lick a pinch of comedy sugar.
Sniff a line of romantic vinegar.

Cut the finger nails, ten crescent moons fall.
Go to the yard to pick the pea pods dried up on the cloth line.

Fast growing orchids loud future sky crying baby
Sun sometimes out sometimes in. Is it some kind of trick?

At the sink, hair by hair you hack at your beard then go out to jog
turning soil left and right from sneakers.

Warm wind leaning south, dragging and twisting
shiny, stringy, dodder hair, your slight grin.

Spring follows like a kite.

                    –R.L. and Z.E.

The Musical Life of Thomas

Every day, the neighbor Thomas
listens to an obscure song walking, in and out,
holding garage key in his mouth

昨天那段婉转的蓝调，就是
蓝礼帽妇人的休止符，颤音振得

像睫毛，尾调收得
臀部一样光滑。

他总是淋漓地喝掉十一罐啤酒，
然后手里夹着颅骨拨片，醉倒在

一堆肥嫩的内衣上。

书房逼仄

1
晴日也显出了邪恶，四周
仿佛更暗，墨水从笔杆
逆流而上，我惊讶于
兰花内部的空旷。

2
你说风会往下掉，于是你将风扇
调高。万物反光，云层略显单薄，
你读法兰克福汇报，忽然响亮地
举起上海的巨幅照：看黑白高架！

3
来读吧，好象参与一起分赃：
那些安闲的怨妇，复仇的苦儿，
伺机捉住词句的首尾，手起刀落，
一碟小菜端上！

4
你说到新疆辣鸡，那小餐馆
退成日渐遥远的历史。如今，

Never tired from anything in this world
Romance, the repeated formula of medicine refreshed

by the water, soup, some other liquid
the chaos of a million varieties drawn from one root

As the girls fell under the strings of his instrument
and he rolled them out into fragrant musical scores.

Yesterday's winding melodious blues
was rest note for the woman with blue top hat, trill trembling

like eye lashes. The coda concludes smooth
as her bottom.

Each time he feverishly guzzles eleven cans of beer,
then sweats, drunk, with a skull bone plectrum in hand

on top a pile of tender fat undergarments.

–R.L. and Z.E.

Narrowing Study

1.
This day, bright and clear, shows evil
the atmosphere seems to darken
and the pen's ink moves upward
I'm surprised by the vacancy in the orchids.

2.
You say that wind falls, so tilt the fan up
higher. Everything reflects light, the cloud layer
looks a little thin. Reading FAZ, your German Daily,
you burst out, holding the full page photo of Shanghai:
"Look at the viaduct in black and white!"

街上有人罢工，麦克风里的
修辞猛烈，却不如孜然熏香。

5
瞧这页被揉、挤、搓的纸，竟有意
重回山林？藤蔓、芽、打猎人的神经，
那些潦草的偏旁，将被好奇的
法布尔，也疏忽……遗忘？

在 ST 城过圣诞节

理发，把发梢剪平。

安静是阅读中的立方体，
或许弥漫着烟雾，或许不。

长辈的想象力有时也能出人意料，核桃
和猕猴桃是如何啾鸣着转变成鸟的，魔术师
都不能说清。

而诗人总爱做些无谓的小事，心怀叵测地
使世间琐事在忙碌中更零乱琐碎。还自以为高明地给京城
发手机短信——殊不知有电子、数码时代，就有行止无定的
故障精英。

幻灯片又布置了另一座时空的迷宫。母亲的私密被
历历再现在儿媳的面前：那些抽烟斗的男友、老式的白凉鞋；
潮润宽敞的甲板、泳衣里丰满的小腹。未见海鸥，却有三两艘
停泊在 60 年代香港的游轮……那会儿耆老的尚处年轻，满面胡髭的
则仍待出生。

礼物是只崭新的音乐盒子，
仿佛具有改造世人的特性：
令你这就去喜欢泡沫波普，

3.

Comes to read, as if divying the stolen goods:
Leisured unsatisfied wives, those revenging gamins,
wait for opportunities to clutch the head and tail of the
sentences, one swoop of the knife,
and the dish is served!

4.

Mentions the chilly chicken from Xin Jiang,
that little restaurant fading daily,
retreating into history. Today
there are strikes on the street, exaggerated
rhetoric amplified by the microphone
can't compete with the hot ZiRan spice.

5.

Would even this crumpled paper would
return to its mountain forest?
Vines, shoots, the nerves of hunters,
rushed illegible radicals omitted by
the curious Fabre and forgotten?

–R.L. and Z.E.

好象谁生来都是一架，沉
浮于酷时尚的塑壳永动船。

Stuttgart Christmas

Hair cut
ends even

Quiet cube of reading
possibly invaded by smoke

Early generations captured
also by walnut and kiwi fruit
as they unexpectedly twitter into bird
how even the magician hasn't got the answer
The poet always loves to do her useless things
bagatelles, plots make worldly busy routine more
chaotic, trivial, self-assuredly sends short cell messages
to capital oblivious toward the fact of electronic disfunction

Slide show installs added maze of time and space. Private secrets
mother replays in front of daughter-in-law: boyfriends smoking pipes,
old fashioned white sandals, moist wide desk, fleshy belly in a swimsuit.
Seagulls unseen, though in Hong Kong, two or three cruise ships come to
port . . . A time when the old are still young, the full bearded yet to be born.

The present is a brand new portable radio
that perhaps rebuilds us earthlings: fall in
love with the pop bubbles right away.
Everyone would be born a plastic boat in perpetual
motion, sinking and floating with cool fashion.

–R.L. and Z.E.

周瓒

张三先生乘坐中巴穿过本城

1
纵情的下午五点钟。目的地不明
在一生中时时遭遇他冷静反省
他一只脚探出，已经预先
了解到行程的代价：引领他的
是招手即停的想象自由
讨价还价的智力操练。而渡船费

交给吆喝者。一段需要以想象充实的
道路，首先他需要寻找到身份认同
的座位。他"在路上"的事实无需交代
像流浪汉小说中的主人公
被群蚁讲述，被唾沫阅读
被印刷机织进文明和艺术史的网结

现在，放好他那标准牌手提箱
把目光移向窗外。视点的
移动代替梦想中的高倍变焦镜头
像一个画家渴望变成机器人
他也宁愿变成一架摄像机，在飞驰中
留下一片后表现主义的油彩擦痕

2
请想象一架机器的轻松心情
改头换面的死神挥舞着它
残缺的肢体 ，但每一部分
都能代表整体说话
是的 ，"如果只是倾听死亡
我的整个生命就不是生命

Zhou Zan

translations by Susan M. Schultz and Jennifer Feeley

Mr. Zhang San Rides through Town on a Minibus

1.
5 p.m. Do what you want to your heart's content. The destination's
unknown: one often meets his sober introspection;
he puts his best foot forward, already knowing
the cost of his travels: what guides him is
an imagined freedom that promptly stops beckoning,
its bargain: mind drills. He gives the hawker

his ferry boat fare. This paragraph requires a path
enriched with imagining; first he seeks out
a seat for his self. Facts of his being on the road needn't
be handed over like those of the official in a picaresque
novel, narrated by an ant army and read by saliva,
knot woven into culture and history by the printing press.

Setting down his drab briefcase,
he shifts his gaze outside the window. His new
p.o.v. replaces the double-sized scorched fantasy photos.
Like a painter who yearns to be a robot,
he'd rather be a speeding camcorder,
discarding a smudged post-Expressionist oil painting.

2.
Please imagine a machine's relaxed mood.
Death, which alters appearances, wields
fragmentary limbs and body, but each part
represents the whole, says, "If it only
listens attentively to death, my entire life
is not life, but suffering." Harboring his cautious

dread, he returns to people: Li Ke Long's second floor
resembles a weary dyspeptic stomach,

411

而是苦难"。怀着审慎的恐惧
他回到人们中间：利客隆的二楼
像一只疲惫的消化不良的胃
正向着对面的双安商场那一对
巨幅民间剪纸式的孩童发出
被汽车喇叭篡改的断断续续的嘟哝

过街天桥僵瘦的犬腹下
道路被分割成等级制的现代平装本
书籍，打开后可供永恒的蓝衣上帝
阅读、分析，重新制定一整套关于
人类行为道德的十诫。他想象
他是以但丁进入丛林的心情踏上了中巴

3
"我们自身就成了正在被书写的诗行……"
这段道路就是例证，找不到任何
可以设想为叙事的情节成份
中巴式的抒情节奏不适合单独面对
后工业时代的大众。他忍受临时性
停车的分行就像忍受激情的放纵

太平庄、农林局、马甸和静安庄
都市中的蚊子或文字飞舞在
噪音的众声喧哗之间；而这丝毫
也不妨碍他使得周围的女性
承受被看的复杂体验。他，张三先生
一个面貌普通的男人的天赋人权

"她们中间谁最热衷于购物，仟村百货
英斯泰克还是燕莎商城？"只能从
衣着上猜想……他家有贤妻，对于
女士们的爱好算是有经验，她们中的一位
爱上叛徒余永泽，就为他的被捕
出自一个与贪吃有关的贤妻的爱好

directly across from Shuang An Department Store,
where one pair of huge kids cut from paper emit
intermittent mutters distorted by car horns.

Cross the street; skywalk the stiff underside of a dog's belly,
the road cut up in paperbacks; open the back cover to offer
sacrifices to the blue-clothed god who reads, analyzes, drafts
anew a complete oeuvre on human behavior in ten moralizing
commandments. He thinks his mood is Dante's
entering the forest, as he steps into the exclusive minibus.

3.
"We ourselves become lines of poetry written by books . . ."
Case in point: at this section of road, we're unable to locate
the imagined components of narrative, a plot.
Alone, the minibus's lyrical rhythm can't lull the post-
industrial masses. He endures his fleeting nature at the bus-
stop, as if it were a self-indulgent fever.

Bus stops: Taiping Zhuang, Nonglin Ju, Madian, Jing'an Zhuang:
they're either the city's mosquitoes or fluttering characters
in the midst of a crowd's raucousness; yet this silk brush
might as well stop him from using women around him
to bear the complicated experience of the gaze. He, Mr. Zhang San,
an ordinary man, is possessed of some natural rights.

"Among women, who is most fond of shopping where: Qiancun Department
Store, Instec, or the Lufthansa Center?" You can only guess
by the clothing . . . his darling wife stays at home, and she knows
her women's hobbies; one among these women was in love with traitor
Yu Yongze; his arrest stems from his dear gluttonous wife's hobby.

4.
Parcel of pig liver and confidential Party materials, love or
revolutionary enterprise,
these are antitheses in the books he's read;
the question he has no time for allegorized
by passengers getting on and off in turn: "Those who want to get on, get on;

413

4

一包猪肝与党的机要，爱情或革命事业
在他阅读过的书籍中构造着对立
他无暇自我论争的问题正被轮流更替
的乘客隐喻着："想上的上来了
到了地儿的就该言语一声" ——历史真谛
就在对于日常语言的过度诠释中

而为什么他得是个身份明确的角色
写作者对他什么也不想演绎，也做不到
他从手提箱里拿出计算器，算一算
他最近的一笔生意能挣得多少
他年轻有为，坐在中巴里也顶多
是个准中产阶级的暴发户？

"面包会有的，一切都会有的"。他赞赏
他夹着万宝路的食指和中指分别代表的
两个国际性的文化雅号：操！胜利在望！而他
把自己准确地定位在香烟的位置
"我正在被我自己的火焰燃尽
并被我自己的烟雾缭绕"

5

"她在一朵云下离开了家"
现在他不能不回忆起他的一个旧情人
这种无聊的时候还能不滋生
后殖民心态的复杂欲望：二等兵王二
不失时机地提醒他往事如烟的愤闷
她如今在地球的另一端扮作情人

幸运的是那时候他们还算认真，而从
某种意义上讲，认真即真诚
一切都已出演了一遍：浪漫、嫉妒
自怜、仇视、乞求、放弃乃至无所谓
由动词和形容词操纵感情世界
成为他们最典型的青春期论文关键词

if it's your stop, say something" — history's meaning
found in excessive annotations of ordinary speech.

But why must his identity be made clear?
Why does the author not want to discover something about him he cannot
    find?
He takes a calculator from his briefcase, checks
how much his business has earned.
His youth is promising; is his seat on the minibus
nothing more than a mark of the nouveau riche?

"Will have bread, will have everything." He admires
the Marlboro pressed between his fingers, distinguished emblem
of two esteemed cultures, characters: Act! Victory lies ahead! Yet he
identifies himself with the cigarette: "I am being burned
to the utmost degree by my own flame
and curl up in my own smoke."

5.
"She left home beneath a cloud."
Now he can't not remember his old love;
this boring era couldn't propagate
the complex desires of postcoloniality: not missing a beat,
Private Second Class Wang Er brings back the past,
like a cigarette's anger and depression;
now elsewhere, she plays the lover's role.

At that time they were thought happily earnest (which, according
to some definitions means "sincere"); it's all been done
before: romance, jealousy, self-pity, hateful eyes, the begging,
giving up no more than indifference with verbs and adjectives —
the emotions they manipulate, keywords of an adolescent thesis.

But always the body first summons wisdom,
prolegomenon of phenomena's ultimate proposition,
inferior to imagination's pleasures as it arrives at the other shore.
Sublimated to her form, however blurred, he draws
the support of a few images: is one woman not all
women? But is he himself?

不过总还是肉体的召唤先于存在
的哲思；现象学的终极命题不及一次
想象中的快感所抵达的彼岸。过犹不及
她的形象却已模糊了，只好借助
一些概念化的图像升华：一个女人不就是
所有的女人？而他是他自己吗？

6
他在具体的风中品尝抽象的雨水
"如果海洋注定要决堤，就让
所有的苦水都注入我心中"
一瞬间他仿佛看见自己手执长矛，冲锋陷阵
弩辛难得晃动着惊人的速度，以终结者
怒吼的错觉，掠过路边的小旅馆和大排档

伸展"我们的睡眠，我们的饥饿"。它拐弯
驰入上帝戒律的法外情，公民规章的试验田
彩灯缠绕树枝，与公益广告牌一同
列队守卫国家的重大节日。"与我相关的世界啊！"
而谁将从他衣冠楚楚的品牌中辨认出
古典的整体性世界观？俄底修斯终将回家

年老、死亡，在一首场景式诗歌中
张三先生从农展馆下车，倒车跳上另一辆中巴
半小时后，鸡窝头的老婆会打开防盗门
迎接他——天色早已昏暗，城市丛林灯红酒绿
下一首诗将记载他遭遇靡非斯陀，而此刻
摆脱路口那三色灯的瞪视，他随我步入夜色

6.

He savors abstract rain water in the concrete wind:
"If oceans are doomed to break dams, then let
the bitter waters empty into my heart."
In an instant, he sees his hand holding a spear;
he charges the enemy position,
this old incompetent swerves with astonishing speed,
his misconceived Terminator screams sweeping past
the small hotel and food stalls beside the road.

He stretches. "Our sleep, our hunger." The corner turns,
he gallops outside God's reasoned commandments, the field of civil rule
colored lights that wind around branches, like ads on public billboards
lining up to guard the country's great festivals.
"The world related to me, oh!"
But who, based on his immaculate dress, gleans his classical
view of the whole world? Odysseus is finally returning home.

Getting along in years, nearing death in a scenic poem,
Mr. Zhang San gets off at Nongzhan Guan, changes buses,
jumps on another minibus;
after half an hour, the mousy-haired missus opens the many-locked door
and greets him — the color of the sky darkened long ago, maze of asphalt
debauched with red lanterns, green wine;
in the next poem he encounters Méphistophélès, but for now
he shakes off the glare of three lights at the intersection, following
me as I trudge into
night's dim territory.

童年的死(组诗选)

唤起记忆即唤起责任。

             ——雅克·德里达

欠债者

他用告别的方式偿清了
他在尘世欠下的钱财　　却把
借来的一根绳子　　永久地拖欠
仿佛所有活人都成了债主
他们暗暗谴责他　　一了百了
而一个初次目击了死亡的孩子
欠下对于人生不变的恐惧
死　　并不可怕　　它只是拉长了
一个人的身体　　把他的影子
张贴在记忆中的土墙上
它还将一个老人在世时的声音
关在了墙缝中……她多次
从梦中惊醒　　听到他的语音
对她唠叨天气　　蜜蜂
和夏天的蚊虫　　(孩子不懂得
厌烦)　　虽然生活正以厌烦的加速度
到来　　容颜易变——死去的老人
永不再老去　　他身形修长
在梦中的路口　　唤起她成长的热情

垂钓者

白天　　老人来河边钓鱼
孩子坐在树下　　惊异于
垂钓者从容不迫　　担心鱼儿
无常的命运　　老人的白天
就这样被孩子目睹　　而他的
夜生活　　她无从猜想
只晓得　　远在一片竹林里

Death in Childhood (selections)

Awakening memory means awakening responsibility.
—Jacques Derrida

Debtor

He used his sign-off to repay
money owed in this world of dust   the rope
borrowed   in perpetual debt
as though everyone alive became his creditor
secretly condemning him   all solutions to follow the one
child   witnessing death   for the first time
in constant fear of life's debt
death is itself   not frightening   it's only prolonged
a person's body posts his shadow
on memory's earthen wall
takes an old man's voice while he lives
shutting it behind the wall . . . she startles
awake from her dreams   hearing the cadence of his speech
his chatter about the weather   about bees
and summer's mosquitoes   (children can't fathom
boredom)   using boredom's quickening, life
arrives   appearances swiftly change – now he's dead
he'll never again grow old   his body slender
at the intersection of dreams   arousing her adult desires

Fisherman

During the day, an old man comes to fish the river
a child sits beneath a tree   surprised
the fisherman is calm, unhurried   unlike the fish
whose fate is changeable   the old man's day
witnessed by the child   though she
can hardly guess at his night-time
she only knows that in a bamboo grove far away
one can barely discern the old man's house   the child never

老人的小屋若隐若现　孩子从未
走近深绿的竹荫　但她
守候过老人　小河边　雨水天
斗笠下的白胡子　闪着银光
犹如鲫鱼的肚皮　鱼儿的命运
装在竹篓里　被他拎走
整个夏天　雨水和小河
顺着老人的身影流淌　树下
孩子的板凳陷到了土里　担心着
鱼儿水下的命运　她们来了又去
把鱼饵含在口中　又吐掉
有时候　她们中的一个
会侥幸地上钩　被老人带走
走上另外的命运　见人　谈话　微笑
有礼貌……孩子聆听老人的教诲
夏天不利于孩子成长　夏天的身体
暴露　蚊虫的热情　像鱼儿从水中
让老人领走　布满死亡烂臭味的夏天
离我们太近　某夜　竹林小屋
老人死于谋财害命
人们传言——太多的鬼魂追上了他

　蛇

源于恐惧　杀戮超越了死亡
施加于我们心灵中的敬畏
像人们亵渎过鬼神
她杀死过一条毒蛇　这意味着
死亡通过她畏惧的双手
实现了威严的能动性　像一张
表情丰富的面孔　死亡
在一条蛇的躯壳上闪现
全部的美　好像它的存在
就是为了她逃避的勇气而生
为在一瞬间　尸体的信念博得
力量的同情　一条蛇的死亡

420

enters the dark green bamboo shelter   keeps watch
for the old man on the small river bank on a rainy day
his white whiskers visible under a bamboo hat   flashing silver
like a crucian carp's belly   the fish meets his fate
is loaded into a bamboo basket   carried off by the fisherman
during this entire day   rainwater and the small river
trace the child's shadow   under the tree
as her bench caves in   she worries
about the fishes' fate as they come and go
grasping the bait in their mouths   spitting it out
sometimes   one among them
luckily takes the bait   scooped up by the old man
who walks into another fate   sees people chatting   smiling
courteously . . . the child listens to the old man's teachings
she cannot grow up during summer   summer's body
unveils   mosquitoes' fervor   like fish out of water
leads the old man away   in summer's foul stench, suffused with death
too near to us   on that night   in the small house in a bamboo grove
the old man was killed for money
though rumor has it too many ghosts kept chasing him

Snake

Dread at the source   slaughter exceeding death
To exact our spirits' reverence
like people blaspheming ghosts and gods
she has killed a poisonous snake   meaning
death has passed through both her dreaded hands
achieving majesty like a face
lined with feeling   death flashes
before a snake's outward form
its entire beauty so it seems existence
depends on evading courage and lives
so for an instant the corpse's conviction gains
the sympathy of physical strength   the death of one snake
persisting in memory, the revenge of legends
cloaked in nightly dreams to emerge, skittering,

存活在记忆中　而传说中的复仇
以夜梦的形式曲折地展现
欲望号街车疾驰在黑暗中　城市的
脏空气搅动了睡眠中的房梁
草叶　沙滩和起劲挥动的头发
当它从梦的舞台上退场　白昼
将为她招魂　风提醒我　用嘴唇

灵魂和她的伴侣

你可以说她是她身体里
开放的一枝花，这意味着
春天和夏天正在经历
一次货真价实的冒险，想一想
青春时代渴望永恒的秘密吧
花朵在衣裙上找到镜像
尽管季节和异邦趣味会影响
本地时装的风格，就像花开花落

你也可以说她是她身体里
安静的一杯水，这等于说
愿望带来的是类似
焦渴的肌体反应，只有
柏拉图相信，杯水风波
可以忽略不计，而她近乎虚无
的呼喊，曾经招致时代的消防车
昂扬的应答，像忠诚的情侣

也可能她只是绣在她
衣襟上的微型风景，代表
分享时尚带给她的临时身份
"我是我自己的。"她说着
以一种狂热和急切的口吻
感到唯有一个激进的上帝倾听着

as a streetcar named desire winds through the darkness   the city's
smoggy air stirring sleep's beams
its leaves of grass   on a sandy beach its wild and waving hair
when it leaves the dream stage   daytime
calls back the spirit of the dead for her   the wind alerts me   use your lips

The Spirit and Her Companion

You could say she's her body's
blooming flower, meaning
that spring and summer engage
their time in risks-taking.
Consider that youth thirsts for perpetual
secrecy, as flowers find mirrored images
on dresses, though the tastes of seasons
and other cultures influence latest
fashions, like flowers blooming and falling.

You could say she's her body's quiet
water glass, which lets us know
what desire brings us is like
the reaction of a parched body; no one
but Plato believed waves in a water glass
could be left unnoticed, uncounted; she's close to shouting
out from nothingness, having recruited high-spirited sirens
of the era's fire engines, like loyal lovers.

It's also possible she's only sewn onto
the tiny landscape of her lapel, denoting
the passing identity offered her by fashion.

"I'm my own self," she says,
feverish and impatient, feeling
there's but one radical god
listening to her forceful, blind words
who soon attempts to encircle her in arms.

她这句有力的、盲目的话
并试图随后用双臂将她环抱

窗外

我时常想象自己抬起头，从书页上
我想象自己，看到了一片海
有蓝色的液体，游过窗棂
但我所能领受的，只是一小片海域
我告诉自己，那从来就不是
全部的深广，况且
我坐在一个固定的地方
它提醒我，想象，也不能是无限的
想象有一个天然的出发点
也许它有自由
如海鸟一样的翅膀
而我们的心灵要能够
提供树枝
供白日的梦想，一个栖息的支点

新雪

雪落下，又好像在飞起
屋顶和地面铺设的一层
神秘地承受并掩埋着
空气中滚过的声音，远处的刹车
和二胡，发动机在楼下低吼
都是落雪的声音，漫天盖过
雪此时就是一切的碎片，万物的回声
是夜的翅膀飞到了白天
或是白天的梦想跳着舞，直舞到暗夜
雪也有翅膀吗？它有
洁白的引擎和冰凉的方向盘
它驶向我的窗口，沿着虚拟的

Outside the Window

Often, I imagine lifting my head from the page.
I imagine seeing a fraction of the sea,
its field of blue, beyond the window's edge.
But all I glimpse is one small part of the ocean.
So I say to myself, that's not
its full depth or expanse —
besides, I'm only sitting in one place.
It alerts me, imagination has limits.
I know it, too, must begin somewhere;
perhaps it has the freedom
of the sea bird's wings —
like those our soul covets —
offering us branches,
feeding our daydreams
on a perched fulcrum.

New Snow

Snow falls, taking flight,
roof and floor compressed to a single story,
mysteriously bearing and suppressing
the sound of the wind's rolling, screech of faraway brakes
and the erhu's melody, the motor growling
lightly below; all are sounds of falling
snow, filling the sky, everything covered over,
splintered, as ten thousand echoes
are night wings flying til morning,
or daydreams dancing til night falls.
Does snow have wings? Has a pure white
engine and ice cold steering wheel; drives
to my window along a blue highway,
but it's more astronaut than race car driver,
one who falls by another planet, toward
earth's weightlessness; it's like
the indulgences of love, fantasies

太空高速路，但它又不是呼啸的飙车手
它更像从另一个星球
降临的宇航员，掉进了地球
失重的气层；它像
正沉溺在爱恋中的人，幻想着
遥远的也就是接近的
它轻叩着我的窗玻璃，说：
"等着，我来接你
去你想去的地方——"
这是春节过后，第一场雪
这是新的雪，落在我的早晨

that what is far is actually close by;
A tap at my windowpane announces:
"Wait, I'm coming to get you
to go wherever you want to go —"
Spring Festival has passed,
the first snowfall — this is new
snow, falling in my morning.

Postface: On the Translation

The translations in this anthology are the result of a two-step process: the literal translation from the Chinese original to an English "raw" or "draft" translation, and then the transformation of these drafts into poetry. This process was accomplished by two groups of individuals whose talent and knowledge complimented each other, each having an intimacy with either the Chinese original text or poetics in English. Chen Dongdong and I made the choice of this two-step strategy before we began the editorial work of selecting poetry for the anthology. This choice was made by necessity. In an ideal world, American poets, equally accomplished as their counterparts in China, would be equipped with sufficient knowledge of the Chinese language to render the translation single-handedly. In the absence of such an ideal, the project brought about the necessary collaboration through a two-year process involving much deliberations and effort. We found that one American poet working with a Chinese poet through a literal translator brought about a high level of an English version of the original Chinese poem. I completely agree with Willis Barnstone, one of the pioneers in translating modern Chinese poetry into English, when he writes "We should not read inferior translations, since they traduce the work of the author." Therefore we should not produce inferior translations.

This process is nothing new in the world of translation, especially in translating Chinese poetry into English. The well-known and influential translation of classical Chinese poetry from Japanese trots by Eza Pound pointed to the possibility of an intellectually productive collaboration of the informative and the creative in translation. A few years back, *New Generation*, the anthology of Chinese poetry in translation edited by Wang Ping, also followed a similar strategy. Yet the process in itself doesn't guarantee successful translation and is as difficult and risky as it is opaque. It would be interesting to publish the final polished poems together with the back and forth revisions from the first draft, negotiating word by word, line by line between the literal/fidelity and the liberal/creativity. On the average, it took the translators four to five revisions to agree on a translation. Between the versions, translators discussed or "talked through" the poems line by line via telephone, in face to face conversation if they happened to live near each other, and most likely for this book, via emails. As translators worked in different styles, it is hard for me here to capture and display a full picture of the working process for all of them. Having said that, let's examine the translation process of a short poem by Chen Dongdong, "Light the Lamp." It is one of the smoother and less problematic translations in the anthology. However, it went through transformations like other poems in the book. The four versions here show the roles of each party and the care given by all involved, particularly the important role of the poet-translator, Joseph Donahue, who "massaged" or "fiddled," as he put it, with every word and every line to make the draft a poem, and further to make the poem sing in the translated tongue.

Draft 1 by Chen Dongbiao (CDB):

> Light the lamp into the stone, let them see
> the stance of the sea, let them see
> fish of the ancient times
> And let them see the bright light too,
> a lamp raised high on a mountain
>
> The lamp should also be lit into the river water, let them see
> living fish, let them see
> the sea without a sound
> you ought to let them see the sunset too
> a firebird bucks up from the forest
>
> Light the lamp. When I block the north wind with my hands
> when I stand between the canyons
> I think they will crowd around me
> they will come to see my words
> like the lamp

Draft 2 by Joseph Donahue (JD):

> Shine the lamp on the stone. Let them see
> the swirling of the sea. Let them see
> the primordial fish.
> Let them see the light itself,
> a lamp raised high on a mountain.

Shine the lamp into the river. Let them see
living fish. Let them see
deep into the silence of the water.
Also, show them what a sunset is like —
a firebird bursting from the forest.

Light the lamp. When I fend off the north wind with my hands
when I stand between the canyons
let everyone crowd around me
let them see my words are
also a lamp

Draft 3 with my modification and notes (ZE):

Shine the lamp <u>into</u> the stone. Let them see[*]
the <u>swirling/posture</u> of the sea. Let them see[†]
the primordial fish.
Let them see the light itself,
a lamp raised high on a mountain.

Shine the lamp into the river. Let them see
living fish. Let them see
deep into the silence of the water.
Also, show them what a sunset is like —
a firebird bursting from the forest.

Light the lamp. When I fend off the north wind with my hands
when I stand between the canyons
let everyone crowd around me
let them see my words are
also a lamp

---

[*]the original word is "li," inside, which is bit odd, most likely he is talking about fossils/rock with primordial fish in it. I like your choice of "primordial."

[†]swirling is fine, the original word is "zishi," means posture/position/stand. Swirling adds the action to it. Your choice.

Final version: Light the Lamp

Shine the lamp into the stone.
Let them see the swirling print of the sea.
Let them see the primordial fish.
Let them see the light itself,
a lamp raised high on a mountain.

Shine the lamp into the river.
Let them see living fish. Let them see
More deeply into the silence of the water.
Also, show them what a sunset is like —
a firebird bursting from the forest.

When* I fend off the north wind
with my hands, light the lamp.
When· I stand between the canyons
let them crowd around me, let them see
my words are a lamp

Here is another example of a little more involved process for the last stanza
of Chen Dongdong's *Waibaidu Bridge*:

Draft version by CDB:

The old pinions of the iron bridge flap with all strength
The volitation lands heavily onto the other bank
The city tentacle stretching out of the space
Joins and stitches centuries with birds' defeat
To penetrate through every road of rebirth
But the numerous and jumbled structure makes it abound ambiguity
The power of delirium, even lifts it up

JD's version 1:

---

*JD replaced "when" in lines 1 and 3 with "while" in the galleys.

The hinges of the bridge rise and fall
What flight there is tumbles onto the other bank
The city is like a tentacle stretching out into space
centuries are held together by the failure of escape
if only to travel down every road of rebirth
the bridge is a prison of ambiguity
delirium passes here for freedom

Email from JD to ZE:
A question: my trouble here is with the word tentacle. Is the bridge compared
here to a tentacle, as in the arm of an octopus? I find it hard to fit that image,
given that DD[*] is not a full-blown surrealist, with the scheme of bird imagery
associated with the bridge. Am I correct that the bridge and not the city is
being compared to a tentacle in line 3, and is there any other words beside
tentacle that I could play with here, or does he actually mean for us to insert
the mental picture of an octopus, or a squid, into our meditation on the bridge?

Email from ZE to JD:
literally he said, "touching hand" of the city. yes, the bridge is the touching
hand which belongs to the city. touching hand in Chinese is clearly
associated with either insect or octopus or machine. not of birds though.
maybe we should go with the "mechanical arm" to fit the bridge's structure,
rather than to animate it.
he is kind of surreal here, half blown.

JD's version 2:

The hinges of the bridge rise and fall
What flight there is tumbles onto the other bank
The bridge is a limb of the city stretching out into space
the centuries are linked by our failure to escape
if only down the road of every rebirth . . .
Ambiguous prison: the bridge is held in air
by the sheer force of our delirium.

---

[*]"DD" is an abbreviation for Cheng Dongdong.

ZE to JD:
here is my two cents:

> The hinges of the bridge rise and fall
> What flight there is tumbles onto the other bank
> The bridge is a limb of the city stretching out into space
> the centuries are linked by its failure to soar *
> if only over the route of every rebirth . . . *
> Ambiguous cumbersome/colossal structure: the bridge is held in air *
> by the sheer force of our delirium.

JD to ZE:

I take it that the "prison" concept is out, which is fine with me. Was it even in the original? Of the three adjectives that now modify "structure" which ones are in the text? Is it "ambiguous" and then something like "cumbersome" or "colossal" ? Are there other possibilities for ambiguous, since it is hard for me to hold together ambiguous and say colossal, since what can really be ambiguous about something so big and obvious? Clearly, what the bridge represents, in terms of aspiration and escape etc. is ambiguous, its just hard, to my ear to apply the term ambiguous to a large metal structure. Could ambivalent work? I'll figure something out. My main concern is I don't want to have too many syllables running around in the penultimate line, it blunts the effect of the last line.

ZE to JD:

you are such a fine poet, Joe, can one get even closer to the words?

No. the prison is not in the original. the 2nd to the last line is literally: but the huge and confused (or numerous and jumbled, or cumbersome) structure make it so ambiguous.

---

*back to the bird image here, the bridge is the bird, its failure to be airborne long enough/flight. Please tweak. Near nearer the peak of perfection.

It is an odd sequence in the Chinese too. cumbersome structure is ambiguous. I think he means that its presence/intention is hard to explain. or its cumbersome structure is unexplainable . . .

I will accept your solution.

JD to ZE:

Here it is, another attempt to climb the mountain of perfection! I have my ice pick, my water bottle, a chocolate bar and of course the holy bible! I fiddled with the third line a bit, substituting reach for limb. My thinking here is merely that the limb image, while it saves us from the intrusive picture of a squid or octopus, still raises questions in the reader's mind. If the bridge is essentially like a bird, then it can't quite be called a limb. Even if it's a limb of a bird, that is a wing. Then it would sound like the city is the body of the bird, and the bridge is its wing. So I've put reach instead, a bit more abstract, but then maybe closer in a way to the Chinese sense of "touch" that you said was in the original. As for the last two lines, I think "so much" gets enough of the sense of colossal, and that iron in air gets the uncanniness of the bridge, and prepares us for the idea that it is "upheld" by collective desire. I realize the word eerie is different from ambiguous, but they are related, and it sets the last two lines more within the perceiving consciousness. I think the sense of eerieness is latent within ambiguous here, and that its a more emotionally effective adjective. Twice the word for half the syllables! Also, while span is different from structure, I believe it conveys the sense of the architectural design, while communicating some of the energy and daring of building any kind of bridge. And at one syllable, it's a bargain!

Anyway, let me know what you think.

JD's final version:

> The hinges of the bridge rise and fall
> What flight there is tumbles onto the other bank
> The bridge is the reach of the city into space
> The centuries are linked by its failure to soar
> if only over the route of every rebirth . . .
> Eerie span: so much iron held in the air

by the sheer force of our delirium.

Here are a few examples of Email correspondence between the translators and from translators to this editor on the process to illustrate the essence of the task at hand:

Between a poet translator (P) and a literal translator (L):

P: For me, the first duty of a translator is to make a version in English that works as English . . . this often requires transpositions not only of language but of fact, culture, etc. What may be coherent, visually, to a speaker of Chinese may be incoherent to an English reader . . . i.e. language is also in the eye. Lord knows, it makes for difficulties. . . . but there are also opportunities for invention, as Pound showed in his Cathay. . . .

L: I totally agree that the final poems should be English poems not clunky translations from the Chinese. Still since we are two people who each knows one language intimately, we have an advantage over Pound . . . i completely trust you on the English version's poetic quality. the revision is not a question of that. it is its distance from the Chinese original. After all we are not here to rewrite the poem for [the Chinese poet]. Especially these are not my own work, i do not have the liberty to disregard/reduce certain layers of the poems (or to add new elements to them).

P: But let's be bold about translation. . . . some things, and sometimes important ones, I have found, will always be discarded and some things added. . . . a boat must be re-fitted to sail in different waters, sometimes radically refitted. . . . our translation will succeed if it advocates the original for which, of course, it cannot substitute. . . . I remember once seeing a kangaroo lost in a snowstorm in Missouri. . . . it had clearly escaped from some local petting zoo . . . we don't want to make a kangaroo in the snow.

L: Yet, we don't want to dress the kangaroo up in wolves' skin in order to match the snow either. . . . Please re-read my last version and see if there is anything that you can incorporate back into the current version. The translation in my mind should expand rather than deduct the poem, because additional energy/efforts from the collective intelligence pool have poured in it. On the other hand, "Leave it all out is another way, perhaps a truer way," quoting Ashbery . . .

Between a potential translator (T, who declined to participate in the project) and the editor (E) on the two step strategy:

T: I confess I have my doubts about anthologies where a bunch of poets who know nothing about the original language or culture are given "trots" to turn into poems. I don't think you have to be an expert in the original language, but you should know something, otherwise it turns into a kind of airport art.

E: I am touched by your concern/doubts. yet, as Mao stated once, "One can only learn the taste of the pear by eating it." i view the process of collaborating translation as a way of crossing the culture/language barrier on the micro-level, as a way of touching the other. In most cases, the "trots" here are much closer to the real thing than what Pound had when he tasted his pear. His poetic invention and his linguistic mistakes are more interesting than most of sinologists' correctness. to me, a bunch of poets who are willing to risk their reputations by venturing into a unfamiliar arena are more attractive than a bunch of sinologists/academics who have no interest in poetry per se.

A literal translator's retrospective comment on the collaboration with a poet translator:

Hard to explain [the process]. Sometimes through [the poet translator]'s misreading my English, I became aware of meanings I didn't realize my words would generate. Also as we went back and forth about individual poems, even lines and words, I could feel [the poet translator] coming closer to what I saw [the original] words meaning. I sensed that the process of gradually discerning the structure of meaning through my sometimes misleading or disorganized English was exciting for [the poet translator]. Finally, [the poet translator]'s questions or word choices often required me to consult [the Chinese poet], which I had done little during the translation phase (when I tried a few times early, I had trouble getting answers I could use). But when I returned with very specific questions I sometimes discovered that I had made silly mistakes in my translation (thank God I caught them!), and I also got much clearer answers from [the Chinese poet].

The translations in the anthology are the result of collaboration of many talented people. This is manifested in the long list of translators at the back of the book. More than twenty Chinese scholars, linguists, graduate students and sometimes the poets themselves contributed in the literal translation. They have an intimate knowledge of the Chinese language. It's either their mother tongue or a main focus of study for many years. They painstakingly translated as accurately as they could the Chinese original poems into English drafts. Many a time, the drafts were accompanied by comments and notes, multiple choices of wordings, to clarify or to point out hidden layers of original work without glossing over it. Many literal translators also participated in the second step of the translation, the transformation of the drafts into poetry. They offered background information on the language and culture in general and chose words, rhythm, voices, personal characteristics of individual poets at hand, as questions often were raised by the poet-translators working from the drafts. Most importantly their feedback are largely responsible for the fundamental accuracy of the translation in the anthology. For poets whose literal translators were not available for the second-step consultation, I would play the role of the "reality" check of the literal translators.

An equal number of poets writing in English (mostly American, one Canadian, one British and one Egyptian) participated in the second step of the translation. These poets are poets whose poetics attracted my attention before or during the project. Many are established poets with multiple volumes of published poetry and are winners of prizes and fellowships in poetry. In most cases, their seriousness in their poetic undertaking was demonstrated by their previous experience in translation. They shared the common belief, as I deduced from reading their poetry even though I never took a formal survey, that language means and therefore translation is possible. Their poetic style varies greatly, yet they tend to be versatile in handling language, employing various strategies, and commanding large vocabularies in their own creative work.

Whenever possible, I attempted to "match" the voice of a poet-translator with that of a Chinese poet. The poet translators have their individualized strategies that they use in treatment of line breaks, rhythm, schemes of extension and contraction of space and pace. It would serve the poetry they are translating better if they would be able to utilize their talent "naturally." So I tried to take this into consideration when choosing which American poets would work with which Chinese poets. Other considerations such as similar social identities, beliefs and poetics sometimes also played into the matching schemes. However, my role as an editor/match-maker figured small in the success of the poem/marriage. The creativity and skills of the poet-translators and their devotion to their charge are entirely responsible for the poetic success of the translations.

The large team of translators who contributed to the anthology offered many diverse voices, many strategies in translation and poetics, to say nothing of abundant energy and intelligence. No effort has been made on my part to standardize the translations, as I saw diversity as an advantage. The reader will find translators with a minimalist approach who intentionally left traces of "raw" material uncovered, translators working with scholarly diligence, documenting their translations with notations and comments, and translators who tweaked every word. Some even tried to make their Chinese counterparts adopt an American accent. "There are many roads to China," says Tony Barnstone, Willis Barnstone's son, in his insightful essay "The Poem Behind the Poem: Literary Translation as American Poetry." I hope this book offers a few useful tips and a road map for those who intend to travel far. Readers would benefit most by examining the bilingual text in detail and accepting the challenge of comparing translators' styles in order to understand the "Chinese" poetics.

In spite of the efforts and deliberations by the translators and this editor, the outcry by Wai-lim Yip remains relevant. In his introduction to *Chinese Poetry*, an anthology of classical Chinese poetry edited and translated by himself, Yip speaks against "gross distortions of Chinese poetry by translators who allowed the target language to mask and master the indigenous Chinese aesthetic, creating treacherous modes of representation." Although this anthology is of contemporary work, Yip's description of the Chinese language and its difference from Indo-European languages remains true: "The Chinese language has articles and personal pronouns, they are often dispensed with in poetry. This opens up an indeterminate space for readers to enter and reenter for multiple perceptions rather than locking them into some definite perspectival position or guiding them in a certain direction." However, difficulties arise in translation from Chinese to English, as I observed during composition of this anthology, not so much from "tyrannical framing functions of the English language" as Yip put it, but from the fact that each language resides in its distinct domain of metaphysics, at least in part, in different epistemologies. In other words, each language offers a different conception of knowledge, therefore the world. The so-called Chinese poetics and the answer to what Chinese poetry offers to world literature are precisely derived from the fundamental stand of Eastern ideology (see my preface).

I want to express my special thanks to Ying Qin, who devoted countless hours of hard and careful work in rendering several poets' poems into "draft" translations and has been such a rich source of council for many poet-translators. Also to John Balcom, Martin Corless-Smith, Daniel Comiskey, and Maged Zaher for taking up the translation on a short notice in the face of pressures of all kinds. To my husband, Leonard Schwartz who recommended several poet-translators for the project, edited this very postface and the my preface, in addition to completing his own translation for the book. To Martine Bellen, who copyedited my preface and postface in addition to her translation for the book. To Richard Sieburth, who advised me on the translation process and the design of the project, and edited my preface. To Leung Ping-kwan, a poet and scholar of Hong Kong, who listened with indulgence to my monologue on the composition of the book's preface at the 2005 Taipei Poetry Festival, and offered valuable feedback. To Wai-Lim Yip for his inspirational scholarly essays on Chinese poetics. Finally to Ed Foster of Talisman House, Publishers, whose unfailing patience and support for the project made the impossible possible.

Zhang Er
November 25, 2005
Olympia, WA

Contributors

Chinese Poets:

Cao Shuying was born in Nov. 1979 in Ha'erbin of Heilongjiang Province. She obtained her Ph.D. from Beijing University in comparative literature and world literature. Her poems have been collected in numerous anthologies and periodicals including *Writers, People's Literature, Star,* and *Poetry,* as well as in many nonofficial poetry journals such as *Wings, Deviation, Selected Poems of 70's Poets, Battlefield,* and *Provinces.* Besides poetry, Cao writes fiction and fairy tales.

Chen Dongdong was born in 1961 in Shanghai and started writing when he was twenty. He graduated from the Chinese Literature Department of Shanghai Normal University. Chen has been a teacher, archive clerk, opera journal editor, website designer and writer, and poetry journal editor. He is the author of multiple volumes of poetry and prose including his most recent poetry collection *Down to Yang Zhou* (2001).

Han Bo was born 1973 in Mu Dan Jiang, Hei Long Jiang Province. He graduated from Fu Dan University in Shanghai with law and literature degrees. He is the author of multiple poetry collections including *No Entry for Minors* (2000) and *A Banquet of Knots* (2002). He won the Li-An Liu poetry prize in 1998. He has also been writing and directing plays since 1996. His short stories have been published in literary journals.

Han Dong, born in 1961, graduated with a bachelor in philosophy from Shan Dong University. He is the author of numerous books of poetry, fiction and nonfiction. He was the editor of the poetry journal *They.* He has been involved in various Internet journals and publication venues since 2000.

Hu Xudong, poet, column writer, was born in 1974 in He Chuan, Chong Qing. He obtained his Ph.D. in Literature from Beijing University. He is an associate professor at the World Literature Research Institute at Beijing University. He visited and lectured in Brazil from 2003 to 2005. He is the author of three collections of poetry, including *From the Water's Edge, Wind Milk,* and *When Love Is a Spreading Disease.* He has been awarded many poetry prizes such as the Liu Li-An poetry prize and the Tomorrow Poetry Prize. His poetry has been translated into many languages including English, Spanish, Portuguese, Japanese, French, German, and Swedish.

Huang Canran was born in 1963 in the ancient city of Quanzhou, Fujian Province, Mainland China. He immigrated to Hong Kong in 1978 when he was fifteen and returned many years later, graduating from Jinan University, Guangzhou in 1988 with a degree in journalism. Since 1990, he has worked at *Ta Kung Pao Daily* in Hong Kong as an international news translator. He has published three books of poetry, a book of essays on poetry and translation, and is currently editing an anthology of Hong Kong poetry. He is also an acclaimed Chinese translator of many Western poets and writers.

Jiang Tao was born in the 1970s and started writing in the 1990s. His work has been published in many poetry journals and poetry collections, including *Sadness*, *Sometimes*, and *Canon of Bird*.

Lan Lan was born in 1967 in Yantai, Shandong Province, China. She graduated in 1988 from Zhengzhou University in Henan Province. She began to publish poems when she was fourteen years old and has since worked as a factory worker and a literary editor. A winner of Anne Kao Poetry Prize in 1996, Lan Lan has published several books of poetry, prose, and children's stories.

Lü De-An was born in 1960 in Fu Zhou, Fu Jian Province. He is a trained painter and interior designer. In the 1980s, he was one of the founding member of the poetry journal *They*. He is the author of multiple volumes of poetry, including *Paper Snake*, *The North from the South*, and *A Stubborn Rock*. He first visited the United States in the early 1990s. He currently lives in New York City and Fu Jian.

Ma Lan is a member of the Hui minority and was born in Meishan County, Sichuan in the 1960s. In 1982 she began working in a bank, where she served as an accountant for ten years. In 1993 she immigrated to the United States, first living in New York, and is currently living at Yale University in New Haven, Connecticut. One of the originators of the major online Chinese literary website *Olive Tree (Ganlan shu)*, Ma Lan is currently editor in chief. Her fiction, poetry, and essays have appeared in magazines and newspapers around the world. A German translation of her short story "Shi cong" (Hearing loss) appeared in 2003 in the anthology, *Das Leben ist jetzt: Neue Erzählungen aus China*. She is the author of the poetry collection *Zuo zai nali (Where Shall I Sit?)* and the short story collection *Hua fei hua (Flowers Are Not Flowers)*.

Mo Fei was born in Beijing on Dec 31, 1960. He began his writing career in 1970s. His main works includes *Palm Trees* (a book-length poem, 1982), *A Band of Mad Men* (a poetic drama, 1985), *Emptiness of the Empty* (a collection of poems, 1987), *Words and Things* (1989-1991), *Spiritual History* (a collection of poems, 1996), *Days Without Description* (a book-length poem, 1995), *Garden Without Time* (a book-length poem, 1996), *Words Without Scenes* (a book-length poem, 1996), *Scissors Without Cutting* (a book-length poem, 1997), *A Collection of Sonnets* (1999), *Record of Passing the Lamp* (a collection of poems, 2000), *Qingliang Mountain* (a collection of poems, 2002). His works has been translated into English, French, German, Italian, Greek, Spanish, Dutch, and Arabic. In November of 1997, he was invited to attend the Fourth International Poetry Festival in Paris, France. He is now living in Beijing.

Qing Ping, born in 1962 in Su Zhou, went to Beijing for college in 1983. He stayed and worked in Beijing after he graduated. He won Li-An Liu prize for his poetry in 1996. His poetry collection *A Kind of Persons* is forthcoming.

Sang Ke was born in 1967. He grew up in Heilongjiang Province and graduated from Beijing Normal University in 1989. He taught writing at Changchun College of Geology, and later became a newspaper editor at Harbin. He has published several collections of poetry, including *Snow at Midnight* (1987), *Untitled* (1988), and *Fifteen Poems* (1997). He is Philip Larkin's and W.H. Auden's Chinese translator.

Shu Cai was born in Fenghua, Zhejiang in1965. He majored in French at Beijing Foreign Study University. From 1990 to 1994 he was a diplomat of the Chinese embassy in Senegal. Since 2000, he has worked in the Foreign Literature Research Institute of the Chinese Academy of Social Sciences. His published works include *A Loner* (1997), a poetry selection and *Peep* (2000), an essay selection. His works have been translated into English, French, Spanish, Italian, and Arabic. He was invited to attend the 4th International Poetry Festival in Paris in 1997. He also translated such books as *Selected Poems of Pierre Reverdy*, *Selected Poems of Rene Char*, and *Selected Poems of Yves Bonnefoy*. He is now living in Beijing.

Tang Danhong was born in November 1965 in Chengdu, Sichuan, and graduated from Sichuan University in 1986. She started to write poetry in the 1990s and won the Li-An Liu poetry prize in 1995. Her work of poetry has been widely published in literary journals and anthologies, and has been translated into Spanish and Swedish, as well as English. She is also a documentary filmmaker.

Yang Jian was born in 1967 in An Hui Province. He started to write poetry in 1986 and won the first Li-An Liu poetry prize in 1995. His poetry collection *Dusk* was published in 2003. He is a Buddhist monk living in seclusion.

Yang Xiaobin, poet and critic, received his B.A. degree from Fudan University (Shanghai, China), M.A. from the University of Colorado, and Ph.D. from Yale University. His major publications include *Chuanyue yangguang didai* (*Across the Sunlight Zone*), which won the 1994 Award for the First Book of Collected Poems in Taiwan, and *The Chinese Postmodern: Trauma and Irony in Chinese Avant-Garde Fiction*. He has served as editor-in-chief of *Xiandaishi* (*Modern Poetry Quarterly*), the most prestigious poetry journal in Taiwan, and editor-at-large of *Qingxiang* (*Tendency*), a leading Chinese journal of humanities and literature based in North America.

Ye Hui was born on November 13, 1964 in Gao Chun County, Jiang Su Province. He is the author of poetry collection *In the Candy Store*. He lives in Gao Chun.

Zang Di was born in Beijing in April 1964. He obtained his Ph.D. in Literature from Beijing University and is an associate professor at Beijing University. He worked briefly as a journalist in Chinese New Agency. He started writing poetry in 1983. He is the author of *Memory of Yan Yuan* (Culture and Art Press, 1998), *Wind Blows and Grass Wave* (Chinese Workers' Publisher, 2000) and *Fresh Thorns* (New World, 2002). He edited several anthologies of poetry and poetics and unofficial poetry journals, as well as the Chinese translation of *The Selected Work of Rilke*.

Zhang Er was born in Beijing in the 1960s and moved to New York City in 1986. She is the author of three collections of poetry in Chinese, *Seen, Unseen* (QingHai Publishing House of China, 1999), *Water Words* (New World Poetry Press, 2002), and *Because of Mountain* (Tonsan, Taipei, 2005). Her most recent chapbooks in translation are *Carved Water*, and *Sight Progress*. *Verses on Bird*, Zhang Er's selected poems (an English bilingual edition) was published by Zephyr Press in 2004. She has worked as a contributing editor for several Chinese poetry journals, such as *First Line*, *Poetry Currents*, and *Oliver Tree*. She teaches at The Evergreen State College in the state of Washington.

Zhang Zao was born in December 1962 in Changsha, Hunan Province. He graduated from the English department in Hunan Normal College and went on to earn his master degree in American and English literature from Sichuan Foreign Language College. He moved to Germany in September 1986 and earned his doctoral degree in literature from Tübingen University. His poetry is collected in *Letters of Spring and Autumn* (1998).

Zhang Zhen in the early 1980s began publishing poems in Chinese literary magazines as well as underground venues in China. While dividing her time between Sweden, China, Japan and United States during the last two decades, she continued to write, publish and take part in public readings. Her book of poetry *Mengzhong louge* (*Dream Mansion*) was published by the Chunfeng Wenyi Publishing House in 1997. Zhang Zhen is also a film scholar, currently teaching cinema studies at New York University. She is the author of *An Amorous History of the Silver Screen: Shanghai Cinema, 1897-1937* (University of Chicago, 2005).

Zhao Xia was born in September 1976 in Shanghai. She was the proprietor of an art gallery in Shanghai, and has edited several Internet poetry journals. She is the author of two volumes of poetry collection, *Seven Lilies in Barbarism* and *Paper-Back Spring*. She translated work of Paul Celan and Gunter Grass into Chinese. She currently lives in Germany, Nanjing, and Hong Kong

Zhou Zan was born in 1968 in Ru Dong, Jiang Su Province. She graduated from the Chinese Department of Yang Zhou University in 1989 and obtained her Ph.D. in Literature from Beijing University. She started writing poetry while attending university and is the author of multiple publications including *Dreaming or Self Questioning* in 1999. She is the editor of poetry journal *Wings*, which is exclusively dedicated to women's writing.

Translators:

John Balcom has been translating modern Chinese literature for a quarter century. He is the head of the Chinese program in the Graduate School of Translation and Interpretation at the Monterey Institute of International Studies as well as the president of the American Literary Translators Association. His *Indigenous Writers of Taiwan: An Anthology of Stories, Essays and Poems* was published by Columbia University Press in 2005.

Joshua Beckman is the author of four books of poetry, most recently *Your Time Has Come* (Verse Press, 2004). He is also a translator of the work of Tomaz Salalmun, and *Five Meters of Poems* by Carlos Oquendo de Amat (Ugly Duckling Press, 2005).

Jody Beenk did her graduate work in Chinese linguistics in the U.S. and in Taiwan. She has collaborated most recently on a translation of Bei Dao's essay "Allen Ginsberg" in *Blue House* (Zephyr Press).

Martine Bellen is the author of six collections of poetry including *The Vulnerability of Order*, Copper Canyon Press; *Tales of Murasaki and Other Poems*, Sun & Moon Press, which won the National Poetry Series Award; and *Places People Dare Not Enter*, Potes & Poets Press. She's a recipient of the New York Foundation for the Arts, the Fund for Poetry, and the American Academy of Poets Award.

Charles Borkhuis' recent books include *Mouth of Shadows* (plays), *Savoir-Fear* (poems) and *Alpha Ruins* (poems), selected by Fanny Howe as runner-up for the William Carlos Williams 2001 Book Award. His book-length poem *Afterimage* was published by Chax Press in 2006. His essays on poetry recently appeared in two books: *Telling It Slant: Avant-garde Poetics of the 1990s* and *We Who Love to Be Astonished: Experimental Women's Writing and Performance Poetics*, both from the U. of Alabama Press. His play *Phantom Limbs* won a Drama-logue Award and Critics Choice from the L.A. Times. He is the former editor of *Theater: Ex Magazine* and has been a curator in the Segue poetry series for 12 years. His screenplay *Undercurrent* was a finalist in the Robert Vague NYU film award. His play *Sunspots* was produced in French in Paris during March and April of 2006.

Chen, Dongbiao was born on Nov. 1967 in Shanghai and was educated in the Foreign Language Department in East China Normal University. He translated the following books published in Chinese: *Speak, Memory* by Vladimir Nabokov, *Jorge Luis Borges: Selected Poems 1923-1967*, *A Jew Today* by Elie Wiesel, *The Agony of Flies* by Elias Canetti, *Journals* by W. B. Yeats, as well as many others.

Chen, Xiangyang is a Ph.D. candidate in the Department of Cinema Studies at New York University. Her research interests include Chinese cinema, Hong Kong cinema, film history/historiography and film genres. She is currently writing her dissertation on Cantonese cinema.

Cheng, Wei was born in Yueyang, Hunan in 1966. He majored in English in Wuhan University in 1984-1988. He graduated from Beijing University with a Master's degree in Comparative Literature. He obtained his Ph.D. in American Literature in 2002. He works now in the Institute of Foreign Literatures of Academy of Social Sciences of China as a professor. He published several books, some of which are novels and essay collections. He lives in Beijing.

Daniel Comiskey is a poet who lives and works in Seattle, Washington. He is a member of the Seattle Research Institute, a group of writers who collaborate on books, lectures and other projects. With Kreg Hasegawa, he edited *Monkey Puzzle*, a magazine of poetry and prose. He was a member of the poetry programming committee for Northwest Bookfest in 2002, and a guest curator for the Subtext Reading Series in the fall of 2003. He used to be the literary manager for The Poet's Theater, which produced readings of dramatic works written by poets including John Ashbery, E.E. Cummings, Joyelle McSweeney and Frank O'Hara. He has also been involved in a series of ongoing art pranks and has collaborated with other poets on a number of works, the most recent of which is the long poem "Crawlspace," written with C.E. Putnam as a chapbook.

Martin Corless-Smith was born in Worcestershire, England. His books include *Of Piscator* (University of Georgia Press), *Complete Travels* (West House Books), *Nota* (Fence Books) and *Swallows* (Fence Books).

Caroline Crumpacker lives with her partner Tom O'Malley and their daughter Colette in upstate New York. She is an editor for *Fence Magazine*, a contributing editor for *Circumference* and *Double Change* (an online magazine of French and American poetries) and curator for the Bilingual Poetry Reading Series at the Bowery Poetry Club in Manhattan. She received a fellowship from the Fine Arts Work Center in Provincetown, MA in 2001/02. Her translations, essays and poems have appeared in the books *American Poets in the 21st Century: Who we are Now* (Wesleyan University Press, 2005); *Talisman Anthology of Contemporary French Poetry* (Talisman, forthcoming); and *Love Poems by Younger American Poets* (Verse Press, 2004) and in literary magazines.

Joseph Donahue's most recent volume of poetry is *In this Paradise: Terra Lucida XXI-XL*. Previous titles include *World Well Broken* and *Incidental Eclipse*, both published by Talisman House. He co-edited the anthologies *Primary Trouble: An Anthology of Contemporary American Poetry* and *The World in Time and Space: Towards a History of Innovative American Poetry in Our Time*. He lives in North Carolina where he teaches at Duke University.

Chris Dusterhoff is founder and editor of Spankstra Press, specializing in limited-run chapbooks. Spankstra has published books by Todd Moore, Harvey Goldner, Eli Richardson, Maged Zaher, David LaTerre and Ira Parnes. He lives in downtown Seattle, Washington.

Jennifer Feeley is a doctoral candidate in modern Chinese literature in the department of East Asian Languages and Literatures at Yale University. Her research focuses on Chinese women poets' negotiations with gender-oriented stereotypes throughout the twentieth century. Her translations have appeared in *Field: Contemporary Poetry and Poetics*.

Gao, Xiaoqin was born in 1973. She graduated from Fudan University in 1995 and currently lives in Shanghai.

Gao, Xing was born in Wujiang, Jiangsu in 1963. He majored in Eastern European Literature in Beijing Foreign Study University and graduated in 1987. He was a visiting scholar at Indiana University from 1995-1996. From 2001-2002, he acted as Consul of the People's Republic Of China in Constatsa. He is now Deputy Editor-in-Chief of *World Literature Magazine*. His works include *A Concise History of Romanian literature* (1993) and *The Drawers of Heart* (2004), an essay selection. He also translated and published such books as *Selected Poems of Ana Blandiana, An Anthology of Romanian Poems, My First Loves, Vincent van Gogh*, among others. He lives in Beijing.

John Gery has published five collections and two chapbooks of poetry— most recently, *Davenport's Version* (Portals Press, 2003), a narrative poem of the Civil War and *A Gallery of Ghosts* (Story Line Press, 2005). He has also published a critical work, *Nuclear Annihilation and Contemporary American Poetry: Ways of Nothingness* (Florida, 1996). Gery has co-translated Armenian poetry and prose with Vahe Baladouni, most notably, Hmayyag Shems's collection of prose poems, *For the House of Torkom* (Cross-Cultural, 1999) and has co-translated Serbian poetry with Biljana Obradovic. A Research Professor of English at the University of New Orleans, Gery is Director of the Ezra Pound Center for Literature at Brunnenburg, Italy.

Sam Hamill has translated Lao Tzu, Chuang Tzu and most of the major poets of ancient China and Japan. His selected poems and translations, *Almost Paradise*, was recently published by Shambhala. He was Founding Editor at Copper Canyon Press from 1972 through 2004.

John High is the author of six books, including his award-winning (Village Voice top 25 books of the year) trilogy of novels, *The Desire Notebooks*, and his recently published selected writings, *Bloodline*. He is the recipient of four Fulbrights, two NEA grants and writing awards from the Witter Bynner Foundation, Arts International and the Academy of American Poets. A translator of contemporary Russian poetry, he was the chief editor of *Crossing Centuries: The New Russian Poetry*. He is the founding editor of the *Five Fingers Review*. He has taught creative writing at San

Francisco State University, Moscow State Linguistics University and Montclair University. Currently, he is on the faculty of the English Department at Long Island University. His most recent book *Here* was published by Talisman House Publishers in 2006. A Zen practitioner, he lives in Brooklyn with his daughter, Sasha, and his girlfriend, Andrea.

Bob Holman's eighth and ninth books are *A Couple of Ways of Doing Something*, a collaboration with Chuck Close (Art of this Century/Pace Editions), and *Carved Water* (Tinfish), his translations of the poetry of Zhang Er. He is Visiting Professor of Writing at Columbia University and Proprietor of the Bowery Poetry Club. He is Artistic Director of Study Abroad on the Bowery, an applied poetics program launched in 2005 and publisher of Bowery Poetry Press.

Ha Jin was born in Xuefei Jin in Liaoning, China. He is the author of three books of poetry, four novels and three collections of stories. *Waiting* received the National Book Award for fiction and the PEN/Faulkner Award, and has been published in more than two-dozen countries. A professor of English at Boston University, Ha Jin's latest novel is *War Trash*.

Karla Kelsey was educated at UCLA, the Iowa Writer's Workshop and the University of Denver. Her work has recently appeared in *Verse*, *Boston Review* and *Fence*.

Ko Kho is a translator and an online poetry journal editor from Singapore.

Jane Lai studied at the University of Hong Kong and the University of Bristol. She taught English literature and translation at the University of Hong Kong for many years, and is now Chair Professor of Translation, director of the Centre for Translation, and Dean of the Arts Faculty at the Hong Kong Baptist University. She has long been associated with the Hong Kong theatre scene, translating plays by Shakespeare, Harold Pinter, Tom Stoppard, Eugene O'Neill, Arthur Miller, Edward Albee, Samuel Beckett, Bertolt Brecht and Jean Genet.

Charles A. Laughlin was born in Minneapolis. He received his B.A. in Chinese Language and Literature from the University of Minnesota in 1988, and went on to complete a Ph.D. in Chinese Literature at Columbia University in 1996. Since then, he has taught at Yale University, where he is currently Associate Professor of Chinese Literature. His first book, *Chinese Reportage: The Aesthetics of Historical Experience*, was published by Duke University Press in 2002, with a Chinese translation forthcoming. He is currently completing a book on the modern Chinese essay entitled *The Literature of Leisure and Chinese Modernity*.

Rachel Levitsky's first full-length volume of poetry, *Under the Sun*, was published by Futurepoem books in 2003. She is the author of five chapbooks of poetry, *Dearly*, (a+bend, 1999), *Cartographies of Error* (Leroy, 1999), *The Adventures of Yaya and Grace*

(PotesPoets, 1999), *2 (1x1)Portraits* (Baksun, 1998) and *Dearly, 3,4,6* (Duration Press, 2005).

Li, Chun born in 1981, a native of Sichuan, China, received his B.A. in English Literature from Nankai University in 2002. He is now a graduate student of Beijing University, specializing in Modern Chinese Literature. He has translated Henry Hobhouse's *Seeds of Wealth* (Macmillan, 2003) from English into Chinese (Beijing University, 2005).

Xiaorong Liu, Ph.D. in Biology from University of Virginia, 2002; B.S. from Beijing University, 1996; Now is a postdoctoral fellow in University of California, San Francisco.

Christopher Mattison graduated with an M.F.A. in Literary Translation from the University of Iowa and is currently managing editor of Zephyr Press and co-director of the series Adventures in Poetry.

Jason Pym holds a diploma for Chinese to English Translation from the Institute of Linguistics, UK. He worked as a professional translator and editor since 2000 for various international journals in China. He also works as a freelance translator.

Meredith Quartermain's books include *A Thousand Mornings*, (with Robin Blaser) *Wanders*, and *Vancouver Walking*. Her work has appeared in *Canadian Literature*, *Prism International*, *West Coast Line*, *Raddle Moon*, *Five Fingers Review*, *Chain*, *Sulfu*, and *Jacket*.

Ying Qin was born in 1975 in Shandong Province, P. R. China. She obtained a Master's degree in Chemistry from Fudan University in Shanghai in 1997. She worked as an editor at Shanghai Far-East Publishing House for a year, and then moved to the United States to study at the University of Rhode Island. She obtained two Master's degrees, one in Computer Science (2002) and another in English Literature (2005).

Bill Ransom 's poetry was nominated for both the Pulitzer Prize and the National Book Award. He's published six novels and numerous short stories, most recently in *Carve* magazine. A CD of his recent poetry collection, *War Baby*, is available from Wordman Production Company. He teaches at The Evergreen State College in Olympia, Washington.

Donald Revell is the author of nine volumes of poetry, most recently of *Pennyweight Windows: New and Selected Poems* (Alice James Books, 2005). A recipient of the PEN Award in poetry (twice) and of the Academy of American Poet's Lenore Marshall Prize (for My Mojave), he has been given fellowships from the NEA as well as from the Ingram Merrill and Guggenheim Foundations. Wesleyan University Press has published two collections of his translations of the French poet Guillaume Apollinaire: *Alcools* (1995) and *The Self-Dismembered Man* (2004). Revell is a Professor of English at the University of Utah, where he also serves as Director of Creative Writing.

Judith Roche, poet, arts educator, editor, arts programmer, is the author of two poetry collections, *Myrrh/ My Life as a Screamer* and *Ghosts*. She received an American Book Award for co-editing *First Fish First People, Salmon Tales of the North Pacific Rim*. She has taught poetry workshops and residencies extensively to adults, students, prisoners and others and was the Literary Arts Director for One Reel, an arts events organization.

Eleni Sikelianos's two new books are *The California Poem* (Coffee House) and *The Book of Jon* (Nonfiction; City Lights). Previous books include *The Monster Lives of Boys & Girls* (Green Integer, National Poetry Series), *Earliest Worlds* (Coffee House) and *The Book of Tendons* (Post-Apollo). She has been conferred numerous awards for her poetry, nonfiction and translations.

Susan M. Schultz is Professor of English at the University of Hawai`i in Honolulu. She is author of three volumes of poetry, most recently *And then something happened* (Salt, 2004) and *A Poetics of Impasse in Modern and Contemporary American Poetry* (Alabama, 2005). She edited *The Tribe of John: Ashbery and Contemporary Poetry* (Alabama, 1995). In 1995 she founded Tinfish Press, which specializes in experimental poetry from the Pacific.

Leonard Schwartz is the author of several collections of poetry, including *Ear And Ethos* (Talisman House, 2005), *The Tower of Diverse Shores, Words Before The Articulate: New and Selected Poems* (Talisman House), *Gnostic Blessing* (Goats and Compasses), *Meditation* (Cloud House), *Objects of Thought, Attempts At Speech* (Gnosis Press) and *Exiles: Ends* (Red Dust Press). He is also the author of a collection of essays, *A Flicker at the Edge of Things: Essays on Poetics 1987-1997* (Spuyten Duyvil).

Mark Wallace is the author of more than ten books and chapbooks of poetry and fiction, including *Nothing Happened and Besides I Wasn't There* and *Sonnets of a Penny-A-Liner*. *Temporary Worker Rides a Subway* won the 2002 Gertrude Stein Poetry Award and was recently published by Green Integer Books. His multi-genre work *Haze* (Edge Books) was published in 2004. His first novel, *Dead Carnival*, was also published in 2004, by Avec Books, which published his first collection of fiction shorts, *The Big Lie*, in 2000. His critical articles and reviews have appeared in numerous publications. He co-edited *Telling It Slant: Avant Garde Poetics of the 1990s* (University of Alabama Press), a collection of 26 essays by different writers on the subject of contemporary avant garde poetry and poetics; and co-edited *A Poetics of Criticism*, a collection of poetry essays in non-standard formats published by Leave Books.

Li-Hua Ying, Associate Professor of Chinese Language and Literature, Director of Chinese Program, Bard College, Chair of the Advisory Board for Calligraphy Education Group. Born in Sichuan; Grew up in Yunnan; Ph. D., Comparative

Literature, University of Texas at Austin, 1992; M.A., English, University of Texas at Austin, 1985; B.A., English, Yunnan Normal University, Kunming, China, 1980.

Maged Zaher was born in Cairo, Egypt. His poems appeared in such magazines as *Columbia Poetry Review, Exquisite Corpse, Ribot* and others. He has two chapbooks: *speculations on a second weather* and *the wholesale approach.*

A CD with several of the poets anthologized in this book reading from their works is available from the publisher for $3.50, including packaging and shipping within the United States. For shipping elsewhere, contact the publisher for details. Checks and money orders should be sent to:

Talisman
PO Box 3157
Jersey City, NJ 07303-3157